Students' Guide
to
Macbeth

KT-458-360

Peter H. Burgess

03 FEB 2001

TYNRON PRESS, SCOTLAND

© *Peter H. Burgess, 1989*

First published in 1989
by Tynron Press
Stenhouse
Thornhill
Dumfriesshire DG3 4LD
Scotland

ISBN 1-871948-45-2
All rights reserved

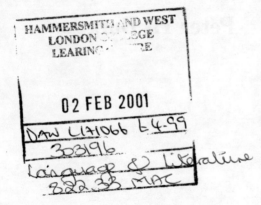

HAMMERSMITH AND WEST
LONDON COLLEGE
LEARING CENTRE

0 2 FEB 2001

DAW LI71066 £4·99
303196
Language & Literature
822.33 MAC

Cover design by Eric Yeo, Trans Graphics
Typeset by AZ Graphic
Printed in Singapore by Lolitho Private Limited

303196

Contents

Foreword

The line numbers used in this book have been taken from Longman's New Swan edition of *Macbeth*. Variations in the line numbering of the play exist in other editions but, as they are usually not very great, they should pose few problems.

Nearly every word and idea in Shakespeare's plays, particularly the great tragedies (and *Macbeth* is one of these), has been analysed, argued about, or queried. So it is impossible to write anything about the play that is definitively correct, in the sense that it can better all other interpretations, past, present, or future. And I am aware that at times my opinions have changed and wavered, as though I cannot make up my mind. For this, I apologise in advance, and my best suggestion is that you the student choose for yourself when a conflict of possible interpretations arises in this book. I can only hope there are not too many.

Use this book sensibly; don't follow it slavishly but let it make you think about the play so that you can generate your own ideas. If you don't agree with me, there's no harm done. If you think Lady Macbeth is really a wonderful woman who deeply loves her husband, while I call her rude names, it doesn't matter, that is, so long as your argument is based convincingly on your reading of the text, rather than on guesswork. We can still be friends.

Peter H. Burgess

1. Shakespeare's Life and Times

William Shakespeare was born on April 23rd, 1564, at Stratford-upon-Avon, some ninety miles north-west of London in the English county of Warwickshire. In those days Stratford was a small, quiet market town surrounded by fertile farmland. Shakespeare's father, a prominent citizen of Stratford, was in the glove-making business, while his mother came from a family of wealthy landowners.

William was the eldest son in a family of six children, and almost certainly attended the local grammar school where he would have received an education that concentrated on the classics — Latin and Greek.

Shakespeare married, perhaps rashly at the age of eighteen, a woman of twenty-five, Ann Hathaway, who came from a village near Stratford. A few months later, their first child, a daughter called Susannah, was born. She was followed by a twin boy and girl, Hamnet and Judith. But Shakespeare was to spend the best part of his married life away from his family, in London where he discovered fame and fortune.

We have little idea what made Shakespeare leave Stratford in the first place. As the eldest son, he would ordinarily have been apprenticed to his father's shop so that he could learn and eventually take over the business. Legend has it that he was running away from a charge of poaching on the land of a wealthy aristocrat. We know that his father's business was not doing well when William was in his teens, and this may well be the reason why he chose to find employment elsewhere. Of course, Shakespeare might have just wanted to explore the broader horizons beyond the small world of his family and Stratford, and London would have been the obvious place for a young man to go in search of adventure and a fortune.

Shakespeare remained almost continuously in London for

over twenty years, until 1609, when he was forty-five; then he returned to Stratford, a wealthy man, to live in semi-retirement with his wife and daughter Judith. Hamnet had died in 1596, aged 11; Susannah married in 1601; and Shakespeare's father died in 1601, his mother in 1608. Shakespeare himself died in 1616 from, so legend tells us, a fever caught after a drinking bout; but we've no way of knowing if this is really true.

We don't know exactly when Shakespeare arrived in London. The first direct reference to him appears in 1592 when another playwright, making an unmistakable pun on his name, calls him contemptuously 'an upstart crow...in his own conceit the only Shake-scene in a country'.

Shakespeare was working as an actor and this was his regular source of income, but he also wrote plays in his spare time and made extra money by hiring them out to the acting company he was working with. Consequently, by 1594 Shakespeare was comparatively rich. In that year he joined an acting company called the Chamberlain's Men, and handed over to his new company the eight or nine plays he had already written. The Chamberlain's Men included some of the best actors of the day: Richard Burbage, Will Kempe and, later on, Robert Armin.

Before 1594 times had been hard for actors and acting companies. Frequent outbreaks of the plague closed down the London theatres with grim regularity, but after 1594 a new prosperity arrived for the London-based theatre companies. For nearly eight years these companies were able to perform continuously without interruption from the plague. During this period, Shakespeare became part-owner of a new playhouse, the Globe, built in 1599 on the south bank of the Thames, and his wealth and reputation grew even greater.

The Chamberlain's Men soon became the foremost acting company in London, and Shakespeare's plays must have been largely responsible for their success. The most popular plays of the day were *Hamlet* (1601) and the three history plays that feature the character of Falstaff: *Henry IV, Part 1, Henry IV, Part 2* (1596-7) and *Henry V* (1599) — although Falstaff is merely referred to in *Henry V*. The Chamberlain's Men, who performed regularly at court, changed their name to the King's Men in 1603, when Queen Elizabeth I died and James I (who had previously been James VI of Scotland) succeeded to the throne of England.

Macbeth was written in or around the year 1606. With its Scottish setting, it seems a conscious attempt by Shakespeare to honour a Scottish king, for it deals with two things of great interest to James I — his own royal ancestry, and witchcraft.

Shakespeare wrote two plays a year for his acting company, one serious and one comic or lighthearted. Over a period of about twenty years, he handed over to them thirty-eight plays. Ben Jonson (another celebrated Elizabethan playwright) and Heming and Condell (two actors in Shakespeare's company) tell us that he wrote with great speed and ease, rarely crossing anything out. Quite probably, Shakespeare took a small part in each play for himself, but his fame and fortune were made by his genius as a playwright and not by any skill he may have had as an actor.

When he retired to Stratford in 1609, he bought the second largest house in the town, called New Place, and several hundred acres of farmland. He wrote a few more plays there (*The Winter's Tale, The Tempest,* and a part only of *Henry VIII*). In these retirement years he probably helped other playwrights by writing the occasional scene for them. In the meantime, he enjoyed being reunited with his family, particularly (or so it seems) with his daughters.

After his death in 1616 (the same year that his youngest daughter Judith got married), his actors gathered his plays together and his two friends, Heming and Condell, arranged for them to be published in 1623 in a single edition known as the First Folio. Had this not happened, the thirty-eight plays of the greatest playwright and poet of the English language would probably have been lost forever.

2. Shakespeare's Theatre

When a play is produced in the modern theatre, the actors cannot see the audience. The house-lights are turned down; the audience sits in virtual darkness, and the powerful beams from the spotlights and footlights allow the actors to believe, if they so choose, that they are alone. The modern theatre-goer is expected to show his approval or dissatisfaction with a performance in a polite and restrained manner. If he likes what he sees on the stage, he will applaud enthusiastically when the final curtain falls; if he doesn't think much of the play or the actors, he will probably clap courteously at the end of the performance, and later on tell his friends that the show wasn't worth the money.

Shakespeare's theatre and his audience were very different. The performances were, by our standards, rushed, noisy and unsophisticated. Shakespeare's acting company, the Chamberlain's Men (renamed the King's Men after 1603), consisted of about twelve leading actors. The parts were cast fairly automatically, because Shakespeare wrote each major part with a particular actor in mind. Richard Burbage always took the leading role (he would have played Macbeth); Robert Armin took any part that required singing or dancing (so he featured more prominently in the comedies and romances, though in *Macbeth* he probably played the porter in II. iii); another actor was always a soldier, another an old man, and so on. Each of the main actors had an apprentice, a young man, and these apprentices took the female roles because it was illegal for women to act on the stage in the public theatres. The parts of Lady Macbeth and Lady Macduff, therefore, would have been played by boys or youths in their early teens (before their voices broke).

There was no scenery apart from a few simple props which

could easily be carried onto the stage; perhaps a wooden throne for Duncan and then Macbeth to sit on; a table and a few chairs for the banquet scene in III. iv. There was little or no attempt made to get the costumes to suit the period in which the play was set. The performances (of any of Shakespeare's plays) rarely lasted more than two hours; so the actors must have rushed through their lines, probably declaiming much more than we are used to in the modern theatre, and because of the absence of props, the scene changes would have been very swift.

Apart from Sundays and a few other days off for Christian festivals, the Chamberlain's Men put on a performance at the Globe Theatre every afternoon of the week, weather permitting. Each play ran for about ten or twelve performances and then had to be changed to keep the audiences coming; so the leading actors had to keep brushing up their parts for the next play before the one they were in at the time had finished its run. Men would be hired on a daily basis to play the walk-on parts, i.e. for crowd scenes, or where an army was being represented, etc. Behind the stage sat a prompter or 'bookkeeper' to remind the actors of their lines if they faltered.

The Globe Theatre was built in London's Southwark region, on the south bank of the River Thames, in 1599. It was jointly owned by Shakespeare, Richard Burbage and a few others. The octagonally shaped outer wall of the theatre enclosed a roofless inner area, known as the yard, into which the stage projected. Around the yard were three galleries, one above the other, the topmost of which was roofed with thatch. Of course, there was no such thing as stage lighting; the only light the actors had was daylight. If rain came during a performance, a blue awning with a design of stars on its underside was pulled across to keep the actors and the audience in the yard dry, so that the play could go on. A flag flying above the Globe signalled that the weather looked good that day and the people could expect a performance in the afternoon. A trumpet was blown to announce that the play was about to start.

The Globe could hold an audience of about two thousand. The poorer citizens paid an entrance fee of a penny each to stand in the yard. That may not seem a lot, but remember that a skilled man in those days earned about a shilling (twelve pence) a day. This section of the audience was called the groundlings. The seats in the galleries were much more expensive. And some wealthy young men of the day used to like showing off by paying a lot extra to sit on the stage on stools, making what mischief they chose for the actors. The audience expected value for their money, and they knew how to insist on getting it, particularly the groundlings, who had to stand packed together for two hours. They expected to be thoroughly entertained by a continuous barrage of words and action. The audience was quick to show its approval or disapproval by cheering, shouting or booing. Meanwhile, within the amphitheatre, hawkers were selling nuts, fruit (particularly oranges which kept the stifling smell of body odour away from more delicate nostrils), beer, flowers, and more. Usually, the actors had to get through their lines against a background of noise which would seem intolerable to the modern actor.

Behind the main stage was a curtained place (marked as N in the diagram of the Globe). This was used for scenes where surprise was required, or else to represent a bedroom. Above this was a gallery (marked O in the diagram), used sometimes by musicians, sometimes for a balcony scene, as in *Romeo and Juliet,* or as the battlements of a castle, as in *Hamlet.* A trap door in the centre of the stage was used for the entrance of ghosts, such as Banquo's Ghost in III. iv.

Apart from the daily performances at the Globe, Shakespeare's acting company was frequently asked to perform at court. The company was particularly popular with James I, who came to the throne in 1603. The Chamberlain's Men sought to honour the new king by changing their name to the King's Men and by performing for him, (he was formerly James VI of Scotland) *Macbeth,* a play set in the King's homeland, which dealt with his ancestry and with the supernatural, two topics of great interest to the new King.

The Globe burned down in 1613, during a performance of Shakespeare's last play, *Henry VIII.* A cannon fired during the action of the play set the thatch roof ablaze, and soon the whole of this wood-built theatre was razed to the ground. This was three years before Shakespeare's death, but he had already retired to Stratford by then, a very rich man. The Globe was rebuilt in 1614, but thirty years later was destroyed by the Puritans. A brewery now stands on its site.

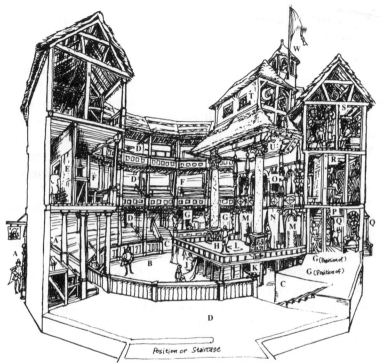

The Globe Playhouse

AA Main entrance
 B The Yard
CC Entrance to lowest gallery
 D Entrance to staircase and upper galleries
 E Corridor serving the different sections of the middle gallery
 F Middle gallery ('Twopenny Rooms')
 G 'Gentlemen's Rooms or Lords Rooms'
 H The stage
 J The hanging being put up round the stage
 K The 'Hell' under the stage
 L The stage trap, leading down to the Hell

MM Stage doors
 N Curtained 'place behind the stage'
 O Gallery above the stage, used as required sometimes by musicians, sometimes by spectators, and often as part of the play
 P Back-stage area (the tiring-house)
 Q Tiring-house door
 R Dressing-rooms
 S Wardrobe and storage
 T The hut housing the machine for lowering enthroned gods, etc. to the stage
 U The 'Heavens'
 W Hoisting the playhouse flag

3.   Plot Synopsis: The Story of *Macbeth*

On a stormy day in the year 1040, two Scottish noblemen, Macbeth and Banquo, are returning victorious from a battle against rebel forces. They meet three Witches on a heath who prophesy that Macbeth will become Thane of Cawdor and King, while Banquo will be the father of kings. The first part of this prophecy comes true when Duncan honours Macbeth for his deeds in battle by giving him the title of the former Thane of Cawdor (a traitor and a member of the rebel forces who has been put to death). This turns Macbeth's thoughts to murder. He writes to his wife telling her all that the Witches have foretold and preparing her for Duncan's arrival at their home, Inverness Castle.

Lady Macbeth is as ambitious as her husband, but she fears that he is 'too full o' the milk of human kindness' to do what has to be done to seize the throne. With much encouragement and goading, she persuades Macbeth to murder Duncan while he is a guest at their castle and drugs two of Duncan's attendants to allow Macbeth access to the King. They plan to leave the attendants' daggers at the scene of the crime to make it appear as if they were the assassins.

Duncan's sons, Malcolm and Donalbain, are wary of Macbeth's version of events and flee the country. Macbeth becomes King of Scotland, but he fears Banquo for his virtuous nature, and because the Witches said Banquo would be the father of kings. He arranges for Banquo and his son to be murdered, but the boy, Fleance, manages to escape.

Meanwhile, Macbeth is haunted by Banquo's Ghost at a banquet. No one else can see the Ghost and Lady Macbeth explains her husband's strange behaviour by telling the guests that he has been seized by a fit.

To bolster his waning confidence, Macbeth returns to the

Witches, who warn him against Macduff. They add that Macbeth has nothing to fear, for 'none of woman born' can harm him and he will never be defeated till "Great Birnam wood to high Dunsinane hill/Shall come against him'. While Macduff is in England, seeking help to depose Macbeth, Lady Macduff and her children are slaughtered.

Lady Macbeth's conscience is deeply troubled and she walks in her sleep, imagining blood stains on her hands. Meanwhile, Malcolm, with support from English forces, is besieging Macbeth's castle. Many of Macbeth's men have deserted him, but he takes comfort from the Witches' prophecy that he has a charmed life and that he will never be defeated until Birnam wood comes to Dunsinane.

His wife dies, and for a moment Macbeth contemplates the futility of life: 'it is a tale/ Told by an idiot, full of sound and fury,/ Signifying nothing'. Then a messenger tells him that Birnam wood is moving towards the castle. The attacking forces are carrying branches as camouflage for their advance, and so it appears as though the wood is moving. Realising that the Witches' words have tricked him, Macbeth leaves the castle to meet his foe and to fight with great courage. When he encounters Macduff, he brags that no man born of a woman can kill him. But Macduff replies: 'Despair thy charm ... Macduff was from his mother's womb/ Untimely ripped.' Macbeth is slain and Macduff hacks off his head and carries it to Malcolm, who invites all to attend his coronation.

4.   The Historical Source of *Macbeth*

A real King Macbeth of Scotland did exist. In the year 1040 he was commander of the forces of King Duncan I. After murdering Duncan, Macbeth claimed the throne and ruled for seventeen prosperous years. In 1057 he was killed in battle by Malcolm Canmore, a son of Duncan I, who was later King Malcolm III of Scotland.

Shakespeare almost certainly read this little piece of history in a book by Raphael Holinshed called *Chronicles of England, Scotland, and Ireland* (published in 1577). However, in writing *Macbeth* for the stage, Shakespeare was out to create entertainment for his audience; he didn't want the play to be a documentary and so he didn't feel in the least obliged to remain faithful to historical facts. To put it another way, Shakespeare was not afraid of exaggerating and distorting history. *Macbeth* is not the only example of this: in another of his tragedies, *Richard III,* Shakespeare took quite a good English king of the Middle Ages and converted him into just about the most base villain who ever lived!

5. *Macbeth* as a Tragedy

If *Macbeth* is not a history play in the strictest sense (in that it makes no attempt to retell history accurately), what type of play is it? The answer is that it is a tragedy.

In the first collected edition of Shakespeare's plays, (called the *First Folio*) Heming and Condell, the editors and former friends of Shakespeare's, placed *Macbeth* in the category they reserved for his tragedies. The other categories they used were for the comedies, the history plays, and the tragi-comedies. *Macbeth* shares a place in the *First Folio* with Shakespeare's other tragedies: *Romeo and Juliet* (1595), *Julius Caesar* (1599), *Hamlet* (1601), *Othello* (1604), *King Lear* (1605), *Antony and Cleopatra* (1606) and *Coriolanus* (1608). *Macbeth* was written in 1606, the same year as *Antony and Cleopatra*. (Although it is safe to say these eight plays are tragedies, four others defy such easy classification; they are *Richard III* (1593), *Richard II* (1599), *Troilus and Cressida* (1602), and *Timon of Athens* (1608). Their central characters lack greatness or tragic stature, and so they fall uncomfortably between the histories and the tragedies in the *First Folio,* seemingly having been cast almost randomly by Heming and Condell into one category or the other.)

But what is tragedy, in the sense in which we use this word in literature? When we refer to a tragedy in our day-to-day speech, we usually mean an event, or a series of events, which has ended sadly. We might read a newspaper headline which says, 'Tragedy of Flight 505: No Survivors in Worst Air Disaster of the Decade'; or someone might say to us, 'It was a tragedy their marriage ended in divorce; they seemed so well-suited.' But sadness is not the defining factor in Shakespeare's tragedies, though elements of it usually appear: we feel sad when Macduff's family are murdered (IV.

ii), and Macbeth's soliloquy (V. v. 17-28) after his wife's death, generates enormous pathos. However, we don't feel at all sad when Macbeth is slain by Macduff at the end of the play. In fact, we feel a sense of relief: that this *had* to happen. A great evil has manifested itself, and our emotions of terror and pity have been excited, but now they are calmed. This is called *catharsis*, a purging of the feelings. We don't leave the theatre with bitterness in our hearts, but with a sensation that things have turned out as they had to.

What we observe in Shakespearean tragedy is the destruction of a great and noble man through some imperfection, some fatal flaw, in his character (what Hamlet refers to as a 'vicious mole of nature', which surfaces and corrupts a once virtuous man). Hamlet's fatal flaw is brooding indecision; Othello is both jealous and gullible; King Lear is vain; and Coriolanus is too proud. Macbeth's downfall is caused by ambition. His virtues, his courage and nobility, his sense of honour and conscience, even his love for his wife, are obvious to us from very early on in the play; but so also is this one imperfection in his personality, and it is this which will destroy him. Macbeth himself is aware of it, referring to it in Act One:

> 'I have no spur
> To prick the sides of my intent, but only
> Vaulting ambition'

(I. vii. 25-27).

Shakespeare makes it clear that his tragic characters have free will. They are each faced with a choice: to follow the course of action which their conscience says is honourable, or to attempt to appease the demands of that one imperfect component in their otherwise worthy natures. In I. vii. 31-35, we see Macbeth wavering between good and evil, honour and ambition, as he wrestles with his conscience:

'We will proceed no further in this business:
He hath honoured me of late; and I have bought
Golden opinions from all sorts of people,
Which would be worn now in their newest gloss,
Not cast aside so soon.'

Here, Macbeth is telling his wife that he doesn't want to continue with their plan to murder Duncan, because he feels grateful to him and doesn't want to run the risk of losing people's good opinions of himself (i.e. his honour).

What is really troubling Macbeth is his awareness that what they are about to do is totally immoral. Nevertheless, his conscience is not a powerful enough brake to halt the driving force of his ambition. So he does murder Duncan — not because Lady Macbeth or the Witches make him (although they do encourage him), but because he freely chooses to do so.

6. The Language and Imagery of *Macbeth*

(i) Poetry and Prose

Shakespeare wrote his plays in both poetry and prose. In *Macbeth,* poetry predominates and there is relatively little prose (more is said about this later on).

The type of poetry most often used by Shakespeare is called blank verse — 'blank' because normally it is unrhymed; although Shakespeare does use rhyming couplets to round off longer speeches neatly, as well as at the end of scenes and acts. E.g:

> 'Whiles I threat, he lives:
> Words to the heat of deeds too cold breath gives'

(the end of a 30 line soliloquy by Macbeth: II. i. 60-61).

> 'Fair is foul, and foul is fair:
> Hover through the fog and filthy air'
>
> (the end of a scene: I. i. 10-11).

> 'Receive what cheer you may;
> The night is long that never finds the day'
>
> (the end of an act: IV. iii. 239-240).

However, rhyme is the exception and not the rule. Instead, Shakespeare's poetry relies on an internal rhythm within the lines, created by stressed and unstressed syllables. What is a syllable? Well, it's a word or part of a word uttered by only one effort of the voice. 'Man', 'cat', 'thirst', 'chalk' are all words of one syllable. 'Kind-ness' has two syllables; 'faith-ful-ness' has three; and 'con-ver-sa-tion' has four. (The hyphens are used by way of example only and do not appear in the normal spelling of these words.)

A syllable is said to be *stressed* when the vowel sound

within it is given a full emphasis. Conversely, a syllable is said to be *unstressed* when we tend to play down its vowel sound in the pronunciation of the word. Here are some examples of stressed and unstressed syllables (the ´ sign indicates a stressed syllable, and the hyphens once again separate the individual syllables within a word): Síng-a-pore, swóll-en, bán-dit, dis-pél, hár-vest, míght-y, pur-i-fi-cá-tion, sánc-tu-a-ry, póck-et, poll-úte. (Most dictionaries show where stressed syllables are placed in much the same way as this, so find some examples of your own.)

The rhythm in Shakespeare's verse is established by a pattern of five stressed to five unstressed syllables in each line:

> 'Wísdom! to léave his wífe, to léave his bábes,
> His mánsion, ánd his títles, ín a pláce
> From whénce himsélf does flý? He lóves us nót'
>
> (IV. ii. 6-8).

Of course, if every line followed precisely the same rhythm, the verse would become monotonous. To avoid this, Shakespeare created different patterns within the standard five-stressed and five-unstressed syllables, as in this example:

> 'Whó can be wíse, amázed, témperate and fúrious,
> Lóyal and néutral, in a móment? Nó Mán:'
>
> (II. iii. 105-106).

Another device he uses to add variety to his poetry is to let one character begin a line and another finish it:

Lady Macbeth

Why did you bring these daggers from the place?
They must lie there; go, carry them, and smear
The sleepy grooms with blood.

> *Macbeth*
> I'll go no more:
> I am afraid to think what I have done;
> Look on 't again I dare not.
>
> *Lady Macbeth*
> Infirm of purpose!
> (II. ii. 47-51).

In this example, line 49 is started by Lady Macbeth and finished by her husband, while he begins line 51 and she ends it.

The formal name for the type of metre (rhythm) Shakespeare employs in his blank verse is *iambic pentameter*. Translated from the original Greek, this grandiose phrase means something like 'A line of poetry with five feet'.

One word of caution before we leave our discussion of Shakespeare's verse: when you read it aloud (as you should), to yourself or in front of the class, don't keep stopping at the end of each line, unless that is what the text clearly indicates. Pause at punctuation marks. We will illustrate this by continuing the example given above:

> *Lady Macbeth*
> 'Infirm of purpose!
> Give me the daggers. The sleeping and the dead
> Are but as pictures; 't is the eye of childhood
> That fears a painted devil. If he do bleed,
> I'll gild the faces of the grooms withal,
> For it must seem their guilt'
>
> (II. ii. 51-56).

After 'Infirm of purpose!', you stop abruptly. The next five lines should flow into each other, with only a slight pause for the punctuation marks in the middle of lines 52-54 and at the end of lines 54-55. Practise this 'flowing method' of reading

Shakespeare's verse for yourself. Two good passages to use for this are Macbeth's soliloquies in I. vii. 1-28 and II. i. 33-61.

Prose is any written or spoken English which isn't in poetry (i.e. where no attempt is made to get the syllables of the words to interact in such a way that a rhythm is established) and which does not have to start with a capital letter at the beginning of each new line.

Generally, poetry is used in Shakespeare's plays by noble characters, or at times of dramatic or emotional intensity.

Some fine lines of verse are given to the first of the three Murderers in III. iii. 5-8, as they lie in wait for Banquo and Fleance:

'The west yet glimmers with some streaks of day:
Now spurs the lated traveller apace,
To gain the timely inn; and near approaches
The subject of our watch.'

The Murderers are far from noble, but this moment in the play is full of tension, hence the use of poetry.

On the other hand, although Macbeth is a 'noble' character, his letter to his wife is in prose, but then it would seem completely artificial if he'd written it in verse. The prose here, with its tone of wonder and tender intimacy, contrasts with Lady Macbeth's sharp and determined response to it in rich verse:

(Macbeth's Letter)

"Whiles I stood rapt in the wonder of it, came missives from the king, who all-hailed me 'Thane of Cawdor'; by which title, before, these weird sisters saluted me, and referred me to the coming-on of time, with 'Hail, king that shalt be!' This have I thought good to deliver thee, my dearest partner of

greatness, that thou might'st not lose the dues of
rejoicing, by being ignorant of what greatness is
promised thee. Lay it to thy heart, and farewell.''

(I. v. 4-12).

Lady Macbeth

Glamis thou art, and Cawdor; and shalt be
What thou art promised. — Yet I do fear thy nature:
It is too full o' the milk of human kindness
To catch the nearest way. Thou wouldst be great;
Art not without ambition, but without
The illness should attend it: what thou wouldst highly,
That wouldst thou holily; wouldst not play false,
And yet wouldst wrongly win; thou'dst have, great
Glamis,
That which cries, ''Thus thou must do, if thou have it'';
And that which rather thou dost fear to do,
Than wishest should be undone. Hie thee hither,
That I may pour my spirits in thine ear,
And chastise with the valour of my tongue
All that impedes thee from the golden round,
Which fate and metaphysical aid doth seem
To have thee crowned withal.

(I. v. 13-28).

The Porter in II. iii speaks most of his lines in prose. He is
the only lowly character in the play with a longish speaking
part. His eccentric wit and ribald humour are carefully
devised by Shakespeare to take the heat out of our feelings
before they are excited again by the discovery of Duncan's
murder later on in the scene. But if the Porter speaks prose
because he is a lowly, comic character, why does Lady
Macduff lapse into prose while talking to her son, just before
the Murderers enter in IV. ii? Probably again to calm our
feelings, to give an appearance of things being normal, even

mundane, before the Murderers come and our passions are whipped up again.

Lady Macbeth speaks prose while sleepwalking in V. i, and so do the Doctor and the Gentlewoman observing her. The subject matter of the scene, Lady Macbeth's crimes and her guilty conscience, is certainly intense; so why is it in prose? Probably because Lady Macbeth is dreaming and her words and thoughts are disjointed, which makes prose more suitable, e.g:

> 'Out, damned spot! out, I say! — One; two; why, then 't is time to do 't. — Hell is murky. — Fie, my Lord, fie! a soldier, and afeard? — What need we fear who knows it, when none can call our power to account? — Yet who would have thought the old man to have had so much blood in him?'
>
> (V. i. 28-32).

There is comparatively little prose in *Macbeth*. There is no subplot with humorous low-life characters speaking predominantly in prose, as we find in so many of Shakespeare's other plays. Nearly all the characters are noble (with the Weird Sisters defying classification) and the plot is unremittingly intense throughout; so it is appropriate that, but for a few instances as mentioned earlier, *Macbeth* should be written in fine, rich poetry.

(ii) Metaphors and Similes

A metaphor occurs when a person or a thing is described in terms not normally associated with that person or thing. For example: 'He is a tiger when angry'; 'a sickly yellow colour'; 'she sailed into the room'; 'you must put a brake on your spending'; 'the company crashed into bankruptcy', etc.

Metaphors enrich our language and we use them in our

everyday speech without thinking much about it. *Macbeth* abounds in metaphors; they can be found on almost every page.

In I. iv, Duncan proclaims his son Malcolm to be his heir and the Prince of Cumberland. Macbeth, in an aside, comments:

'The Prince of Cumberland! — That is a step
On which I must fall down, or else o'erleap,
For in my way it lies'

(I. iv. 48-50).

In this metaphor, Macbeth compares Malcolm to a step lying across his path on the way to the throne. If he trips against it, then all his hopes are dashed; but if he can leap over it, then it will lead him to higher things.

Lady Macbeth, a mother (although we never learn how many children she has), is fond of metaphors which compare nursing and milk to unwanted tenderness and kindness. What is being emphasised, of course, is Lady Macbeth's unnaturalness as a woman. After receiving her husband's letter in I. v, she chides him in her thoughts for not being ruthless enough to seize the throne by murdering Duncan:

'Yet I do fear thy nature:
It is too full o' the milk of human kindness
To catch the nearest way'

(I. v. 14-16).

A little later on in the same scene, she appeals to the spirits to 'unsex' her, to take away her milk (which stands for kindness or pity) and to replace it with gall (bitterness):

'Come to my woman's breasts,
And take my milk for gall, you murdering ministers'

(I. v. 45-46).

In 1. vii, while scolding her husband again for having doubts about their plan, she metaphorically compares her own ruthlessness and determination to the ability to pluck a nursing child from her breast and dash its brains out:

> 'I have given suck, and know
> How tender 't is to love the babe that milks me:
> I would, while it was smiling in my face,
> Have plucked my nipple from his boneless gums,
> And dashed the brains out, had I so sworn as you
> Have done to this'
>
> (I. vii. 54-59).

A simile is a figure of speech in which a person or thing is compared to something else, using 'like' or 'as', e.g: 'he is as strong as an ox'; 'the wind cut me like a knife'; 'the truth is as clear as daylight', etc. Just as there are numerous metaphors in *Macbeth*, so there are also many similes and it would be impossible to list them all here. But to give you an idea what to look for, here are three examples:

When the Murderer tells Macbeth in III. iv that Banquo is dead but that Fleance has escaped, Macbeth, very agitated, replies:

> 'Then comes my fit again: I had else been perfect;
> Whole as the marble, founded as the rock,
> As broad and general as the casing air'
>
> (III. iv. 21-23).

Macbeth is saying that if Fleance had been killed as well as Banquo, and all things had gone as planned, then he would be as composed as a marble statue ('Whole as the marble'); firm in his purpose, like a rock that can't be shifted ('founded as the rock'); and as free as the air around him to go and do as he chooses ('As broad and general as the casing air'). So in these similes, composure or peace of mind is likened to a statue; firmness of purpose is likened to a rock and freedom to the air.

In another example, Macbeth says in a soliloquy:

> 'this Duncan
> Hath borne his faculties so meek, hath been
> So clear in his great office, that his virtues
> Will plead like angels, trumpet-tongued, against
> The deep damnation of his taking off'
>
> (I. vii. 16-20).

In this simile, Duncan's virtues are likened to, or compared to, angels with tongues as loud as trumpets. The figure of speech emphasises the point that Macbeth is making: that Duncan's murder will be deeply deplored throughout the land because he is such a virtuous king.

One final example: in V. vii, Macbeth knows that all is lost; many of his men have deserted him, his castle is surrounded, and he is fighting alone on the plain:

> 'They have tied me to a stake: I cannot fly,
> But, bear-like, I must fight the course'
>
> (V. vii. 1-2).

The allusion is to the popular Elizabethan sport of bear-baiting, in which a bear was chained to a stake and cruelly tormented. In this simile, Macbeth compares himself to the bear tied to the stake, for, like the bear, he cannot run but must stand and fight to the death.

(iii) The Recurrent Imagery of *Macbeth*

Metaphors and similes form the main part of the imagery of *Macbeth*. What we mean by 'imagery' in literature is the formation of mental pictures, pictures in the mind's eye, by the use of language. To bind all the elements of the play together and to give each its own distinctive character, Shakespeare quite often repeats an idea in his imagery: this is what is called 'recurring imagery'.

In *Macbeth*, one particular idea that gets repeated has to do with clothing or covering something with cloth. This image is first introduced clearly in I. iii, when Macbeth is met by Rosse and Angus and told that the King has made him Thane of Cawdor. He replies:

> 'The Thane of Cawdor lives: why do you dress me
> In borrowed robes?'
>
> (I. iii. 108-109).

And as Macbeth muses over the Witches' prophecy coming true so soon, Banquo tells the others:

> 'New honours come upon him
> Like our strange garments, cleave not to their mould
> But with the aid of use'
>
> (I. iii. 144-146).

Later on in the play, in Act V, this image of a man in ill-fitting garments is repeated by Angus, one of the Scottish nobles fighting for Malcolm:

> 'now does he feel his title
> Hang loose about him, like a giant's robe
> Upon a dwarfish thief'
>
> (V. ii. 20-22).

The clothing image can be interpreted in more than one way: that Shakespeare looked on his hero Macbeth as a small man taking too much upon himself, hence the idea of him wearing garments that are too large for him; or else we may see the garments as stolen, just as Macbeth has stolen the crown; or the garments may symbolise the hypocrisy to which Macbeth is committed once he embarks on his criminal career (for Macbeth is a criminal, despite his rank and nobility).

The clothing/cloth image appears throughout *Macbeth*. Three more examples are given here, but the student will find others in the text:

(a)   *Rosse*
                                   Will you to Scone?

                                        Macduff
No, cousin; I'll to Fife.

                                        Rosse
                                   Well, I will thither.

                                        Macduff
Well, may you see things well done there: —
                                   adieu! —
Lest our old robes sit easier than our new!
                                   (II. iv. 35-38).

(b)   'Come, seeling Night,
Scarf up the tender eye of pitiful day'
                                   (III. ii. 47-48).

(c)   'Come, thick night,
And pall thee in the dunnest smoke of hell,
That my keen knife see not the wound it makes,
Nor heaven peep through the blanket of the dark
To cry, "Hold, hold!"'
                                   (I. v. 48-52).

Another group of images is concerned with babies, milk and breast-feeding. This was largely dealt with in the previous section ('Metaphors and Similes'), but a few more examples will not go amiss here. In I. vii, Macbeth, debating with himself whether or not to murder Duncan, says:

'And pity, like a naked new-born babe,

Striding the blast, or heaven's cherubin, horsed
Upon the sightless couriers of the air,
Shall blow the horrid deed in every eye'

(I. vii. 21-24).

And in IV. iii, when Malcolm is testing Macduff by pretending
to be villainous, these lines appear:

'Devotion, patience, courage, fortitude,
I have no relish of them; but abound
In the division of each several crime,
Acting in many ways. Nay, had I power, I should
Pour the sweet milk of concord into hell'

(IV. iii. 94-98).

In these passages, and in the examples given in the previous
section, the baby symbolises pity; the milk, humanity and
tenderness.

Yet another important group of images draws on the
related ideas of sickness and medicine. Significantly, they
come in the last three acts of the play, after Macbeth has been
crowned and Scotland is suffering from the disease of
tyranny — a disease which can only be cured, as fever was
thought to be cured in Shakespeare's day, by bleeding. (The
Elizabethans and Jacobeans thought that fever was caused by
an excess of certain bodily fluids, either blood itself or other
fluids carried in the blood; so drawing blood out of the body
by the process of bleeding a person was thought to cure him.)

Macbeth, himself, uses the imagery of sickness. In III. i.
106, he tells the Murderers that he wears his 'health but sickly'
so long as Banquo is alive. When he hears of Fleance's escape
in III. iv, he says in an aside, 'Then comes my fit again' (line
21). And, referring to Duncan in his grave, in III. ii. 23, he
says, 'After life's fitful fever he sleeps well', suggesting that
life itself is one long illness cured only by death. Macbeth

believes that Scotland's illness is caused by the presence of Malcolm and the English forces, and so he asks the Doctor in V. iii:

> 'What rhubarb, senna, or what purgative drug,
> Would scour these English hence?'
>
> (V. iii. 55-56).

The opposition, in contrast, see Macbeth's evil as the cause of Scotland's sickness, and Cathness refers to Malcolm as 'the medicine of the sickly weal' (V. ii. 27).

Finally, there is the imagery in which night and darkness are associated with evil, and day and daylight stand for what is good. Many scenes are set in gloomy light or darkness: there is the 'fog and filthy air' of I. i; Duncan approaches Inverness castle in I. vi as darkness is falling; Macbeth weighs up the consequences of killing him in I. vii, while it is dark; Duncan is murdered that same night in II. ii, and after Duncan's murder, the overcast sky is seen as the result of the sun's being strangled by darkness:

> 'by the clock 't is day,
> And yet dark night strangles the travelling lamp.
> Is 't night's predominance, or the day's shame,
> That darkness does the face of earth entomb,
> When living light should kiss it?'
>
> (II. iv. 6-10).

Banquo is killed as night is falling. The First Murderer's lines here are memorable:

> 'The west yet glimmers with some streaks of day:
> Now spurs the lated traveller apace,
> To gain the timely inn; and near approaches
> The subject of our watch.'
>
> (III. iii. 5-8).

Both Macbeth and Lady Macbeth invoke night to quash pity and fear, and to conceal their crimes:

Lady Macbeth

Come, thick night,
And pall thee in the dunnest smoke of hell,
That my keen knife see not the wound it makes,
Nor heaven peep through the blanket of the dark
To cry, "Hold, hold!"

(I. v. 48-52).

Macbeth

Come, seeling Night,
Scarf up the tender eye of pitiful day,
And, with thy bloody and invisible hand,
Cancel, and tear to pieces, that great bond
Which keeps me pale!

(III. ii. 47-51).

Macbeth refers to the Witches as 'black and midnight hags' (IV. i. 48), while earlier, Banquo had warned against the evil trickery of these 'instruments of darkness':

'oftentimes, to win us to our harm,
The instruments of darkness tell us truths,
Win us with honest trifles, to betray 's
In deepest consequence'

(I. iii. 123-126).

In the scene set in England (IV. iii), and in the last act, with the exception of the sleepwalking scene (V. i), light predominates over darkness, as the forces of good begin to overtake those of evil.

7.   Scene Studies

Act One Scene I

The year is 1040. On a piece of open land somewhere in
Scotland, during a storm and while a battle is raging in the
distance, three Witches discuss how they will meet Macbeth
upon a heath, before sunset, 'When the battle's lost and won'
(line 4).

The Witches exit, chanting:

> 'Fair is foul, and foul is fair:
> Hover through the fog and filthy air'
>
> (lines 10-11).

Commentary

Although very short in duration, this little scene is a powerful opening to the play. Shakespeare certainly knew how to
capture his audience's attention. An atmosphere of chaos,
confusion and suspense is created, and there is no mistaking
that evil influences are afoot.

Shakespeare's audience believed in witches and witchcraft.
Indeed, a witch-hunting mania obsessed Europe from about
1050 until the end of the seventeenth century. All witches
were supposed to have a mark somewhere on their bodies,
made by the devil, which was insensitive to pain. So one test
for a witch was to prick her all over to see if that spot could
be found. In another test, a suspected witch was thrown into
water. If the woman sank and drowned, she was supposed
innocent; if she stayed afloat, she was considered guilty and
therefore burned to death!

Witches were thought to have a whole host of powers
deriving from their relationship with the devil: to cause or

cure illness, or transfer it from one person to another; to raise storms; to produce impotence in men and sterility in women; to cause crops to fail, animals to be barren, and milk to go sour; to make people fall in and out of love through the use of charms; and to do harm or even bring about death with just a glance, or by sticking pins into a wax image of the victim.

They could supposedly become invisible and fly, sometimes with the aid of a broom. It was also alleged that witches could foretell the future, revive the dead, conjure up spirits, and transform themselves and others into animals, particularly into cats.

All this might sound like just so much hocus-pocus to us, but it was all very real to Shakespeare's audience at the Globe. The punishment for witchcraft in those days was to be burned at the stake, so you can see that witchcraft was taken very seriously indeed.

Shakespeare put the four Witch scenes in the play (I. i; I. iii; III. v*; and IV. i) because he knew the fascination which his audience, and King James I, had with the supernatural. And there may well have been other Witch scenes in the original *Macbeth* since the play as it appears in our texts (copied from the First Folio of 1623) seems to have been shortened, perhaps for the purposes of a court performance, from the version which Shakspeare wrote in 1606.

There is an important point that should be made right at the start of our study of the play: the Witches do not *make* Macbeth do anything. He is never under any spell cast by them. He has, as all Shakespeare's tragic heroes have, freedom of will. He is influenced by them, no doubt, and tricked by them, but the evil which results is of his own

---

* Most editors agree that Shakespeare didn't write this particular scene, but he may have asked someone to write it for him. See Commentary to III. v.

making. So, if the Witches are anything, they are an external symbol of that evil, not the cause of it.

Consider line 10, the Witches chant, 'Fair is foul, and foul is fair'. Literally, the line can be taken to mean that the day is fair because they know the right side will win the battle which is raging, and it is foul because of the bad weather. On another level, however, the chant outlines Macbeth's nature; he is both 'fair' and 'foul'. That is, he is courageous, noble, loves his wife, and has a highly developed sense of moral awareness; yet, coexisting with this 'fair' side to his character is something 'foul' — something which will first corrupt all the virtue in him and then destroy him — 'Vaulting ambition' (I. vii. 27).

Although these evil women are referred to as Witches in the *Dramatis Personae* and in the stage directions to the scenes in which they appear, elsewhere in the play (with the exception of I. iii. 6) they are called the 'weird sisters', possibly because their powers are considerably more potent and they themselves are very different in type from the women (usually the victims of gossip) who were labelled witches in Shakespeare's day.

Act One Scene II

At a camp near Forres, King Duncan, with his sons Malcolm and Donalbain, hears a report of the battle from a wounded sergeant (though he is called Captain in the stage directions). The Captain says that things stood in the balance for a while, neither army gaining the advantage. Then one of the rebel leaders, Macdonwald, received reinforcements of mercenaries from Ireland and the Hebrides (an archipelago of about 500 islands west of Scotland).

At first luck seemed to be on Macdonwald's side, but Macbeth was undaunted. Ignoring the odds, he carved his way forward with his sword until he faced the traitor, and then he cut him open from his navel to his throat. Following this, Macdonwald's troops retreated, but the King of Norway launched a fresh attack. Macbeth and Banquo did not lose heart, however, and fought back twice as hard as though they wished to swim in blood. At this point in his narration, the Captain almost faints and he is taken off to receive medical treatment.

Rosse and Angus, two Scottish nobles loyal to the King, enter. They bring news from Fife of the uprising. There, the Thane of Cawdor, backed by the King of Norway's large army, launched a massive attack, but Macbeth triumphed yet again. He fought in hand-to-hand combat with the treacherous Thane and took him prisoner.

Now the King of Norway is suing for peace, and he has been forbidden to bury his dead until he has given ten thousand dollars in reparation. Duncan orders the immediate execution of the Thane of Cawdor, and he tells Rosse to ride out and greet Macbeth with Cawdor's title.

Commentary

The main purpose of this scene is to allow Macbeth's virtue to be defined. His reputation as a valiant warrior, a loyal subject and a truly noble and honourable man is made to precede his appearance in the play. The Captain describes him as 'brave Macbeth (well he deserves that name)' in line 16; then he gives his account of how Macbeth single-handedly tipped the balance of the battle in favour of the King's forces by slaying the 'merciless Macdonwald':

'Disdaining Fortune, with his brandished steel,
Which smoked with bloody execution,
Like Valour's minion, carved out his passage,
Till he faced the slave;
Which ne'er shook hands, nor bade farewell to him,

> Till he unseamed him from the nave to the chaps,
> And fixed his head upon our battlements'
>
> (I. ii. 17-23).

Macbeth dealt with his opponent ruthlessly and summarily, because he was a traitor and didn't deserve to be shown the courtesies of war ('ne'er shook hands, nor bade farewell to him', line 21).

Duncan's plaudit at line 24, 'O valiant cousin! worthy gentleman!', tells the audience something else they need to know about Macbeth: he is related to the King. The word 'cousin' was used rather loosely in those days to describe a variety of family relationships (Olivia calls Sir Toby Belch 'cousin' in *Twelfth Night,* though he is actually her uncle). Later on, in I. vii. 13, Macbeth describes himself as Duncan's 'kinsman and his subject', but we get no further in discovering just how they are related.

Rosse flatteringly refers to Macbeth as 'Bellona's bridegroom' (line 56), figuratively marrying him to the Roman goddess of war, and therefore declaring Macbeth to be a great warrior. But Rosse's remark in lines 55-57 is interesting in another way:

> 'The Thane of Cawdor, began a dismal conflict;
> Till that Bellona's bridegroom, lapped in proof,
> Confronted him with self-comparisons.'

The phrase 'lapped in proof' means clothed in proven and trusted armour. Clothing forms an important part of the recurring imagery of the play (see Section 6 iii, 'The Recurrent Imagery of *Macbeth*'). Notice how from I. iii onwards, the idea conveyed is of Macbeth wearing clothing that is someone else's and which doesn't fit him well, but here, where his courage and loyalty seem beyond question, his clothing suits him admirably and is described as a mark of his honour. It is interesting that after Macbeth's honour has been lost, he appears to have difficulty getting into his armour (see V. iii. 33-58).

But why does Shakespeare heap praise in this scene on a man who is to become, after all, the great villain of the play? Why build him up to bring him crashing down? Most Elizabethan and Jacobean audiences were quite prepared to accept the idea that a tragedy could simply be a play about the downfall of an evil man with no redeeming qualities whatsoever (*The Jew of Malta* by Christopher Marlowe, 1564-93, is a good example of this, with its odious central character, Barabas). However this did not suit Shakespeare at all. So, with the exception of Richard III, all Shakespeare's tragic heroes and heroines start out as noble and virtuous souls, who then veer towards damnation when some imperfection in them surfaces. (This point is dealt with more fully in Section 5, '*Macbeth* as a Tragedy'.) Shakespeare didn't want our feelings towards Macbeth to remain static; that is the point. He saw his tragic heroes as a mixture of good and bad. Consequently our response to them, to Macbeth, fluctuates. We admire him in this scene; deplore his actions, though still like him a little in Acts II and III; detest him in Act IV, after the cowardly killing of Lady Macduff and her family; and admire him again for his courage and stoicism in the latter part of Act V (from V. v. 46 onwards).

Act One Scene III

The Witches are waiting for Macbeth on a heath, while there is thunder in the air. After some discussion about what they have been doing since they last met, the weird sisters hear a drum being beaten. Knowing Macbeth is on the way, they join hands and dance in a circle. Their charm is now ready.

Macbeth enters with Banquo and says: 'So foul and fair a day I have not seen' (line 38; see Commentary to I. i for 'foul and fair'). Banquo notices the Witches. Their strange appearance, particularly their beards, makes him suspect that they are not human. Macbeth demands to know who they are, and they greet him as Thane of Glamis, Thane of Cawdor, and, 'Macbeth! that shalt be king hereafter' (line 50). Banquo asks Macbeth why he appears so shocked and frightened by this news ('Good sir, why do you start, and seem to fear/ Things that do sound so fair?' lines 51-52). But Macbeth is lost in his own thoughts; so Banquo asks the weird sisters what the future holds in store for him. They reply that he will be the father of kings, but not King himself. Macbeth, believing the Thane of Cawdor to be alive, orders the Witches to say how they came by this strange news, but they vanish into the air.

Rosse and Angus enter. The King's pleasure is conveyed to Macbeth for his part in putting down the rebellion, and the Thane of Cawdor's title is bestowed upon him. Macbeth, confused, replies, 'The Thane of Cawdor lives: why do you dress me/ In borrowed robes?' (lines 108-109). Angus explains that the Thane of Cawdor was part of the rebel faction and so he has been put to death.

In an aside, Macbeth wonders at the way the Witches' prophecy is coming true and his thoughts turn to the crown. He asks Banquo if he hopes his sons will become kings, but Banquo is cautious, replying that these evil, unearthly creatures often win our trust in small ways only to trick us when it comes to something important. He then turns to speak to Rosse and Angus.

Now, Macbeth reveals his thoughts in a soliloquy. He cannot decide whether the Witches wish him well or otherwise. If their intentions are bad, why would they fulfil the first part of their prophecy by making him Thane of Cawdor without his asking for it? And if they mean only good, why should his thoughts turn to the possibility of murdering Duncan? After all, if fate wants him to be King, then he will be, no matter what he does.

Banquo, observing Macbeth's musings, remarks to the others how deep in thought he seems, and compares the honours the King has bestowed on Macbeth to new clothes that do not fit very well until they have been worn in.

Macbeth's meditation ends with the thought that the right opportunity to do something always comes along, no matter how difficult things may appear. He thanks the others for waiting for him, and asks Banquo to think about what has happened and to discuss it with him later.

Commentary

In line 37, just before Macbeth and Banquo enter, the Witches chant in unison, 'the charm's wound up' (i.e. 'the charm is ready'). Are we to assume from this that Macbeth is to be put under some sort of spell? No, for if this were the case then he wouldn't be acting freely and we would not be entitled to condemn his behaviour in the subsequent scenes. Shakespeare wants us to know that from the first to last Macbeth acts through choice; he is not compelled, by the Witches or anyone else, to do what he does. The charm referred to here is more likely to be their supernatural ability to peep into the future, and at the same time into Macbeth's mind. Thus when they greet Macbeth with promises of future glory, we can assume that they are merely putting into words what they have read in his thoughts, not promising something as the result of working their magic. This interpretation fits in nicely with what happens a little later on, in lines 50-52:

3 Witch
All hail, Macbeth! that shalt be king hereafter.

Banquo

Good Sir, why do you start, and seem to fear
Things that do sound so fair?

Macbeth is startled and frightened by the suggestion that he
will become King because secretly he has already considered
the possibility of usurping the throne by murdering Duncan.
The Witches, of course, don't mention murder, but Macbeth
does (lines 139-140):

'My thought, whose murder yet is but fantastical,
Shakes so my single state of man.'

It's a subject that has been locked in his mind for a long time;
all the Witches have done is to show that he can succeed in it,
or so he now thinks.

Just as the Witches can foretell Macbeth's future, so they
can do the same for Banquo. In lines 58-60, while Macbeth is
lost in thought, Banquo asks the weird sisters:

'If you can look into the seeds of time,
And say which grain will grow, and which will not,
Speak then to me'.

The Third Witch obliges and tells him: 'Thou shalt get kings,
though thou be none' (line 67). But Banquo is wise; he knows
the Witches are evil and that their prophecies are designed to
confuse, confound and damn people's lives, rather than
benefit them:

'But 't is strange:
And oftentimes, to win us to our harm,
The instruments of darkness tell us truths,
Win us with honest trifles, to betray 's
In deepest consequence'

(I. iii. 122-126).

Banquo calls the Witches 'The instruments of darkness', meaning that they are evil, unearthly creatures, linked to the devil. Throughout the play, darkness symbolises evil and light symbolises good (see Section 6 iii, 'The Recurrent Imagery of *Macbeth*'). By making Banquo wise as well as virtuous (see III. i. 48-53), Shakespeare was deliberately flattering King James I, a distant relative of Banquo's. (Though not written specifically for James I, it is generally acknowledged that *Macbeth* received its première performance before him in 1606, at the Palace of Whitehall.)

Despite the obvious wisdom of Banquo's words in lines 122-126, Macbeth doesn't heed the warning. He goes on placing trust in these malevolent creatures right up until the very last moments of his life; only then does he realise he's been tricked by them:

'... be these juggling fiends no more believed,
That palter with us in a double sense,
That keep the work of promise to our ear,
And break it to our hope'

(V. viii. 19-22).

Could it be then that Macbeth is gullible or credulous? That is almost certainly oversimplifying things, for Macbeth is not stupid. The point is that from the moment he begins to seriously contemplate murdering Duncan (I. iii), he is wracked by feelings of guilt and he knows that he is on the verge of selling his soul to the devil. Banquo guesses the Witches might trick him, because they are on opposing sides: he is virtuous, while they are evil forces. Macbeth on the other hand, feels he is in league with them and that they are united by a common bond of evil, which is one reason why he trusts them. Equally, because the Witches can read his thoughts, they tell Macbeth precisely what he wants to hear. He experiences periods of doubt and failing courage, so it is scarcely surprising then that he should trust the Witches who speak to him so reassuringly.

In this scene, the Witches tell Macbeth what he wants to hear most — that he will be King. But they don't tell him how this will be accomplished. Which leaves Macbeth in the classic situation of a Shakespearean tragic hero — with a choice between good and evil. He can ignore his conscience and murder Duncan, or, if it is inevitable that he will become King whatever he does, leave everything to fate. The first option is considered in lines 134-142:

> 'why do I yield to that suggestion
> Whose horrid image doth unfix my hair,
> And make my seated heart knock at my ribs
> Against the use of nature? Present fears
> Are less than horrible imaginings.
> My thought, whose murder yet is but fantastical,
> Shakes so my single state of man, that function
> Is smothered in surmise, and nothing is,
> But what is not.'

Macbeth, at this stage at least, is no hardened villain. He thinks about murdering Duncan, but recoils from the idea in horror ('function/ Is smothered in surmise', i.e. the thought of committing the crime is horrible enough to keep him from doing it). He is no coward: just look at the way he dealt with the treacherous Macdonwald (I. ii. 9-23). Essentially, he is a virtuous, courageous, honourable man who has one corrosive vice; an obsessive ambition, which will eventually eat into his fineness like acid into bright metal.

In lines 143-144, it almost seems as if Macbeth might settle for the second option which is to leave everything in the hands of fate:

> 'If Chance will have me king, why, Chance may crown
>   me,

Without my stir.'

At first glance this appears commendable, as if he has decided not to murder Duncan, and we might be tempted to assume from this that it is Lady Macbeth's influence (from I. v. onwards) which breaks this resolve. Not so! Look at lines 146-147:

> 'Come what come may,
> Time and the hour runs through the roughest day.'

Translated, this means: 'Whatever happens, an opportunity always presents itself to get something done, no matter how difficult the situation is.' Effectively, he is leaving his options open. If fate doesn't make him King, then he will simply wait until the moment is right to murder Duncan. Lady Macbeth will be responsible, perhaps, for speeding the murder up, but she doesn't corrupt her husband. As we can see here, he is making his own way towards damnation.

Just before the scene ends, Macbeth turns to Banquo and, out of the hearing of Rosse and Angus, says:

> 'Think upon what hath chanced, and at more time,
> The interim having weighed it, let us speak
> Our free hearts each to other'
>
> (I. iii. 153-155).

Macbeth wants Banquo to think about the Witches' prophecy and to discuss it with him later. Why? The obvious answer is that this is another expression of Macbeth's guilty conscience. Of course, he has no intention of telling Banquo that he is thinking of murdering Duncan. Rather, he just wants to talk things over in more general terms because the matter is weighing heavily on his mind. Or could it be that he wants to gauge from Banquo, a man he respects for his wisdom, what his chances are of becoming King if he remains passive? Both interpretations seem possible, and neither necessarily excludes the other.

The main recurrent imagery of clothing appears again in this scene, after its introduction in I. ii (see Commentary to I. ii). The main examples are dealt with in Section 6 iii, 'The Recurrent Imagery of *Macbeth*', so we need not re-examine them here. However, one subtle example of the clothing imagery, not mentioned in Section 6, deserves attention. It occurs in line 112:

> 'Whether he was combined
> With those of Norway, or did line the rebel
> With hidden help and vantage'
>
> (I. iii. 111-113).

In the expression 'line the rebel', Angus is saying that the Thane of Cawdor may have strengthened the rebel forces in a covert way, just as the lining of a coat strengthens it without being seen from the outside.

Act One Scene IV

At Forres Castle Duncan asks his son Malcolm if the Thane of Cawdor's execution has been carried out as he had ordered. He is told that Cawdor confessed his treason, begged the King's pardon, and went to his death with great courage and dignity. Duncan considers the difficulty of telling from a man's face what is going on in his mind:

> 'There's no art
> To find the mind's construction in the face:
> He was a gentleman on whom I built
> An absolute trust — '
>
> (I. iv. 11-14).

In mid-sentence Macbeth enters, along with Banquo, Rosse,

and Angus. Duncan continues speaking, straight away switching his attention to Macbeth and praising him loudly. He says that Macbeth has achieved so much in such a short time that his gratitude cannot keep pace with the debt he owes him. He wishes that Macbeth had deserved less so that he might have been able to reward him adequately. Duncan acknowledges that more is due to Macbeth for his loyal service than he can ever repay. In reply, Macbeth says that his service and loyalty to his King is its own reward; adding that Duncan must accept that service as his rightful due, for he is owed love and honour by his subjects. Duncan welcomes Macbeth and says he will see him prosper, then turns to Banquo, embracing him and saying that he deserves equal thanks.

At this point, Duncan is overwhelmed to the point of tears. Charged with emotion he announces to everyone that he has chosen Malcolm, his eldest son, to be his successor and that from now onwards Malcolm will be called the Prince of Cumberland. Duncan then says he will go to Macbeth's castle at Inverness, and Macbeth decides to ride ahead to give his wife the joyful news of the royal visit.

Now, in an aside, Macbeth considers Malcolm's advancement to Prince of Cumberland and Duncan's heir, realising that this is a serious obstacle in his way to the throne and that he must find a way around it or his ambitions will be thwarted. He implores the stars to stop shining so that darkness might hide his wicked desires; at the same time he wishes that his eyes might not see the cruel deed his hands must do. Macbeth leaves the stage.

Meanwhile, Duncan has been conferring with the others and agrees with Banquo that Macbeth is valiant, comparing the good reports he has had of Macbeth to the abundant meat and drink of a banquet. He tells the others he will follow Macbeth to Inverness, knowing that Macbeth is thinking of

his welfare by riding ahead in order to prepare a welcome.
Duncan pronounces Macbeth to be a kinsman without equal.

Commentary

The fact that those sent by Duncan to order the execution
of the Thane of Cawdor have not yet returned, indicates that
little time has passed since the end of I. ii. Malcolm's
eloquent description of Cawdor's death in lines 5-11 is praise
for a man who lived corruptly but redeemed himself by dying
nobly:

> 'very frankly he confessed his treasons,
> Implored your highness' pardon, and set forth
> A deep repentance. Nothing in his life
> Became him like the leaving it: he died
> As one that had been studied in his death,
> To throw away the dearest thing he owed
> As 't were a careless trifle.'

Why does Shakespeare introduce this inconsistency in
Cawdor's character? If he was a villain, an evil, treacherous,
self-serving man, why are we made to admire the noble
manner of his death? Shakespeare is preparing us for
Macbeth's entrance a few lines later on, and Cawdor's death
reminds us of something about Macbeth: that a sense of
honour and nobility can co-exist with great evil in a man. So,
outward appearances can be deceptive; Duncan makes this
point immediately after Malcolm has finished speaking:

> 'There's no art
> To find the mind's construction in the face'
>
> (I. iv. 11-12).

A phrase crosses our minds from earlier on in the play, 'Fair
is foul, and foul is fair' (I. i. 10). Men like Macbeth and

Cawdor are a deceptive mixture of opposing moral and immoral clements; the fair and the foul, the noble and the ignoble.

Nevertheless, Duncan is too trusting. This becomes more obvious in II. i, when he retires to bed in Macbeth's castle at Inverness with no more than two attendants to guard him. There is considerable irony when Duncan says that Cawdor was 'a gentleman on whom I built/ An absolute trust' (lines 13-14) and at that very moment Macbeth enters — another man on whom Duncan is about to place 'an absolute trust'. Duncan hasn't learnt to be more cautious in his judgements after his mistake over the Thane of Cawdor. He seems too ready to take others at face value.

Macbeth's speech at lines 23-27, in which he emphasises the King's right to receive and the subject's duty to give service which maintains the harmony of the state, sounds forced and a little too glib:

>   'Your highness' part
> Is to receive our duties: and our duties
> Are, to your throne and state, children and servants;
> Which do but what they should, by doing everything
> Safe toward your love and honour.'

This is a royal occasion, a gathering of the court, and Macbeth would be expected to speak formally, even though Duncan is his relative ('kinsman'). Nevertheless, we know Macbeth well enough by now to recognise the self-conscious tone in his words here. His thoughts are now less on serving his monarch than on serving his own interests.

Duncan may be too trusting, but he certainly is gracious (and Macbeth testifies to his virtues himself, later on at I. vii. 16-20). Using a gardening metaphor, he assures Macbeth that he will advance him:

'I have begun to plant thee, and will labour
To make thee full of growing'

(I. iv. 28-29).

We take this to be no idle promise, for Duncan has already shown his gratitude for Macbeth's service against the rebel forces in a tangible way, by giving him the late Thane of Cawdor's title (and with a title in those days went land). But if Macbeth imagines for one moment here that Duncan is about to pronounce him his heir (and we remember Macbeth's words at I. iii. 143, 'If Chance will have me king, why, Chance may crown me'), then he is soon to be disappointed; fate is not going to make things that easy for him. Duncan offers thanks to Banquo and then turning to the assembled lords and thanes, with tears of joy in his eyes (lines 33-35), names his eldest son Malcolm, Prince of Cumberland and his heir. He then gives the appearance of trying to please everyone:

'honour must
Not, unaccompanied, invest him only,
But signs of nobleness, like stars, shall shine
On all deservers'

(I. iv. 39-42).

Duncan seems to be man more prone to emotion than cool, hard reasoning. He has just come close to losing his throne to the ambitious Thane of Cawdor; so this should be a time for caution, not for waving a blank cheque of gratitude in the air to whet an appetite for power in his followers, as he seems to be doing at lines 39-42. He is a virtuous King, a fair and generous King, but perhaps an unwise one.

He then announces that he will honour Macbeth by going to stay at Inverness Castle, giving Macbeth the perfect opportunity to overthrow him, having only moments earlier given him the motive for doing so (Malcolm's promotion to heir apparent). A cautious and wise King would have sensed the possibility of Macbeth becoming dangerously disappointed at the news of Malcolm's elevation, when he himself deserved so much for preserving the realm. Duncan's speech, naming Malcolm his heir and thereby placing yet another obstacle in Macbeth's way to the throne, angers Macbeth and strengthens his resolve to do whatever is necessary. Gone is the agonising and soul-searching that we saw in I. iii; now the sharp monosyllabic words of the verse pound like dagger blows:

> 'Stars, hide your fires!
> Let not light see my black and deep desires;
> The eye wink at the hand, yet let that be,
> Which the eye fears, when it is done, to see'
>
> (I. iv. 50-53).

What the eye (and so the conscience) fears, Macbeth is saying, has got to be done. It is not that Macbeth is now free of his conscience (he never really is throughout the play), but that he is more determined to act now. Macbeth realises that conscience must not be allowed to hold him back; he must detach himself from it and the feelings of guilt and shame which it prompts long enough for Duncan's murder to be committed — only then, when this has been achieved, should he try to come to terms with himself.

Act One Scene V

At Inverness Lady Macbeth is reading a letter from her husband. He tells her how he met the Witches on the last day of his successful campaign against the rebels, and that since then he has learned, from a reliable source, of their supernatural powers. He recalls how they vanished into the air when he wanted to question them further and that while he stood in wonder at this, messengers arrived from the King, greeting him as the Thane of Cawdor. Macbeth explains that the weird sisters had addressed him by this title and predicted that he would one day wear the crown. All this, Macbeth says, he is telling her so that she can share in the good news.

Lady Macbeth responds by saying that although her husband is now Thane of Glamis and Cawdor, she fears he is too gentle and not ruthless enough to become king by assassination:

> 'Yet I do fear thy nature:
> It is too full o' the milk of human kindness
> To catch the nearest way'
>
> (I. v. 14-16).

She knows that he wants to be great and that he is not without ambition, but he lacks the evil nature which is required; he wants to get ahead by honourable means preferably, but he doesn't mind winning unfairly. Great Glamis, she says, you want something that can only be got one way — by a certain deed (i.e. murder) — and yet you are scared to do what has to be done. She urges Macbeth in her thoughts to hurry to her so that she may stir him to action. She vows to inspire him with brave words so as to overcome the inhibitions which prevent him from seizing the crown — the crown which fate and supernatural powers seem to have chosen as his destiny.

A Messenger enters, interrupting Lady Macbeth's speech. He announces that the King will arrive at Inverness that evening. At first she thinks he is crazy and asks where Macbeth is, saying that if it were true, he would have warned her to get things ready. The Messenger explains that Macbeth is on his way and that a fellow-servant had ridden ahead to bring the news of the royal visit. The Messenger leaves.

Lady Macbeth knows that Duncan will never leave Inverness Castle alive. She calls on the spirits to rid her of feminine tenderness and to fill her with cruelty. She prays that conscience may not stand in her way and asks the spirits who attend on murders to turn her breast-milk to gall. Lady Macbeth urges night to come and hide from her eyes and heaven's the wound her knife will make in Duncan.

Macbeth enters, and Lady Macbeth greets him rapturously as 'Great Glamis! worthy Cawdor!/ Greater than both, by the all-hail, hereafter!' (lines 52-53). She is so overwhelmed by what has been promised that she feels it is already theirs. Macbeth greets her tenderly and tells her again that Duncan will arrive that evening, with the intention of leaving the next morning, but she says that he will never see the morning sun. She can read fear in her husband's face and worries that others will see it as well and begin to wonder. So she tells Macbeth to look and behave normally that evening among their guests. Lady Macbeth says that she will arrange Duncan's murder, and once again she tells her husband to play the innocent and not to give himself away by showing his feelings.

Commentary

However much we may despise Macbeth and Lady Macbeth for what they intend to do, we cannot miss, nor can we fail to admire, the strong bond of affection that exists between them. We feel it in the letter at the beginning of this scene, where it is clear that Macbeth doesn't have this dream of greatness for himself alone; he wants very much to share it with his wife:

'This have I thought good to deliver thee, my dearest partner of greatness, that thou might'st not lose the dues of rejoicing, by being ignorant of what greatness is promised thee'

(I. v. 8-11).

Later on, when Macbeth enters, the first words we hear him speak directly to his wife indicate his love for her:

> 'My dearest love,
> Duncan comes here tonight'

(I. v. 56-57).

This tenderness stands in sharp contrast to the wealth of cruel feeling in the play, and ultimately it deepens the tragedy for us by giving it a much more personal dimension. We see it in other places: Lady Macbeth coming to her husband's defence by fainting at II. iii. 115, when he is in a tight spot after Duncan's murder; and again when she makes excuses for him during the Banquet scene, from III. iv. 53 onwards; then there is Macbeth's powerful speech of dejection towards the end of the play when he has learned of his wife's death (V. v. 17-28).

In the scene we are discussing here, what comes across very clearly, emphasising Lady Macbeth's love for her husband, is her deep understanding of his nature. She knows he is gentle: 'too full o' the milk of human kindness' (line 15); that he is ambitious without being ruthless, and that he is basically an honourable man:

> 'Thou wouldst be great;
> Art not without ambition, but without
> The illness should attend it: what thou wouldst highly,
> That wouldst thou holily'

(I. v. 16-19).

And Lady Macbeth knows two other things about her husband very well: firstly, that she has the power to influence him:

'Hie thee hither,
That I may pour my spirits in thine ear,
And chastise with the valour of my tongue
All that impedes thee from the golden round'

(I. v. 23-26).

Secondly, she knows that he is not a good liar, and that his face mirrors all his thoughts:

'Your face, my thane, is as a book'

(I. v. 60).

Some may argue that Lady Macbeth is sufficiently evil to despise her husband's virtues, seeing them as detestable weaknesses in his character, but there is really no direct evidence for this, here or elsewhere in the play. However there is little doubt that Lady Macbeth is evil; a point which is emphasised three ways in this scene. Firstly, there is her contempt for religion, implied in the lines:

'what thou wouldst highly,
That wouldst thou holily'

(I. v. 18-19).

Secondly, there is the grotesque plea to the spirits to 'unsex' her, to fill her with cruelty, to remove all capacity for remorse from her, and, using an image which stresses her unnaturalness, to take all tenderness from her and fill her with bitterness instead:

'Come to my woman's breasts,
And take my milk for gall, you murdering ministers'
(I. v. 45-46; see Section 6 ii, 'Metaphors and Similes').

Then thirdly, when Macbeth enters, her greeting to him is almost an exact echo of the Witches' greeting at I. III. 48-50:

'Great Glamis! worthy Cawdor!

Greater than both, by the all hail, hereafter!'

(I. v. 52-53).

This last point is an obvious ploy of Shakespeare's to make Lady Macbeth sound like the Witches, so that instinctively we associate her evil nature with theirs.

Lady Macbeth may be her husband's equal in terms of ambition, but she is more ruthless and determined than he is. Macbeth's letter to her at the beginning of the scene makes no mention of murder, nonetheless her thoughts run to it soon enough. She is caught off guard for a moment by the Messenger who announces that Duncan will arrive at Inverness that evening; she hadn't expected an opportunity for the murder to present itself so soon, but she is undaunted nevertheless. She is totally unsqueamish and visualises herself plunging a dagger into Duncan:

'Come, thick night,
And pall thee in the dunnest smoke of hell,
That my keen knife see not the wound it makes'

(I. v. 48-50).

She is absolutely determined that Duncan will die that very night:

'O! never
Shall sun that morrow see!'

(I. v. 58-59; 'sun' means the King).

Macbeth, at the end of the scene, is still hesitating: 'We will speak further' (line 69). He wants encouragement and re-assurance; his nerves are showing badly and Lady Macbeth has to tell him not to give himself away:

'Only look up clear;
To alter favour ever is to fear'

(I. v. 69-70).

She is now in control, and has told Macbeth to leave everything to her:

> 'you shall put
> This night's great business into my despatch'
> (I. v. 65-66).

Lady Macbeth has no doubts, misgivings, or scruples at this stage (although her conscience returns to haunt her in V. i); she knows Macbeth is wavering but she wants to be queen too much to leave things to chance and so she becomes the driving force. She is fixed and insensitive in her purpose, and having started out towards her objective, is completely incapable of turning back.

(A less charitable view of the relationship between Macbeth and Lady Macbeth is taken elsewhere in this book, for example, in the character study of Lady Macbeth on pages 204-210, and in the Specimen Essay Answer to Question 12 on pages 233-236. It is up to the student to decide which interpretation he or she prefers.)

Act One Scene VI

King Duncan, with his sons Malcolm and Donalbain, Banquo and other lords, arrives at Inverness Castle. Duncan comments on the pleasant position of the place and the agreeably fresh air. Banquo agrees, observing that house-martins (birds of summer) have nested in every part of the building and they only do this where the air is sweet.

Lady Macbeth enters and bids her guests welcome. Duncan says that his subjects' love is sometimes tedious, although he is still grateful for it, but the inconvenience he is putting Lady Macbeth to now is intended to show his regard for her. She replies that she cannot do enough to thank Duncan for the great honours he has bestowed on her family, both in the past and recently. Duncan asks where Macbeth is, saying that he had hoped to arrive at Inverness before him but that Macbeth's love has spurred him on to get there first. He then announces that he is Lady Macbeth's guest for the night. Very formally Lady Macbeth replies that she, her servants and everything she possesses are his to command. Taking Lady Macbeth's hand, Duncan asks to be taken to his host, professing his love for Macbeth and promising to continue showing him favour.

Commentary

This short scene stands in marked contrast to what has gone before. We have had the raging battle, the Witches, and the 'fog and filthy air' of I. i; Macbeth's dark machinations in I. iii and I. iv; Lady Macbeth summoning 'thick night' and 'the dunnest smoke of hell' to hide her evil intent in I. v; but now the tension is relaxed for a moment. The scenery is pleasant, the air salubrious, and Duncan's easy conversation with Banquo (about the tranquil beauty of Inverness Castle) contrasts with the murderous and intense scheming of the Macbeths in the previous scene. But there is considerable irony here as well, in both Duncan's and Banquo's remarks before Lady Macbeth enters. Duncan says:

'This castle hath a pleasant seat; the air
Nimbly and sweetly recommends itself
Unto our gentle senses'

(I. vi. 1-3).

But we, the audience, remember just how wrong Duncan can be in judging appearances (i.e. the Thane of Cawdor, and Macbeth: see I. iv. 11-14, and I. iv. 54-58). Banquo's description of the castle as the 'procreant cradle' of the house-martin (line 8) creates an image of fertility, but the word 'martin' meant 'dupe' in Shakespeare's day, someone easily fooled by appearances; the idea being that the castle invites a false sense of security. Both Duncan and Banquo are horribly wrong. Inverness Castle, like its tenants, is both 'fair and foul' — fair on the outside yet housing foul treachery on the inside. While house-martins peacefully nest on the castle's external walls, inside, a raven 'croaks the fatal entrance of Duncan' (I. v. 36-37); rather than the castle inspiring fertility, we recall Lady Macbeth in the previous scene summoning the spirits to unsex her and to replace her breast-milk with gall (I. v. 39, and 45-46). Images of evil, blackness and death created in the last scene are now juxtaposed with other images of harmony, peace and fertility, producing a powerful sense of irony. And the irony deepens the sensation of foreboding within us.

Lady Macbeth enters to greet Duncan. Macbeth is not with her; yet Duncan knows that Macbeth has arrived before him and he is not suspicious. He asks where Macbeth is, but Lady Macbeth dodges the question at lines 25-28. Duncan is too trusting, and his remark about Macbeth's 'great love, sharp as his spur' (line 23) produces shivers as an image of death, like a dagger plunged into soft flesh. Macbeth, we assume, is too nervous to appear, fearing, as Lady Macbeth warned him in I. v, that his guilt will be seen written on his face (see I. v. 60-61). Another explanation for Macbeth failing to appear in this scene is that his conscience is troubling him and he is isolated by guilty reflections, brooding alone, as we see him do at the beginning of the next scene. As Duncan takes Lady Macbeth's hand and is led off to meet his host, irony is felt again; for Duncan suspects nothing and yet we know he is being conducted to his death.

Act One Scene VII

A banquet is in progress at Inverness Castle, and servants

pass across the stage carrying dishes of food. Macbeth enters, having left the banquet, and in a soliloquy of 28 lines he thinks about the plot to murder Duncan. If it could be done without any further consequences, he meditates, then it would be best to get it over with quickly. He seems prepared to risk the damnation of his soul in the next life if Duncan's death alone could guarantee him success in this life. Macbeth considers how people get what they deserve in this world and how, if by example we teach others to murder, we should not be surprised if in turn we become murder victims. He continues in this way, weighing up the various reasons why he should spare the King's life, especially in view of the fact that Duncan is entrusted to him in two ways. Firstly, Macbeth is his relative and his subject — both strong reasons against murdering him and secondly, since Duncan is Macbeth's guest at Inverness, he should be given Macbeth's protection. Also, Duncan is a good King, gentle and virtuous, and for this reason his murder would be impossible to justify on any grounds. The only thing spurring Macbeth on is ambition, but that in itself, he knows, is dangerous and can lead to a man's downfall.

Lady Macbeth enters and tells her husband that Duncan has almost finished eating. She wants to know why he has left the banquet, saying that Duncan has asked for him. Macbeth announces that he is going no further with the murder plan, for Duncan has honoured him recently and he has earned the respect of all sorts of people — a respect that he wants to enjoy now and not throw away so soon. Lady Macbeth scornfully asks if his ambition was merely a display of bravado, for now, she says, he is showing weakness and fear. She taunts him, saying that from now on she will assume that his love for her is a weak thing as well. She asks if he is afraid to match his desire with the action necessary to achieve it, and accuses him of cowardice, comparing Macbeth to the cat in a proverb who wanted fish but didn't dare get his paws wet. Macbeth silences her, saying that he is as courageous and daring as any man, but she asks bitterly why he revealed his plans to her in the first place if he is now backing out. Macbeth was only a man, she insists, when he had the courage to commit the murder; ambition is the very measure of a man. Before, she points out, the time and place were wrong for such a deed and yet Macbeth wanted to arrange these to suit his purpose; now when he has the ideal opportunity, he is losing his nerve.

In a gruesome image, Lady Macbeth says that she knows what it is to love a baby sucking milk at her breast, but she would have pulled the nipple from his mouth and dashed his brains out if she had sworn as strongly to do this as Macbeth has sworn to kill Duncan. Macbeth is worried that they might fail, but Lady Macbeth mocks the idea; if he has courage, she tells him, they won't fail. Then she reveals her plan.

The murder will be done later that night while Duncan is sleeping deeply after his hard day's journey. First she will ply the guards of his bedchamber with drink, to make it easy for them to get to him and then, when the guards wake up, the blame for Duncan's murder will be put on them. Macbeth tells her to bear only sons, for her fearless nature is better suited to rearing male children. He adds the idea of using the grooms' daggers and smearing them with blood to cast suspicion on them. Lady Macbeth then explains that when the murder is discovered they must give the impression of feeling great sorrow so that no one will suspect them. At this, Macbeth says that his mind is made up; he will do the deed, and deceive his guests in the meantime with a happy face.

Commentary

At the beginning of the scene, Shakespeare creates an

obvious contrast of situation and mood: while waiters cross the stage carrying dishes of food for Duncan and his attendant lords, who are merrily wining and dining in another room, Macbeth is caught up in guilty and fearful reflections (a similar contrast is achieved in I. iv and, possibly, in I. vi). Unable to choose between good and evil, Macbeth is trapped in miserable isolation, missing out on the fruits of either course of action.

In his great soliloquy, we see Macbeth gnawing away at his own soul. Here he feels that if by his act of murder this whole episode came to a neat conclusion, with no further consequences resulting from it, he could face the prospect of eternal damnation calmly:

'If it were done when 'tis done, then 't were well
It were done quickly: if the assassination
Could trammel up the consequence, and catch
With his surcease success; that but this blow
Might be the be-all and the end-all here,
But here upon this bank and shoal of time,
We'd jump the life to come'

(I. vii. 1-7).

But he is filled with the realisation that murdering the King will mark the start of his reckless venture, not the end of it. Murdering the King, God's regent on earth, will not only damn his eternal soul, it will also bring retribution here on earth — 'in these cases,/ We still have judgement here,' (lines 7-8) — and so Macbeth devises excuses why he should not carry out his plan. He says: (i) that we get our just desserts in this world, and teaching the art of bloodshed will only make us victims of our own lessons (lines 7-12); (ii) that as Duncan is his King and relative, he is entitled to protection (lines 12-14); (iii) that as Duncan's host, he should be shutting his murderer out, not bearing the assassin's knife himself (lines

14-16); and (iv) that Duncan has been a good and virtuous King (lines 16-25).

This last excuse for not murdering Duncan deserves greater analysis, for it draws Macbeth back to the question of damnation, which he claimed to be willing to risk. Perhaps it weighs more heavily on him than it at first seemed:

> 'Besides, this Duncan
> Hath borne his faculties so meek, hath been
> So clear in his great office, that his virtues
> Will plead like angels, trumpet-tongued, against
> The deep damnation of his taking-off;
> And pity, like a naked new-born babe,
> Striding the blast, or heaven's cherubin, horsed
> Upon the sightless couriers of the air,
> Shall blow the horrid deed in every eye,
> That tears shall drown the wind'

(I. vii. 16-25).

The vision is of heaven turned into tumultuous anger by Duncan's slaying. Duncan's virtues are compared (in a simile in lines 18-20) to angels, which will loudly proclaim Macbeth's damnation for the murder. At first pity is compared to a baby, something weak and powerless (line 21). The helplessness of pity against evil is contained in the image of the baby exposed to the storm: 'And pity, like a naked new-born babe,/ Striding the blast' (lines 21-22). But then in line 22, pity is associated with 'heaven's cherubin' (the angelic children of heaven), which invests it with divine strength; strength capable of conquering and destroying the evil-doer by turning popular opinion against him: 'heaven's cherubin, horsed/ Upon the sightless couriers of the air,/ Shall blow the horrid deed in every eye,/ That tears shall drown the wind' (lines 22-25). Macbeth fears divine intervention and the destruction of his body in this world and of his soul in the next, if he offends God by murdering Duncan.

By the end of this soliloquy, we can see that while Macbeth's ambition is as compulsive as ever, he still lacks the strength of purpose to do what has to be done, because he is all too aware of the consequences:

'I have no spur
To prick the sides of my intent, but only
Vaulting ambition, which o'erleaps itself
And falls on the other — '

(I. vii. 25-28).

He is about to say 'side' when Lady Macbeth interrupts him. The image is of a man who, over-eager to mount his horse, leaps and misses the saddle, only to fall on the other side. Macbeth is saying that he has nothing to spur him on but his soaring ambition, which, unless it is exercised with caution and skill, (both of which are denied him by his lack of courage and determination) will lead to his downfall.

Lady Macbeth immediately asks, 'Why have you left the chamber?' (line 29). Macbeth doesn't give a direct answer; he doesn't want her to know he is scared and wavering, and, more to the point, he doesn't want her to know, or he feels he cannot explain, the spiritual nature of his fears. When he tells her that he doesn't want to go on with the murder, he gives her a rather superficial reason for abandoning it:

'I have bought
Golden opinions from all sorts of people,
Which would be worn now in their newest gloss,
Not cast aside so soon'

(I. vii. 32-35).

Why does he do this? Why doesn't he just tell her that he is. terrified of the consequences, both in this life and the next? Probably because Macbeth knows that his wife, being more ruthless and determined, will scoff at the idea and see it as an excuse for physical cowardice. And cowardice is exactly what Lady Macbeth then accuses him of. Macbeth, using a clothing image, has said that he wants to wear the 'Golden opinions' he has won from others 'in their newest gloss' (lines 33-34). Lady Macbeth contemptuously flings this image back at him: 'Was the hope drunk,/ Wherein you dressed yourself?' (lines 35-36), i.e. 'Was the ambition in which you clothed yourself false?' (drunk). She continues to goad him, doubting his courage, calling him a coward, and, very cruelly, since she knows it is her husband's other sensitive area (his manhood and honour being the first), expressing doubts about his love for her:

> 'hath it (i.e. your ambition) slept since,
> And wakes it now, to look so green and pale
> At what it did so freely? From this time
> Such I account thy love'
>
> (I. vii. 36-39).

> 'Wouldst thou have that
> Which thou esteem'st the ornament of life,
> And live a coward in thine own esteem,
> Letting "I dare not" wait upon "I would,"
> Like the poor cat i' the adage?'
>
> (I. vii. 41-45).

Macbeth defends himself by making a moral point: 'I dare do all that may become a man;/ Who dares do more is none' (lines 46-47), i.e. 'I dare do anything worthy of a man, but he who does more than that is no man at all.' This falling back on morality seems something of a last-ditch stand, for Macbeth, as we observed, tends to shy away from discussing the moral and spiritual aspects of the plot with his wife, lest she pour scorn on him — which she does. With the words, 'What beast was 't then,/ That made you break this enterprise to me?' (lines 47-48), she is saying, if it wasn't a man who suggested this plan — and from your behaviour now I have my doubts about this — what animal was it? Not only does she imply that he lacks manly valour, she suggests that even a dumb animal would show more determination than he. This is a very cruel attack, not what you would expect of a wife or close relative, which is why here, Lady Macbeth uses the formal 'you' and not the familiar 'thou' of earlier speeches.

The baby image which symbolises pity and which appeared earlier on in the scene (lines 21-22), reappears here. Lady Macbeth uses it to show how little of that quality she has, how ruthless she can be, and in so doing, demonstrates how unnatural a woman she is:

'I have given suck, and know
How tender 't is to love the babe that milks me:
I would, while it was smiling in my face,
Have plucked my nipple from his boneless gums,
And dashed the brains out, had I so sworn as you
Have done to this'

(I. vii. 54-59).

What she is saying is that if *she* had sworn to kill someone — even if it was one of her own babies — as he has sworn to kill Duncan, she would do it, no matter what feelings urged her not to. (This speech also raises an interesting question, though not essential to our understanding of the play, namely, where is Macbeth's son? How many children does he have? We never see them, and so we never find out. It may seem a little odd, but as Macbeth's children are not so fundamental to the plot as the other offspring, Malcolm and Donalbain, Fleance, and Macduff's son, Shakespeare seems to have felt that a passing reference to his (or their) existence was sufficient. On the other hand, some students will spot the

obvious inconsistency in the plot — this is not unusual in
Shakespeare's plays — when they get to IV. iii; Macduff,
mourning the death of his family, says of Macbeth in line
216, 'He has no children'.)

In response to his wife's cruel goading Macbeth can only
whimper, 'If we should fail', at which point Lady Macbeth
switches from abusing him to reassuring him. She offers him
her strength by scorning the idea of failure and by smoothly
taking over the management of the murder plot. Macbeth is
in awe of his wife's courage and strength of purpose, which,
because he sees these as essentially male virtues, makes him
say:

> 'Bring forth men-children only!
> For thy undaunted mettle should compose
> Nothing but males'
>
> (I. vii. 72-74).

Macbeth, now drawing strength from his wife, adds his own
suggestion to the efficient accomplishment of the murder —
using the grooms' daggers and smearing the grooms with
Duncan's blood (lines 74-77). And as the scene closes, all his
doubts and fears seem to have evaporated:

> 'I am settled, and bend up
> Each corporal agent to this terrible feat'
>
> (I.vii. 80-81).

We remember Lady Macbeth's words at I. v. 23-26:

> 'Hie thee hither,
> That I may pour my spirits in thine ear,
> And chastise with the valour of my tongue
> All that impedes thee from the golden round'.

She has kept this promise in this scene, pouring her fiery
spirits into Macbeth's ear to purge him, for the moment at

least, of his scruples.

How do Lady Macbeth and Macbeth know that Duncan will only post two grooms as guards at the bedchamber door? Perhaps this is Duncan's usual practice whether he is at home or away, but more likely they realise that the King trusts them and so does not feel any need to mount a heavy guard while he is staying at Inverness.

Act Two Scene I

A few hours later on, in a courtyard at Inverness Castle, Banquo enters with his son Fleance, who is carrying a torch. Banquo asks what time it is; Fleance replies that he hasn't heard the clock strike but the moon has gone down. Banquo says that the moon goes down at midnight, but Fleance thinks it is now later than that. Banquo hands Fleance his sword, and observes that the stars are not shining in the night sky. He is tired but tells his son that he is afraid to sleep, for he is frightened of the terrible thoughts which haunt his dreams.

Suddenly, Banquo hears a noise and, taking his sword back from Fleance, he calls out 'Who's there?' Macbeth enters with a servant. Banquo is surprised to find Macbeth still up. He tells his host that the King is already in bed, having enjoyed his evening so much that he has rewarded the servants. Then Banquo produces a diamond which Duncan wants Lady Macbeth to have for being such a kind hostess. Macbeth says that they were unprepared for Duncan's visit but did the best they could for him.

Banquo abruptly changes the topic of conversation to the three Witches. He tells Macbeth that he dreamt of them the previous night, and observes that their prophecies have started to come true for Macbeth. Macbeth replies that he hasn't thought about them, but asks Banquo to spare him a moment of his time later on to discuss the matter. Then Macbeth subtly attempts to get Banquo's support by saying that if they can come to some agreement on the Witches' prophecies and join sides, it will be to Banquo's advantage. Banquo cautiously replies that he will follow Macbeth's advice so long as he can remain honourable and loyal to the King. They say goodnight and Banquo exits with Fleance.

Dismissing his servant, Macbeth is left alone on stage, deep in thought. He looks up and staring into space, begins to hallucinate, seeing a dagger hovering in the air, the handle towards him. Macbeth tries to seize it, snatching at the empty air, but there is nothing there. Yet he can still see it. He wonders if the dagger can be felt as well as seen, or whether it is just an imaginary dagger; the product of a sick and troubled mind. He draws his own weapon from its sheath, observing that the ghostly dagger looks just as real as the one he is now holding. Then he realises that the dagger, which is just like the one he intends to use for the murder, is pointing the way for him to Duncan's bedchamber. Macbeth doesn't know whether to trust his eyes (which tell him the dagger is real) or his other senses (which tell him that it is an hallucination). Now, drops of blood appear on its blade and handle. Macbeth is convinced he is imagining things because he is so troubled by thoughts of the murder. Half the world, he reflects, is sleeping; dreams are creeping into men's minds; witches are performing their strange rites; the murderer, woken by the sound of howling wolves, stalks his victim with swift, silent steps, like a ghost. Macbeth says that he must move silently or he will give himself away, just when the time is right for the murder. All this thinking and soul-searching, he says, just prolong Duncan's life; talk cools a man's courage. A bell rings. It is the signal arranged between himself and his wife and Macbeth says it is inviting him to commit the murder and summoning Duncan to heaven — or to hell.

Commentary

An atmosphere of impending evil predominates. Evil is symbolically associated in the play with darkness. It is past midnight; the moon is set and the stars no longer shine — we recall Macbeth's words in I. iv. 50-51, and Lady Macbeth's in I. v. 48-52:

> 'Stars, hide your fires!
> Let not light see my black and deep desires;'

> 'Come, thick night,
> And pall thee in the dunnest smoke of hell,
> That my keen knife see not the wound it makes,
> Nor heaven peep through the blanket of the dark
> To cry, "Hold, hold!"'

Banquo hands Fleance his sword and one other unspecified item. Perhaps it is his dagger: 'Take thee that, too'. (line 5) This seems a reasonable interpretation: Banquo is innocently giving up his dagger for the night and thinking of going to bed, while Macbeth on the other hand is about to do just the opposite. Evil, in the form of the Witches' prophecy, is disturbing Banquo's sleep, when his conscious mind, which is governed by virtue, honour and loyalty to the King, has no resistance to it. Unlike Macbeth who freely chooses to pursue evil for his own ends, Banquo prays for complete protection from it, asking heaven to purge its malign influence from his dreams:

> 'merciful powers!
> Restrain in me the cursèd thoughts that nature
> Gives way to in repose!'

> (II. i. 7-9).

The disturbing effects of evil on sleep, and the idea that sleep is the reward of innocence, are seen later on in the play:

the voice that Macbeth hears, after he has murdered Duncan, calling out, '"Glamis hath murdered sleep, and therefore Cawdor/ Shall sleep no more, Macbeth shall sleep no more!"' (see II. ii. 41-42); the 'terrible dreams' that Macbeth tells his wife 'shake us nightly' (III. ii. 18-19); Lady Macbeth's diagnosis of her husband's disturbed state at the end of the banquet scene, 'You lack the season of all natures, sleep' (III. iv. 141); and Lady Macbeth's sleep-walking in V. i.

There is a cruel irony in the way that Duncan has gone to bed feeling so grateful to the Macbeths for their hospitality ('shut up/ In measureless content', lines 16-17), even going to the extent of sending Lady Macbeth a diamond ring as a reward for her being a 'most kind hostess' (line 16). Once again in the play we see the way appearances often contradict reality (particularly Duncan's interpretation of appearances: see I. iv. 11-14, I. iv. 54-58, and I. vi. 1-3).

Lady Macbeth is absent in this scene, for a reason that becomes obvious in II. ii: she is busy plying the grooms outside Duncan's bedchamber with drugged wine.

Banquo's frankness in admitting that he has dreamt about the Witches (lines 20-21) shows his open nature and this is made to stand in contrast to Macbeth's dishonesty when he replies, 'I think not of them' (line 21). But the suddenness of the change in the conversation by Banquo (from Duncan's visit to the Witches), must tell us something more. There is an urgency in his words and line 21 sounds more like a challenge or a question than a statement of fact: 'To you they have showed some truth.' Either this is a veiled accusation that Macbeth is in league with evil forces, or it is an implied question whose answer Banquo hopes will unravel the 'cursed thoughts' of his dreams, i.e., tell him what is in store for him from the Witches, or more precisely, for his sons. Macbeth seems to take lines 20-21 both ways: firstly as an accusation, hence his evasive reply, 'I think not of them'; then as a question arising out of Banquo's interest in these dark forces, which would explain why Macbeth immediately tries to solicit Banquo's support between lines 22-26:

Macbeth

Yet, when we can entreat an hour to serve,
We would spend it in some words upon that business,
If you would grant the time.

Banquo

At your kind'st leisure.

Macbeth

If you shall cleave to my consent, when 't is,
It shall make honour for you.

In this case, a pause would be in order at the end of line 21 ('I think not of them:'), just long enough for Macbeth to move from being on his guard at Banquo's remarks (lines 20-21), to seeing the possibility of exploiting Banquo's interest. Banquo's reply is that he will not seek any advantage for himself which would compromise his honour or bring into question his loyalty to the King (lines 26-29). The point being developed here was introduced by Macbeth in I. vii. 46-47: 'I dare do all that may become a man;/ Who dares do more is none.' In other words, when a man uses dishonest means to increase his honour, he loses his honour instead.

By the time Banquo exits with Fleance, he must have severe misgivings about Macbeth's intentions. Macbeth has effectively given himself away to Banquo, and his death, after Duncan's, is inevitable.

The last time Macbeth asked Banquo to discuss the Witches' prophecies with him was in I. iii. 153-155, when his thoughts of murder were just forming ('My thought, whose murder yet is but fantastical', I. iii. 139). Now, in II. i. 22-24, he has asked Banquo again, but for an entirely different reason.

Macbeth has steeled himself to go through with the murder and he is more interested, at this stage, to use a private conversation with Banquo about the Witches to secure him as an ally, than he is in exploring the moral issue of his actions (which was what he was after in I. iii. 153-155).

In the soliloquy, we see Macbeth's nerves are taut, stretched almost to breaking point (we recall Lady Macbeth's words in I. vii. 60, 'screw your courage to the sticking-place'), yet he remains in control of himself. He has dismissed the servant, telling him to get Lady Macbeth to ring the bell when his drink is ready, a prearranged signal that all is ready — Duncan asleep, the grooms unconscious.

The imagery of the speech at first indicates that Macbeth is more troubled by the horror of the deed than by the moral or spiritual issues involved. Because he is in control of himself (albeit a very shaky self-control) and has firmness of purpose, he can separate fact from fancy and so he guesses quite early on that the image of the dagger is a mere hallucination; the product of mental strain:

> 'A dagger of the mind, a false creation,
> Proceeding from the heat-oppressèd brain?'
>
> (II. i. 38-39).

The dagger is not posing a symbolic question to him — should he do the deed or not? Instead it is pointing the way to Duncan's bedchamber and telling him to get on with it:

> 'Thou marshall'st me the way that I was going;
> And such an instrument I was to use'
>
> (II. i. 42-43).

The dagger, then, is telling Macbeth that the murder has to be done, no matter how he feels about it. Once he has his own weapon in his hand and he sees the hallucinatory dagger covered with blood, he has all the reassurance he needs that it will finally be done; at which point, he no longer needs the imaginary dagger to prompt him into action and so can dismiss it:

> 'There's no such thing.
> It is the bloody business which informs
> Thus to mine eyes'

(II. i. 47-49).

Most producers nowadays like to show the dagger to the audience, but it has to be remembered that it isn't a ghost; it is something created by Macbeth's imagination or subconscious. On the one hand, it is an expression of his horror, a visual representation of Macbeth's feeling of ghastliness at the deed he is about to do; on the other hand, because the dagger can be seen, contemplated, and finally dismissed, the episode enables Macbeth to come to terms with his fear for a moment, leaving him even firmer in his purpose.

Images of unnaturalness and evil fill the last ten lines or so of this scene. First, sleep is compared to (i) the death of nature, and (ii) a curtain:

> 'Now o'er the one half world
> Nature seems dead, and wicked dreams abuse
> The curtained sleep'

(II. i. 49-51).

Nature seeming to be dead reinforces the idea that the deed Macbeth is about to do is unnatural, while 'curtained sleep' refers to the fact that beds in those days used to be curtained to give privacy to their occupants. Thus, sleep is also a curtain shutting out worldly cares, though evil can penetrate through its flimsy cover to haunt dreams (as we saw earlier with Banquo in lines 7-9). The image continues with witches making offerings to their chief goddess, Hecate, as though celebrating the evil they have released upon the world:

'witchcraft celebrates
Pale Hecate's offerings'

(II. i. 51-52).

Macbeth slowly merges with the night, with the forces of evil, losing his identity to become the personification of a murderer, 'withered Murder' (line 52). The word 'withered' suggests both the ugliness and sterility of evil. The fruits of murder, Macbeth will learn, are as illusory as the dagger his mind has just conjured. Macbeth, continuing with the personification, describes his movements in the third person: he moves 'with his stealthy pace ... towards his design.... like a ghost' (lines 54-56). By uniting with evil, Macbeth has become part of a huge force and is no longer an individual.

Ironically, as Macbeth steals off to slay Duncan, he is still carrying the diamond meant for Lady Macbeth, Duncan's symbol of love and gratitude.

Act Two Scene II

Later that same night, as Macbeth is moving 'like a ghost' towards Duncan's bedchamber, Lady Macbeth enters and waits close by downstairs. She has been drinking to give herself courage. In her tense state, she is startled by an owl shrieking, and she compares its call to Duncan's death knell. Macbeth, she knows, is doing the deed at that very moment. She has left the doors to the bedchambers open and the attendants (the grooms), who are supposed to be guarding Duncan, are snoring away, for Lady Macbeth has drugged their drinks.

Macbeth calls out from upstairs, 'Who's there? — what, ho!', and Lady Macbeth is once again startled, fearing Macbeth has woken the grooms and been caught. She pauses, listening carefully. The grooms' daggers, which were to have been used as the murder weapons (see I. vii. 76), have been placed by her where Macbeth cannot miss them. She admits that if Duncan hadn't looked so much like her father as he lay sleeping, she would have killed him herself.

Macbeth enters, his hands stained with blood, carrying two daggers. He tells Lady Macbeth that Duncan is dead and asks if she heard a noise; she replies that she heard an owl scream and the sound of crickets. Their conversation becomes swift and nervously laconic for a moment (lines 16-17). Then Macbeth asks who is sleeping in the room next to Duncan's, and she tells him it is Donalbain.

Looking at his blood-stained hands with horror, Macbeth says what a sad sight they are. Lady Macbeth chides him for speaking foolishly, but Macbeth hardly seems to hear her. One of the grooms/princes, he says, laughed in his sleep; the other cried 'Murder!'. They woke each other up, but then they said their prayers and went back to sleep again. But one of the grooms/princes had cried out 'God bless us!' and the other had responded with 'Amen', as though they could see Macbeth with his hands covered with blood and knew he was listening to them. Hearing them calling out in fear, Macbeth couldn't say 'Amen' when they said 'God bless us'. Lady Macbeth tells him not to think so deeply about it. But Macbeth wonders why the word 'Amen' stuck in his throat when he was most in need of a blessing. Lady Macbeth cautions him, saying that if they keep thinking morbid thoughts, it will drive them mad. Nevertheless, Macbeth continues, adding that he thought he heard a voice crying out: 'Sleep no more!/ Macbeth does murder sleep' (lines 34-35). Lady Macbeth asks whose voice it was, but he doesn't reply.

In an attempt to calm her husband, Lady Macbeth tells him to go and wash the blood off himself. Then she asks why he has brought the grooms' daggers back with him, when they should have been left next to Duncan's body. Macbeth is told to take them back to the bedchamber and to smear the grooms with blood, but he refuses, saying he's afraid to look again at what he has done. Lady Macbeth accuses her husband of cowardice and, taking the daggers from him, she goes off in the direction of Duncan's bedchamber. Suddenly, there are sounds of someone knocking at the castle gate. Macbeth is frightened; every noise, he says, frightens him. He looks again at his hands and wonders if there is enough water in the oceans to wash them clean. It is more likely, he thinks, that his hands would stain the vast, green seas blood-red.

Lady Macbeth re-enters. Her hands are also covered with blood now and she pours scorn on her husband's fearfulness.

The knocking is heard again and Lady Macbeth says they should go back to their room. Unlike her husband a few moments earlier, she is confident that a little water will wash away all suspicion from them. She tells him to put his nightgown on, so that everything will appear normal if they are called for.

The knocking from outside becomes more insistent. Lady Macbeth tells her husband not to be so lost in gloomy thoughts, but he replies that he cannot avoid thinking about what he has done. As the knocking is heard once more, Macbeth wishes that its sound could wake Duncan from the sleep of death.

Commentary

The murder occurs offstage in this scene. Why? Later on in the play we see Banquo murdered, Lady Macduff's son mercilessly cut down (although Lady Macduff also dies offstage, as she flees from the murderers) and Macbeth hacked to death before our eyes, quite apart from the grisly spectacle of his severed head being carried onto the stage. So Shakespeare plainly isn't worried about his audience being squeamish. Then why don't we actually see Macbeth slay Duncan? Probably because Shakespeare wants to control our feelings towards his tragic hero.

He is creating the overall effect of a man caught up in a moral dilemma, rather than just portraying a beastly and savage killer. He wants us to go on liking the man for as long as possible — liking him but deploring certain things about him. Obviously, Duncan's murder, thrust too insensitively in front of the audience at this stage, would strongly prejudice its feelings against Macbeth: he would appear only as a butcher, and all the finer feelings we have observed in him in the last eight scenes would be as nothing. Instead, in II. ii, an atmosphere of suspense is made to predominate, rather than a macabre and gruesome sensation of brutality (although elements of this, of course, are unavoidable: we see Macbeth's bloodstained hands, for example, but at this stage we tend to pity him for his feelings of horror, e.g. lines 20, 58-62, rather than condemn him).

At the end of II. i, we saw Macbeth moving off as though in a trance towards Duncan's bedchamber, but we have seen him do enough soul-searching to know, at the beginning of II. ii, that he might still fail to go through with the murder; that scruples will get in the way and he will fail to match his ambition with his deeds (which is exactly what Lady Macbeth accused him of in I. vii. 39-41: 'Art thou afeard/ To be the same in thine own act and valour,/ As thou art in desire?'). So suspense is now created by Lady Macbeth nervously pacing the stage, waiting for her husband to return with his mission accomplished. Will he go through with it or not? She is startled by an owl shrieking ('Hark! — Peace!', line 2). She must think at first, just for a split second, that it is something more ominous — one of the grooms waking up, perhaps. Then she reassures herself that Macbeth won't fail, comparing the owl's cry to a bell announcing Duncan's death ('the fatal bellman', line 3). She sounds confident when she then says, 'He is about it' (line 4), but moments later that confidence is shaken when Macbeth calls out. Her response shows her fear:

> 'Alack! I am afraid they have awaked,
> And 't is not done: — the attempt, and not the deed,
> Confounds us'
>
> (II. ii. 9-11).

Recrimination flows from her:

> 'I laid their daggers ready;
> He could not miss them. — Had he not resembled
> My father as he slept, I had done 't'
>
> (II. ii. 11-13).

She is saying: 'How could he have bungled it? All he had to do was pick up the daggers, which I left so conveniently for him, and use them. I could easily have done it myself, but for the fact that Duncan looked like my father as he lay sleeping.' This is immediately followed by a cry of relief and praise, 'My husband!' (line 13). She has spotted Macbeth, his hands and arms covered with Duncan's blood, testifying that the murder is done. He has not bungled it, hence Lady Macbeth's tone of relief. She is full of admiration for him (possibly for the first and only time in the play), hence her tone of praise.

Some critics take the view that Lady Macbeth appears more human in this scene, for two reasons: she has been drinking to bolster her nerves; and she expresses a reluctance to kill Duncan herself (lines 12-13) because he reminded her of her own father as he lay sleeping. Another view is that Lady Macbeth appears more ghoulish than ever, as the lines about her father can equally be read this way: that although she wouldn't have the stomach to do it herself, she would willingly have someone else slaughter her father if he were standing in her way to becoming Queen. Either view is possible, though the 'Lady Macbeth as more human' one is more popular.

Macbeth's first words, 'I have done the deed' (line 14), are said almost automatically, for his thoughts are elsewhere than with his wife. The clipped dialogue in lines 14-20 suggests that he is deeply abstracted and that his spirit is still haunting Duncan's bedchamber, for he has walked away only in a physical sense. In another sense, neither the horror nor the consequences of the crime he has committed against Duncan, will ever leave him. It is true however that the sensation of horror at his own evil does eventually fade somewhat. Compare what Macbeth says in this scene (e.g. 'How is 't with me, when every noise appals me?', line 57) with his words in V. v. 9-15:

'I have almost forgot the taste of fears.
The time has been, my senses would have cooled
To hear a night-shriek; and my fell of hair
Would, at a dismal treatise, rouse and stir,
As life were in 't. I have supped full with horrors:
Direness, familiar to my slaughterous thoughts,
Cannot once start me.'

Macbeth clearly learns to live with horror (i.e. bloodshed as a means of advancing or protecting his own interests), but he is forced to pay its price. The lines just quoted from V. v are spoken in Dunsinane Castle, while Macbeth is surrounded by hostile forces, only moments before his world begins to fall in on him (the death of his wife, V. v. 16, and the realisation that the Witches have deceived him, V. v. 33-46, and V. viii. 13-22). It goes without saying that the ultimate price he pays for bloodshed is his own death (V. viii) and we recall his earlier words:

'we but teach
Bloody instructions, which, being taught, return
To plague th'inventor'

(I. vii. 8-10).

Macbeth has heard a noise, which is why he called out
'Who's there? — what, ho!' in line 8. He asks Lady Macbeth
if she heard it (line 14) and she tries to reassure him by suggesting that it could have been the sound of the owl or the
crickets (line 15). At first Macbeth wonders if it was Lady
Macbeth who spoke (line 16), then the occupant of the 'second
chamber' (Donalbain, line 19). Suspense mounts, and it isn't
until lines 34-35 that he describes exactly what it was he
heard:

'Methought I heard a voice cry, "Sleep no more!
Macbeth does murder sleep"'.

Lady Macbeth asks, 'Who was it that thus cried?' (line 43)
but the question is never answered. The voice, like the dagger
at the end of II. I, is clearly an hallucination, the product of
Macbeth's distraught mind. The difference is that Macbeth
knew the dagger was unreal: he had some control over his
imagination at that time, but now he has none. Effectively,
Macbeth has put a curse both upon himself and (as we shall
see in V. i) Lady Macbeth. Because he has murdered Duncan
in his sleep, Macbeth's susbconscious mind is telling him that
he has murdered sleep; so he believes it will never again come
to him, to soothe life's cares away. By telling Lady Macbeth,
he is transferring the same suggestion to her:

Macbeth

the innocent sleep;
Sleep, that knits up the ravelled sleave of care,
The death of each day's life, sore labour's bath,

Balm of hurt minds, great nature's second course,
Chief nourisher in life's feast; —

Lady Macbeth
What do you mean?

Macbeth
Still it cried, "Sleep no more!" to all the house:
"Glamis hath murdered sleep, and therefore Cawdor
Shall sleep no more, Macbeth shall sleep no more!"
(II. ii. 35-42).

It is patently clear by the end of the scene that Macbeth bitterly regrets what he has done: 'Wake Duncan with thy knocking: I would thou couldst!' (line 73). The first indication of this regret comes at line 20, when Macbeth looks at his blood-stained hands and says: 'This is a sorry sight.'

We have always known that there are two sides to Macbeth: firstly, the side that values honour and fears damnation; and secondly, the side which craves advancement and puts worldly considerations before divine ones. We might say that the first side is controlled by his conscience; and the second by his ambition. So when Macbeth looks at his hands again in line 58, it is as if the first side is trying to disassociate itself from and destroy the second side: 'What hands are here? Ha! they pluck out mine eyes.' The full extent of Macbeth's horror is felt in these lines:

'Will all great Neptune's ocean wash this blood
Clean from my hand? No, this my hand will rather
The multitudinous seas incarnadine,
Making the green one red'

(II. ii. 59-62).

Lady Macbeth's response throughout the scene is to tell her husband not to think too deeply about things. She is concerned only with practical issues, and her comment, 'A little water clears us of this deed' (line 66), makes an obvious contrast between her pragmatism and Macbeth's intensely spiritual preoccupations. What is horrifying Macbeth is not just the act of murdering Duncan, but the realisation that his soul is now damned:

Macbeth

One cried, "God bless us!" and, "Amen," the other,
As they had seen me with these hangman's hands.
Listening their fear, I could not say, "Amen,"
When they did say, "God bless us!"

Lady Macbeth
                    Consider it not so deeply.

Macbeth

But wherefore could not I pronounce "Amen"?
I had most need of blessing, and "Amen"
Stuck in my throat.

(II. ii. 26-32)

Macbeth was unable to say *Amen* ("let it be so") to the princes' prayer asking for a blessing, because he feels that he is excluded from God's mercy. (According to the ancient doctrine of the divine right of kings, sovereigns were representatives of God and derived their right to rule directly from God. Therefore, killing a king was deemed a great affront to God.) Macbeth, as we see in lines 59-62, considers his guilt to be so great that all the water in the immense oceans can never wash it away.

It isn't entirely clear who Macbeth is referring to in the prayer incident. At line 19 Macbeth asks, 'Who lies i' the second chamber?' and Lady Macbeth replies, 'Donalbain'. A little later, after Macbeth has described hearing the prayer being spoken, Lady Macbeth says, 'There are two lodged together' (line 25). If both princes occupy the second chamber, why does Lady Macbeth only mention Donalbain at line 19? Some editors believe it is the grooms who awake and pray; as they are drugged, this seems unlikely. A better interpretation is that the princes awake because of a premonition of evil near at hand. However, who awakes remains ambiguous and it is even possible to speculate that the whole incident is another of Macbeth's hallucinations, like the dagger at the end of II. i and the ghostly voice calling out 'Sleep no more' (line 34). Lady Macbeth heard nothing and she had been listening carefully. Macbeth lost his grip on reality in Duncan's bedchamber; his imagination ran wild and his fear of damnation, deeply impressed upon his subconscious mind, expressed itself in this waking nightmare.

Consistent with this loss of control is his bringing the grooms' daggers back with him. As Lady Macbeth says, 'Your constancy/ Hath left you unattended' (lines 67-68); in other words, 'Your loss of nerve and self-control has left you defenceless.' But it seems strange that it takes Lady Macbeth 34 lines to notice them (Macbeth enters at line 13 and she spots the daggers in line 47). Perhaps this is an indication that Lady Macbeth's coolness and firmness of purpose are ebbing away as well.

The knocking at the castle's south gate is first heard in line 56. It continues to be heard, growing more insistent, until the end of the scene. Its sound serves to heighten the tension at the end of the scene and emphasises Macbeth's terror:

> 'Whence is that knocking? —
> How is 't with me, when every noise appals me?'
> (II. ii. 56-57).

But it has two other purposes. In the next scene we switch to the Porter opening the gate to Macduff and Lenox. This gives the Macbeths the opportunity to leave the stage for a while, wash the blood from their hands, and change into their night-gowns. Then consider how we have been caught up in the claustrophobic world of Inverness Castle since I. v. (we stepped outside its walls briefly in I. vi). Our focus of attention has been narrowed down to what is going on primarily in Macbeth's mind. Now the outside world is demanding to be heard. It can't be held at bay: it won't be held at bay. It has its own values too and the knocking signifies its insistence that those values should be heard and reasserted.

Act Two Scene III

The scene shifts to an outer courtyard of the castle. A Porter, somewhat hungover from drinking until three that morning, is on his way to answer the knocking at the gate. 'Who's there, in the devil's name?' he calls out. Then he guesses who it might be. Perhaps it's a farmer who horded grain in the hope of making a huge profit, but who hanged himself when a bountiful harvest forced prices down. Knock, knock! Perhaps it's a devious lawyer who could use words to twist the truth in any case he was arguing, but who couldn't argue his way into heaven. Knock, knock! Or, perhaps it's an English tailor, a dishonest man, who has been sent to hell for being miserly in the amount of cloth he used to make showy (French) trousers. Knock, knock, knock! The Porter invites the tailor in, saying he can heat his clothes-iron on the fires of hell inside. Then the Porter complains that he never gets any peace and that the place is too cold for hell. He had planned to open the gates, the gates of hell he calls them, to all those who have cheated to get ahead in life, but now the job no longer interests him. He opens the gate and lets Macduff and Lenox in.

Macduff asks if the porter got to bed so late that he has overslept and neglected his post. The Porter explains that they were drinking until very late. Humorously, he describes the effects of drinking on a man: it results in red noses, sleep, and urine; it also gives a man the urge for sex but prevents its performance. Macbeth enters and Macduff asks him if the King is up yet, adding that he was told to wake him early. Macduff is shown the door to Duncan's bedchamber and goes in.

Meanwhile, Lenox comments on how stormy the night has been. Chimneys were blown down. People say they heard wailing, strange screams of death, and frightened voices fore-telling disruption and revolution in the land. Bad times seem to be on their way. The owl, the bird of darkness, screeched all night long, and some say they felt earth tremors. Macbeth mutters a reply; Lenox says he can't recall a night like it, when Macduff rushes in yelling 'O, horror! horror! horror!' He has found Duncan murdered. Macbeth and Lenox run off to Duncan's bedchamber, while Macduff orders the alarm bell to be rung. As it clangs, Lady Macbeth enters, followed by Banquo. They are told the dreadful news. Macbeth and Lenox return. Macbeth shows sorrow by wishing he were dead.

Malcolm and Donalbain enter, asking what all the commotion is about. Learning that their father has been killed, Malcolm asks who did it; Lenox says that it seems to have been the grooms, for they were smeared with blood and their daggers were found, still unwiped, on their pillows. They looked insane, he adds, and no one was safe in their presence. Macbeth expresses regret at losing his temper and killing them, which prompts Macduff to ask why he did it then. Macbeth claims that he was overwhelmed with passion on seeing Duncan's body bleeding from fatal wounds, and the grooms nearby with their daggers dripping blood, and lost control of himself. He asks if any man, with courage and love in his heart, would have acted differently.

Lady Macbeth draws attention away from her husband by pretending to faint. While she is being attended to, Malcolm asks Donalbain in an aside why they have nothing to say, since it is their loss more than anyone else's. Donalbain asks what can be said; their lives are in danger, he adds, and they should flee since some of the sorrow being expressed is obviously false.

Banquo orders the servants to look after Lady Macbeth, telling the others to go away, get dressed, and meet later to discuss the murder and the motives for it. He knows they all have their own doubts and fears, but he puts himself into God's hands, saying, from that position of strength, he is ready to fight against any secret plot or act of treason. They all agree with him and everyone leaves to get dressed except Malcolm and Donalbain, who remain on stage. They both know their lives are in danger, and whoever killed their father is now making a pretence of sorrow while carrying a dagger beneath his cloak for them. Without telling anyone, they decide to leave Scotland: Malcolm for England, Donalbain for Ireland.

Commentary

The Porter interlude, with its scurrilous humour (particularly the part about drink and sex) provides a moment of light relief for the audience's feelings after the emotional intensity of the scenes leading up to the murder, with its terrible culmination in II. ii. The tension returns and gradually mounts after Macbeth enters (line 37) and Macduff asks if the King is up and then goes off to wake him. But for a few moments we are allowed to relax while this earthy character, speaking in prose appropriate both to his lowly status and the subject matter, grumbles away as he opens the gate to Macduff and Lenox.

In the meantime, Macbeth and Lady Macbeth are somewhere else, washing the blood away, changing into their nightgowns, and trying to compose themselves in readiness for their entrances a little later on (for they know it won't be long before the crime is discovered).

The Porter styles himself the 'porter of hell-gate' (line 1) and 'devil-porter' (line 15), which seems an ironically suitable title for the keeper of the gate of Inverness Castle, where the dark forces of evil have so recently been active. The satirical humour in the first part of the Porter's speech (line 1-18) cannot be dismissed as only having held a topical interest for a Jacobean audience. The Porter's remarks in these lines comment on the action of the play, or to be more precise, they allude to Macbeth, and then the Witches' promises. The farmer who horded grain and then hanged himself when prices fell, the tailor who stinted on cloth in the making of tight-fitting trousers and the lawyer who used words in a misleading manner, all have one thing in common: they tried to take a short cut to success but failed. They are examples of what the Porter calls, 'some of all professions that go the primrose way to the everlasting bonfire' (lines 16-17). They are like Macbeth in this respect; he, too, is going 'the primrose way to the everlasting bonfire', for he has also tried to get ahead by cunning, and will eventually overreach himself.

The reference to the lawyer as 'an equivocator' points again to a central, recurring theme in the play, 'appearances versus reality'. The lawyer 'could swear in both the scales against either scale' (lines 7-8). He could swear to tell the truth in court but then represent either side in a legal dispute, for he had the ability to use language cunningly so as to mislead others. He wouldn't compromise himself by actually

lying, but he wouldn't be telling the whole truth either. Truth
has an appearance and a reality; there is what *seems* to be
true, and what is *actually* true.

The Witches never lie to Macbeth. They tell him he will
become King, and he becomes King. In IV. i, they tell him
that, 'Macbeth shall never vanquished be, until/ Great Birnam
wood to high Dunsinane hill/ Shall come against him' (lines
92-94); a few lines before this, in IV. i, comes this promise:
'laugh to scorn/ The power of man, for none of woman
born/ Shall harm Macbeth' (lines 79-81). The truth, as it
seems to Macbeth, is that he has been granted invulnerability,
but he has been tricked by words, ambiguous words, and the
reality (the actual truth) starts coming clear to him in Act V,
when Birnam wood appears to be approaching Dunsinane
Castle:

> 'I pull in resolution, and begin
> To doubt th' equivocation of the fiend,
> That lies like truth: "Fear not, till Birnam wood
> Do come to Dunsinane"; — and now a wood
> Comes toward Dunsinane'
>
> (V. v. 42-46).

The confrontation with Macduff in V. viii completes
Macbeth's disillusionment with the Witches' promises. When
he learns that 'Macduff was from his mother's womb/
Untimely ripped' (lines 15-16), i.e. that Macduff is not 'of
woman born', he realises that what the Witches gave him was
not truth, but false hope. Like the Porter's 'equivocator',
they have juggled with words, using them in a double sense to
make promises which are kept in a literal sense, but not in the
sense in which they knew Macbeth would take them:

> 'And be these juggling fiends no more believed,
> That palter with us in a double sense,

That keep the word of promise to our ear,
And break it to our hope'

(V. viii. 19-22).

When Macduff and Lenox are let in, the Porter's cheeky
remark that drink provokes a desire for sex, but takes away a
man's ability to perform ('it provokes the desire, but it takes
away the performance', lines 25-26) echoes something that
Lady Macbeth said about desire in I. vii. She was accusing
Macbeth of desiring the crown but failing to act in order to
fulfil his desire: 'Art thou afeard/ To be the same in thine
own act and valour,/ As thou art in desire?' (lines 39-41). At
that stage Macbeth wanted the crown but couldn't bring
himself to do what had to be done to take it. With the benefit
of hindsight now, it seems that the attack on Macbeth's lack
of valour at I. vii. 39-41 has a strongly mocking sexual
overtone to it — as if Lady Macbeth was comparing her
husband's failure to act with sexual impotence.

There are no stage directions indicating when the Porter
exits. As he has nothing more to say after line 36, and his
continued presence on the stage as a comic character would
be severely out of tune with what happens in the rest of the
scene, we must assume that he shuffles off almost immediately
after he finishes speaking; that is, just as Macbeth enters.

The exchange of 'Good morrow' between Lenox and
Macbeth in line 39 reminds us that it is now morning, but it is
still dark (see II. iv. 5-10). The forces of evil are symbolically
associated with darkness in the play (see Section 6 iii, 'The
Recurrent Imagery of *Macbeth*'), but the forces of good
(associated with daylight) have yet to reassert themselves.

Macbeth enters and tries to act nonchalantly. His short
responses, first to Macduff and then to Lenox, up until
Macduff's return from the bedchamber at line 60, are an
attempt to hold himself in check, so that he doesn't give

himself away by revealing his nervousness. Lenox's description of the strange happenings of the stormy night that has just past demonstrates the Jacobean belief that the murder of a king is a violation of the natural order; Nature is therefore thrown into confusion:

> 'The night has been unruly: where we lay,
> Our chimneys were blown down; and, as they say,
> Lamentings heard i' the air; strange screams of death,
> And prophesying with accents terrible
> Of dire combustion, and confused events,
> New hatched to the woeful time.
> The obscure bird clamoured the livelong night:
> Some say the earth was feverous, and did shake'
>
> (II. iii. 49-56).

Macbeth's response (mentioned a few lines earlier) is terse: ''T was a rough night' (line 57). When Macduff rushes back in, the nature of the murder as an act of sacrilege is emphasised; it is a crime perpetrated against God's representative on earth — a violation of something consecrated (made holy) by Him:

> 'Most sacrilegious murder hath broke ope
> The Lord's anointed temple, and stole thence
> The life o' the building!'
>
> (II. iii. 63-65).

In this image, the King's body is compared to a temple anointed by God. The murderer has broken open the temple, violated its sacredness, and destroyed it. Macbeth pretends to be confused by this image, replying as though he doesn't understand what has happened: 'What is 't you say? the life?' (line 65). When Macduff calls out to wake the rest of the house, the spectacle of Duncan's murdered body is likened to an image of the day of judgement, or Doomsday: 'see/ The great doom's image!' (lines 73-74). (According to the Book of Revelations in the Bible, this is the time at the end of the world when God's forces will do battle with and overcome those of Satan.) The idea being conveyed is that the murder will provoke God's wrath, leading first to chaos, then to Armageddon — a final conflict between the forces of good and evil. Macduff summons Malcolm and Donalbain, telling them to wake up and calling out, 'As from your graves rise up' (line 75), echoing the part in Revelations where the graves will give up their dead to witness the day of judgement.

In line 76, the alarm bell starts to ring, taking over from the knocking which began the scene, as the symbol of the outside world pressing its way in. When Lady Macbeth enters, asking what has happened, there is a certain irony in the way Macduff refuses to tell her for fear of upsetting her delicate, female sensibilities:

> 'O gentle lady,
> 'T is not for you to hear what I can speak:
> The repetition, in a woman's ear,
> Would murder as it fell'
>
> (II. iii. 79-82).

She hears Macduff give Banquo the news and her response, which presumably she has had time to think about and rehearse, seems somewhat inept:

> 'Woe, alas!
> What! in our house?'
>
> (II. iii 83-84).

Banquo's retort in line 84, 'Too cruel anywhere', seems to be either a rebuke at Lady Macbeth's ineptitude, or impatience with her because he suspects her complicity in the murder and so feels she is being grossly insincere.

Macbeth's profession of grief in lines 87-92 sounds, in

contrast, very sincere, probably because he does genuinely regret killing Duncan. Because these lines draw on the combined power of grief, guilt and regret, they are very rich poetry:

'Had I but died an hour before this chance,
I had lived a blessed time; for, from this instant,
There's nothing serious in mortality;
All is but toys: renown, and grace, is dead;
The wine of life is drawn, and the mere lees
Is left this vault to brag of.'

The sentiment expressed here, that life is no longer worth living, can probably be accepted at face value; Macbeth has achieved what he wanted, but he is no longer sure he wants it.

No one has yet asked the obvious question, but it does get asked, when Malcolm and Donalbain enter:

Macduff
Your royal father's murdered.

Malcolm
O! by whom?

(II. iii. 96).

Malcolm's apparent lack of emotion is not to be interpreted as insensitivity. Both he and his brother mistrust gushing displays of grief, knowing they can be hypocritical attempts to conceal guilt: 'To show an unfelt sorrow is an office/ Which the false man does easy' (lines 134-135).

Lenox describes the circumstantial evidence which linked the grooms to the crime: their hands and faces covered with blood, the unwiped daggers upon their pillows, and the 'distracted' (insane) expression on their faces. Lenox is cautious though about these appearances; the phrase 'as it seemed' in line 97 indicates this: 'Those of his chamber, as it seemed, had done 't.' The 'distracted' expressions, of course, were caused, not by insanity, but by fear and confusion. It must surely be obvious to everyone that the grooms had no real motive to murder Duncan; that if they had done it, they wouldn't have given themselves away so easily.

Macbeth uses the opportunity presented by Lenox's remark, 'no man's life/ Was to be trusted with them' (lines 101-102) to reveal that he has slain the grooms. He expresses a regret, of course a false regret, at having done so:

> 'O! yet I do repent me of my fury
> That I did kill them'
>
> (lines 103-104).

Macbeth means he regrets killing them, not because their lives were worth sparing, but because he has destroyed the most important piece of evidence. Macbeth wants to be seen as a man carried away on an impulse by his love for Duncan: 'The expedition of my violent love/ Outran the pauser reason' (lines 107-108). If we think back to I. vii, we will recall that killing the grooms was not part of the plan hatched by Lady Macbeth. This is the first she has heard of it. Nervous, Macbeth killed them for fear that they may have seen him and to prevent them from even trying to prove themselves innocent. When Macduff asks 'Wherefore did you so?' (line 104), he is not saying, 'If you regret killing them, then why did you do it?'; he's expressing suspicion, not curiosity. Macbeth launches into expressions of grief and love for Duncan to explain his actions. But he comes close to getting carried away:

> 'Here lay Duncan,
> His silver skin laced with his golden blood;
> And his gashed stabs looked like a breach in nature
> For ruin's wasteful entrance: there, the murderers,

Steeped in the colours of their trade, their daggers
Unmannerly breached with gore. Who could refrain,
That had a heart to love, and in that heart
Courage to make 's love known?'

(II. iii. 108-115).

The emotional power of these lines (as with lines 87-92) comes
from a combination of bitter sorrow and intense regret. The
part about the grooms, of course, is a lie, but the words
expressing the anguish he feels at having seen Duncan's
butchered corpse again (presumably still by lamplight, for
morning refuses to break, see II. iv. 5-10) are sincere; so lines
108-111 are heartfelt:

'Here lay Duncan,
His silver skin laced with his golden blood;
And his gashed stabs looked like a breach in nature
For ruin's wasteful entrance:'

The line, 'silver skin laced with his golden blood', emphasises
Duncan's majesty (the adjectives 'silver' and 'golden' suggest
the idea of Duncan's skin and blood being precious); the rest
refers to nature wasting away into ruination with the death
of the King, the fixed point on which the Jacobeans believed
the natural order pivoted.

Lady Macbeth, sensing that her highly-strung husband is
saying too much and might give himself away, faints at line
115 to draw attention away from him. Another point of view
is that the faint is genuine, because she, too, is suffering from
the emotional strain of guilt, concealment, and fear of discovery. Either opinion is acceptable.

Banquo dominates the rest of the scene, while Malcolm
and Donalbain seem, in contrast, rather pathetic figures.
They plan to sneak out of Scotland, fearing themselves to be
the murderer's next victims; but Banquo, aligning himself

with God, will stay and fight the traitors who have slaughtered his King:

> 'In the great hand of God I stand; and thence
> Against the undivulged pretence I fight
> Of treasonous malice'

(II. iii. 128-130).

Act Two Scene IV

The scene shifts to outside Inverness Castle, where Rosse is talking to a seventy year-old man. The old man says that in all his years he cannot remember anything like the supernatural events of the night before. Rosse replies that the heavens are angered by man's bloody deeds, so darkness hides the sun as though day is ashamed to show itself. The old man compares the unnaturalness of darkness during daytime to the recent murder.

Other strange disturbances in nature have been seen: a falcon (a bird of prey) was killed by an owl (a much weaker bird) and Duncan's thoroughbred horses turned wild, broke free from their stalls and ate each other.

Macduff enters. Rosse asks if they know yet who killed Duncan. Macduff says it was the men that Macbeth has slain. They were paid to do it, Macduff adds, and as Malcolm and Donalbain have fled the country, suspicion falls on them. It is another unnatural act, Rosse says, for a man to be murdered by his own sons; their ambition has destroyed what gave them life in the first place.

Macbeth has been chosen as the next King and will be crowned at Scone, while Duncan's body will be carried to the small island of Iona, to lie in the family tomb there. Macduff says he won't attend Macbeth's coronation, for he fears that things have changed for the worse.

Commentary

We are now outside the castle, breathing fresh air at last, for we have been trapped inside its closed walls, which have exuded evil, since the end of I. vi. (Or, to be more precise, since the beginning of I. v, with a brief break from its claustrophobic atmosphere in I. vi.)

The old man inspires confidence. Because he is old, we assume he is wise, and because he is unnamed, we take him to be the voice of the people.

Darkness still prevails, although it is already daytime and Rosse, at first, takes this to mean that God's judgement still hangs over the slaying of Duncan:

> 'Thou seest, the heavens, as troubled with man's act,
> Threatens his bloody stage: by the clock 't is day,
> And yet dark night strangles the travelling lamp'
>
> (II. iv. 5-7).

Notice the stage metaphor: the world is compared to a stage upon which men and women act out their lives like players, while God and the heavenly host are compared to the audience. The same metaphor occurs again in V. v. 24-28, where it is used to suggest the idea of life's futility. Here, though, the idea of divine judgement and God as a critical observer of man's affairs is being stressed. Then, rather than the notion of God suspending daylight to show his anger, Rosse says that it is either the forces of evil associated with darkness that are still prevailing, or else the sun (associated with virtue) is ashamed to look on the deed that has been done:

> 'Is 't night's predominance, or the day's shame,
> That darkness does the face of earth entomb,
> When living light should kiss it?'
>
> (II. iv. 8-10).

Rosse moves from a religious interpretation of the darkness

to a supernatural explanation for it. There is nothing particularly contradictory about this, for religion and the supernatural were much more linked in the Jacobean mind than they are in our own.

More images of the disorder in nature brought about by the King's murder follow. A falcon being killed by an owl mirrors the idea of something strong, majestic, and supreme in the natural order (the falcon/Duncan) being destroyed by a creature which is vastly inferior to it and associated with the evil forces of the night (the owl/the murderer):

> 'A falcon, towering in her pride of place,
> Was by a mousing owl hawked at, and killed'
> (II. iv. 12-13).

The cannibalism of Duncan's horses presents us with an image of Nature in chaos, preying and feeding upon itself. There is also the idea of Nature at 'War with mankind' (line 18), because of the outrage committed against her.

Macduff, after his entrance, gives what might be called the official view of Duncan's murder: that 'Those that Macbeth hath slain', line 23 (i.e. the grooms) did it; that they were hired as assassins by Malcolm and Donalbain, upon whom suspicion has fallen because they have fled Scotland. Macbeth, as Duncan's nearest kinsman after the princes, will now become King. Rosse seems to accept this interpretation of events, hence his remark about the unnaturalness of 'Thrift-less Ambition', line 28, (i.e. reckless ambition) when it destroys the source of its own existence — in this case, sons (allegedly) murdering a father for the sake of advancement. But if this view of the murder is accepted by Rosse and the other lords, it is not shared by Macduff. He has merely reported what others are saying.

Macduff's suspicions were obvious to us in the previous scene when he asked Macbeth why he killed the grooms (II.

iii. 104), and while he won't accuse Macbeth openly, he won't
go to Scone to attend the coronation either; instead he will go
home to his castle in Fife. Using the clothing image, Macduff
expresses his reservations about the future; he tells Rosse,
who is going to Scone:

> 'Well, may you see things well done there: — adieu! —
> Lest our old robes sit easier than our new'
>
>   (II. iv. 37-38).

Things may have changed for the worse, Macduff is saying,
again carefully avoiding any direct accusation against
Macbeth. But if Malcolm and Donalbain were rash in
running away, thereby drawing suspicion upon themselves,
isn't Macduff being equally unwise here? (At least the princes
have the excuse of youth and inexperience.) Macduff's absence
at the coronation cannot go unnoticed by Macbeth; it would
be tantamount to challenging his legitimacy as King, and
Macbeth could easily guess why Macduff is withholding his
allegiance. As it turns out, Macbeth becomes more
preoccupied in Act III, after his coronation, with the danger
posed by Banquo (see III. i. 53-54: 'There is none but he/
Whose being I do fear'). Macduff is spared for a while, giving
him time to flee to England. But the Witches warn Macbeth
of the threat from Macduff in IV. i (though he begins to be
aware of it in III. iv. 128-130, when Macduff skips the
banquet) and soon after, in IV. ii, Macduff's family, which
he has naively or irresponsibly left in Fife, are massacred.
Macduff should know better than to make himself conspicu-
ous by his absence (both at the coronation and at the banquet
in III. iv), thereby dropping heavy hints of Macbeth's guilt,
while at the same time leaving his family exposed to
Macbeth's wrath. Macduff might be virtuous, but he hardly
seems wise, (Rosse, on the other hand, calls Macduff 'noble,
wise, judicious' at IV. ii. 16.)

Act Three Scene I

The coronation at Scone is over and we are now back in the royal castle at Forres. Banquo enters alone. In a ten line soliloquy, he reflects that Macbeth now has everything the Witches promised, but Banquo suspects that Macbeth has acted wickedly to get it. He remembers that the Witches made him a promise, too: that Macbeth's children would not succeed him to the throne, but that he, Banquo, 'should be the root and father/ Of many kings' (lines 5-6). Banquo hopes that if the Witches have spoken the truth for Macbeth, they will do the same for him.

A trumpet sounds and Macbeth and Lady Macbeth enter as King and Queen, accompanied by Lenox, Rosse and other lords. Macbeth, using the royal plural ('we' rather than 'I'; 'our' rather than 'my', etc.) greets Banquo as 'our chief guest' (line II), and invites him to a banquet that evening. By engaging him in what seems to be casual conversation, Macbeth learns that Banquo is going for a ride that afternoon and will be back by supper time or a little after dark. Macbeth insists that Banquo attend the banquet. Then he mentions 'our bloody cousins' (line 29), Malcolm and Donalbain, who are in England, and Ireland. They refuse, Macbeth says, to confess their crime and are making up wild stories to tell others. But Macbeth postpones any further discussion of the matter until the next day, when matters of mutual concern to all will be dealt with. Banquo is just about to leave for his ride when Macbeth asks if Fleance, Banquo's son, is going with him. He is, Banquo says, and Macbeth bids him farewell. Macbeth dismisses the lords until seven that evening, saying that he wants to be on his own until supper time. They all exit, following Lady Macbeth off the stage, but Macbeth calls one attendant back and sends him to fetch two men who have been waiting outside. He is alone on stage and, in a soliloquy, he contemplates what has to be done next.

Macbeth knows that being King is not enough; he must be safe from danger and insurrection as well, and so fears Banquo for his naturally virtuous disposition. (Banquo is brave and daring, and he combines this quality of fearlessness with wisdom, which guides him to act cautiously.) Macbeth says that he fears Banquo only, and while he is around he feels threatened (as Caesar felt threatened by Mark Anthony). He remembers how Banquo scolded the Witches when they told Macbeth he would be King, ordering them to speak to him and how they then foretold that Banquo would be the father of a line of Kings. Macbeth resents wearing a crown that will not be passed down to his sons. He reflects with bitterness, that then, all his wicked deeds would benefit Banquo's offspring; for them he would have murdered Duncan, lost his peace of mind, and given away his immortal soul to the devil. Rather than Banquo's sons becoming kings, Macbeth asks fate to champion him and change the future.

The attendant comes back in with the two Murderers and is told to wait at the door. Macbeth reminds the Murderers of a conversation he had with them the day before, when he explained to them that it was Banquo who had treated them badly and not himself, as they had thought. Macbeth convinced the two men that they had been deceived and their plans thwarted; he explained by what means this had been done, who had conspired against them, and everything else that would tell even a stupid man that Banquo was responsible for their miserable plight. Macbeth now asks if they are going to be patient and accept this mistreatment; if they are such good Christians that they will pray for Banquo and his children, even though it was Banquo who made beggars out of the men's own families.

The First Murderer replies that they are only human (and can only take so much). Macbeth scornfully mocks the two men, saying that just as there are different breeds of dogs, each with its own natural talent, so it is with men; each man has a special gift, bestowed on him by nature. He says if they believe themselves better than the lowest form of humanity, he will give them a job to do, which, when it is done, will rid them of their enemy and win his strong regard for them. Macbeth adds that while Banquo lives, he feels unsafe, but with him dead everything would be perfect. The Second Murderer replies that life has been so hard on him that he doesn't care what he has to do to revenge himself; the First Murderer says that he'd rather be dead if he can't find a way to improve his quality of life.

Macbeth says that although he wants Banquo dead as much as they do, he must not be seen to be involved in his death; he uses the excuse that he and Banquo have mutual friends, whose loyalty he doesn't want to lose. So the truth must be hidden from public view. The Murderers agree to do whatever Macbeth commands. Macbeth shows he is pleased with them. Within an hour he will advise them on where to lay their deadly ambush and when it should be sprung . It has to be done, Macbeth insists, that very night and away from the palace. Once again he reminds them that he can't be seen to be involved. Then Macbeth says that Fleance must die as well; his death is just as important to him as Banquo's. The men are told to wait for him in another room. After they have left, Macbeth feels relieved and he says that Banquo's soul will find its way to heaven that night.

Commentary

If Macduff was rash in provoking Macbeth by not attending his coronation, at least he was being honest with himself: he suspects Macbeth of murdering Duncan and so he won't be a hypocrite and help Macbeth celebrate his ascend-

anoy to the throne (all this we saw in the previous scene).
Banquo also suspects Macbeth:

> 'Thou hast it now, King, Cawdor, Glamis, all,
> As the weird women promised; and, I fear,
> Thou playedst most foully for 't'
>
> (III. i. 1-3).

But Banquo doesn't do anything about it. What can he do?
He has no hard evidence, only suspicions based on observing
Macbeth's reaction to the Witches in I. iii, his conversation
with him shortly before the murder at II. i. 20-30, and what
he witnessed along with the others immediately after the
murder in II. iii. That would seem to be enough to convince
him of Macbeth's guilt, but it is all circumstantial evidence.
In other words, Banquo has no actual proof that Macbeth
murdered Duncan; until he has, he can't expose him, and he
must resign himself to accepting him as the *de facto* King.
Banquo is a wise man, as Macbeth acknowledges:

> 'He hath a wisdom that doth guide his valour
> To act in safety'
>
> (III. i. 52-53).

So he won't do anything in haste which might compromise
his own safety. How do you expose the King and bring him to
justice even if you have got solid evidence against him?
Macbeth is speaking the truth when he tells the Murderers:

> 'I could
> With bare-faced power sweep him from my sight'
>
> (III. i. 117-118).

Of course, Macbeth doesn't want to 'sweep' Banquo away
from him with 'bare-faced power' because he knows this will
draw suspicion upon him.

Another view to consider is that Banquo's virtue, defined

in glowing terms by Macbeth in lines 48-55, has become a little tarnished with the Witches' promises and he is actually pleased that Macbeth has become King. The enthusiasm with which he pledges his undying loyalty to his new King in lines 15-18 seems genuine:

> 'Let your highness
> Command upon me, to the which my duties
> Are with a most indissoluble tie
> For ever knit.'

This is obviously very much in contrast to Macduff's refusal even to go to the coronation. Could it be that lines 2-3, 'I fear,/ Thou playedst most foully for 't', are not meant as a criticism but as an ironic statement of fact; that Banquo is glad Macbeth is King, whatever he has done to get there, since it proves that the Witches' prophecies are coming true, and, although he won't actually embrace evil himself, he will now wait in hope of those promises coming true for his own family? This might explain why, in his opening soliloquy, Banquo allocates only three lines to Macbeth's rise to power and the other six lines to what all this means (i.e. the Witches' prophecies proving to be accurate) for himself and his offspring:

> 'yet it was said,
> It should not stand in thy posterity;
> But that myself should be the root and father
> Of many kings. If there come truth from them
> (As upon thee, Macbeth, their speeches shine),
> Why, by the verities on thee made good,
> May they not be my oracles as well,
> And set me up in hope?'
>
> (III. i. 3-10).

Could it also explain in some measure why Banquo is quite

vague about his plans for the day? Perhaps the purpose of his ride is really to visit the Witches so that they can look into the 'seeds of time' for him once more. Now, the reality of Macbeth's success offers a promise of success for himself also, and so he could well be interested to know in detail what he can expect from the future. The fact that Banquo says that the business also requires the presence of his son ('our time does call upon 's') suggests he's not just off for an afternoon ride; then again, there is always the possibility that he doesn't trust Macbeth with his son's life. All these points must lead us to wonder whether Banquo, like Macbeth, is not both 'fair and foul'.

There is irony in Macbeth's insistence that Banquo should not miss the banquet, when he knows Banquo will be dead before that:

> *Macbeth*
>   Fail not our feast.
> *Banquo*
> My lord, I will not.

(III. i. 27-28).

Banquo doesn't 'fail' Macbeth. He turns up at the banquet alright, but as a ghost (III. iv).

As soon as Banquo has gone, Macbeth claims that he wants to be left alone, 'to make society/ The sweeter welcome', lines 41-42, (i.e. to make the company of the lords more enjoyable when they meet again later), but he has the Murderers waiting outside and that is his real reason for dismissing everyone.

Macbeth has only recently been crowned and so he wants to make the right impression. He uses the royal plural extensively to emphasise his royalty. Does he also want the others to think that he is going to use this time alone in solemn prayer? It seems possible. But Macbeth has now sold his soul to the devil and, as we see later on in the scene (lines 87-90), he is scornful of Christianity and the Christian doctrine of forgiveness:

> 'Are you so gospelled
> To pray for this good man, and for his issue,
> Whose heavy hand has bowed you to the grave
> And beggared yours for ever?'

Macbeth wants Banquo dead for three reasons: (i) because he is virtuous; (ii) because he knows too much; and (iii) because he resents the idea that Banquo's sons and not his own will inherit the crown (which is why Fleance has to die as well).

Banquo's virtue is stated in these lines:

> 'in his royalty of nature
> Reigns that which would be feared; 't is much he dares;
> And, to that dauntless temper of his mind,
> He hath a wisdom that doth guide his valour
> To act in safety. There is none but he
> Whose being I do fear: and under him
> My genius is rebuked'

> (III. i. 49-55).

Banquo is the perfect man, according to Macbeth (although we questioned that assumption earlier in this section). He is a man blessed by nature with a balanced make-up of courage, wisdom and virtue. Macbeth is a man flawed by nature, and he fears Banquo because his evil guardian spirit is too weak to resist Banquo's good angel: 'under him/ My genius is rebuked.'

Macbeth effectively gave himself away to Banquo in II. i. 20-30. Macbeth had asked, in rather general terms, for Banquo's support when the time is right, saying it would be to Banquo's advantage if he did so. Banquo replied that he would accept Macbeth's advice and lend him his support so long as he didn't lose his honour in doing so. This conversation took place immediately after reference had been made to the Witches and not long before Duncan was found murdered. Banquo must have guessed at the time (either in II. i. or after the murder in II. iii) what Macbeth was talking about. Here in III. i, in lines 56-57, Macbeth says:

> 'He chid the sisters
> When first they put the name of king upon me.'

This, of course, isn't true. Banquo did not chide the Witches for putting evil ideas into Macbeth's head; all he did was to ask about his own future. Anyway, Macbeth is assuming here that Banquo has made the connection between the meeting with the Witches in I. iii and who murdered Duncan (and, quite clearly, Banquo has).

Macbeth devotes lines 60-69 to expressing his bitterness at the thought that everything he has done to gain the throne will eventually benefit Banquo's sons and not his own:

> 'Upon my head they placed a fruitless crown,
> And put a barren sceptre in my gripe,
> Thence to be wrenched with an unlineal hand,
> No son of mine succeeding'
>
> (III. i. 60-63).

Does Macbeth have a son, or sons? Lady Macbeth in I. vii. 54-58 mentioned the male infant she had 'given suck' to. We never meet Macbeth's child (or children) but it seems important to the plot that he has a son, otherwise this particular reason for killing Banquo as well as Fleance is no longer valid. So we assume that Macbeth's son exists (despite the inconsistency in IV. iii. 216, where Macduff says of Macbeth, 'He has no children').

Macbeth is going to try to stop the part of the Witches'

prophecy dealing with Banquo from coming true by asking fate to be his champion and fight on his behalf to change the future:

> 'come, fate, into the list,
> And champion me to the utterance'

(III. i. 70-71).

But Macbeth is not making sense here. The Witches told Macbeth and Banquo what fate had in store for them. Fate is predetermined, fixed, unalterable; it cannot be knocked off course, like the knight suggested in the image here being knocked off his charger. It is absurd for Macbeth to think that immutable fate will do his bidding. He cannot stop Banquo's children from becoming kings; it is already decided. As Banquo seems ready to give his allegiance to Macbeth as his new King (lines 15-18), Macbeth would be more sensible doing what he started to do in II. i, trying to secure Banquo as an ally. Indeed, the promise made to Banquo in II. i. 25-26 may be the reason why he now appears so co-operative and unwilling to expose Macbeth.

The Murderers enter. They are obviously ragged, disaffected soldiers. Macbeth doesn't seem to have done a very good job of convincing them that Banquo is the cause of all their woes; the First Murderer's response, 'You made it known to us' (line 83) sounds very noncommittal and more like, 'So you said' than 'We believe you'. When Macbeth tells them, 'Both of you/ Know Banquo was your enemy', they reply tersely, 'True, my lord' (line 114), but this is because Macbeth has been haranguing and insulting them, so they will tell him what he wants to hear. They are in no position to contradict their King or disobey his commands. This whole episode with the Murderers is vile and Macbeth is stripped of all nobility during it. He was not (for the obvious reason of his criminality) a prepossessing or convincing figure as King at the beginning of the scene despite his regal manner of speaking; now he seems no better than the Murderers themselves, like a thug manipulating and inciting other thugs to carry out the dirty deeds he doesn't want to be associated with.

Act Three Scene II

We are still in the royal castle at Forres. Lady Macbeth is thinking about Banquo. She is told by a servant that he has left for his ride and will return that evening. While she waits for her husband, Lady Macbeth reflects that they have gained nothing, lost everything; they have got what they wanted but it has not brought them peace of mind. She says she would rather be the murder victim than spend her life worrying like this.

Macbeth enters and, slightly hypocritically, she chides him for keeping to himself and dwelling on morbid thoughts which should have died along with Duncan. She tells him that what is done is done, and there is no point in his turning problems over in his mind for which there are no solutions. Macbeth replies that they have wounded the snake (i.e. the forces opposing them) but not killed it. It can heal itself and so they still live in danger of its bite. He would rather heaven and earth fell apart than they continue to eat their meals in fear and suffer nightmares. Macbeth adds with bitterness that it would be better for them to be dead, and share the peace Duncan has found in death, than for them to continue in mental agony. Duncan is in his grave, sleeping soundly after life's turmoil. Treason has done its worst and can no longer hurt him. He cannot be touched now by sword, or poison, internal rebellion, or foreign armies; he is free at last.

Lady Macbeth tries to calm her husband; she tells him not to look so careworn. He must appear bright and jovial to his guests (at the banquet) that evening. Macbeth promises that he will be cheerful then, and tells Lady Macbeth to be the same. He asks her to pay special attention to Banquo; she should show him the highest respect in the way she looks at him and speaks to him. So long as they are both unsafe, he says, they must hide behind flattery; their faces must be masks, disguising what is in their hearts. Lady Macbeth, seeing that her husband is becoming overwhelmed by fear and suspicion again, tells him to stop thinking like this. Macbeth replies that his mind is full of terrible fears ('scorpions', line 36). He reminds her that Banquo and Fleance are still alive, but she tries to reassure him by saying that they are not immortal. This comforts Macbeth. He says that Banquo and Fleance can be dealt with; so he tells her to cheer up. Macbeth says that before the night is old, a dreadful deed of great importance will be done. Lady Macbeth asks what it will be. Macbeth says that it is better she doesn't know about it just yet, but he adds that she will praise him once it is done.

Macbeth calls on night to cover the tender eye of pitying day; he asks it to use its bloody and invisible hand to destroy the life that keeps him pale with fear. Night is falling. The crow flies home to its nest in the wood. The good creatures of the day begin to feel sleep coming on, while the evil creatures that prey at night are beginning to stir. Macbeth sees that his wife is surprised by his words, but he tells her not to worry. Those who have committed bad deeds, he tells her, grow stronger and more secure by resorting to further evil.

Commentary

It is later in the same day as III. i. Lady Macbeth, once so ambitious to become Queen and only very recently crowned, is already disenchanted with her new life. There is no happiness for them, she says, without safety:

'Nought's had, all 's spent,
Where our desire is got without content'

(III. ii. 4-5).

She doesn't say exactly where she perceives the threat coming from, but the fact that she asks where Banquo is in the first line would suggest that she shares Macbeth's obsession with him. When Macbeth enters, she hides her fears, but her words, 'Things without all remedy/ Should be without regard' (lines 11-12) seem to say that she has thought about the trap, the tunnel of evil they are now caught in, and can find no way out of it. They are, she knows, forced to go on, for there is no way back now. The phrase 'what's done is done' (line 12) echoes earlier lines from Macbeth: 'If it were done when 't is done, then 't were well/ It were done quickly' (I. vii. 1-2); but in I. vii, Macbeth still had a choice between good and evil; now, the only option remaining to him is further evil, and this point, that the forces of virtue have to be outstripped by piling on more and more evil, forms the scene's conclusion:

'Things bad begun make strong themselves by ill'

(III. ii. 56).

The whole mood of this scene is of both Macbeths being aware that they have irrevocably lost everything that makes life worth going on with. Lady Macbeth, for fear of unnerving her husband, says little (in comparison with him) and her reticence in this scene, when she knows they have made a mistake, is in strong contrast to the aggressive volubility we saw from her when she was trying to goad Macbeth on in I. vii.

Macbeth uses the image of a snake to represent the forces of virtue which are opposing him:

'We have scotched the snake, not killed it:
She'll close and be herself; whilst our poor malice

Remains in danger of her former tooth'

(III. ii. 13-15).

The snake, from the Book of Genesis onwards, has always symbolised evil. The inversion of the snake image to symbolise virtue must indicate Macbeth's state of confusion. Macbeth 'hath murdered sleep' (II. ii. 41) and the 'terrible dreams' (line 18) which now haunt him remind us of this. 'Sleep, that knits up the ravelled sleave of care' (II. ii. 36) is no longer the 'Chief nourisher in life's feast' (II. ii. 39) for him, but a torment instead. Macbeth compares his mental agony as he lies in bed to being placed on the torture rack:

'Better be with the dead
Whom we, to gain our place, have sent to peace,
Than on the torture of the mind to lie
In restless ecstasy'

(III. ii. 19-22).

It is not just Banquo that is troubling Macbeth, it is guilt as well. The only escape from guilt is death, which is why it appeals so much to him. Macbeth compares life to a fever and death to sound, untroubled sleep:

'Duncan is in his grave;
After life's fitful fever he sleeps well'

(III. ii. 22-23).

Lady Macbeth had nerves of steel right up to the murder in II. ii, but now she is beginning to lose her composure. Her lines at the beginning of the scene, before Macbeth enters, are an indication of this:

'Nought's had, all's spent,
Where our desire is got without content:
'T is safer to be that which we destroy,

'Than by destruction dwell in doubtful joy'
(III. ii. 4-7).

Her mental deterioration starts here, leading on to her state of nervous exhaustion at the end of III. iv, her sleep-walking in V. i, and culminating with her suicide in V. v. Some critics have argued that the first indication of her loss of nerve is when she faints in II. iii. 115; that she has already used up all her fortitude in holding both herself and Macbeth together and so collapses after the murder from sheer mental strain. In our Commentary to that scene we took a different view: that the faint is a pretence, a device to distract attention from Macbeth whom she thinks is about to be forced into an awkward corner by Macduff. Either view is acceptable (i.e. that her deterioration is first seen here, in III. ii, or in II. iii). In III. ii, she still puts on a brave face in front of Macbeth, however much she is cracking up inside. After his 'better to be dead' speech at lines 13-26, she tells him:

'Come on;
Gentle my lord, sleek o'er your rugged looks;
Be bright and jovial among your guests tonight'
(III. ii. 26-28).

The gentle, affectionate tone belies her real fear that Macbeth will lose control of himself and give them both away by saying something, or showing his guilt, at the banquet planned for that evening. Lady Macbeth knows that her husband's face is an open book: 'Your face, my thane, is as a book, where men/ May read strange matters' (I. v. 60-61). She gently chides Macbeth with the words, 'You must leave this' (line 35), when he is both instructing her and complaining to her of the need for them to hide behind flattery:

'... we

> Must lave our honours in these flattering streams,
> And make our faces vizards to our hearts,
> Disguising what they are'

(III. ii. 32-35).

Then when Macbeth seems about ready to break, exclaiming in lines 36-37:

> 'O! full of scorpions is my mind, dear wife!
> Thou know'st that Banquo and his Fleance lives',

Lady Macbeth comes to his rescue again, giving her husband the reassurance that Banquo and Fleance are not immortal: 'But in them nature's copy's not eterne' (line 38).

Why does Macbeth tell Lady Macbeth to flatter Banquo at the banquet ('Let your rememberance apply to Banquo:/ Present his eminence, both with eye and tongue', lines 30-31) when he knows Banquo will be dead? Because, as he does himself in III. iv, he wants Lady Macbeth to flatter Banquo in his absence to draw suspicion away from them for Banquo's murder.

Whatever we feel about Lady Macbeth for her cruelty and callousness, we can't help admiring her for the way she supports her husband. While her strength is slowly wasting away inside her, she is expending what reserves of energy she has left on him. Lady Macbeth was worrying about Banquo when the scene opened, but she doesn't mention her fears to Macbeth because she doesn't want to make him any more excitable than he already is, although line 38 can be read as a subtle hint that Banquo and Fleance must be dealt with. In response, Macbeth then drops a hint of his own about the 'deed of dreadful note' (line 44) which will take place that evening.

Macbeth has become aware of his wife's heightened state

of anxiety; the faint in II. iii. 115 passed without comment from him, but he presumably saw it as the result of mental strain. He, in turn, now wants to protect her from further anxiety by keeping her in the dark about the plot to murder Banquo and Fleance:

> 'Be innocent of the knowledge, dearest chuck,
> Till thou applaud the deed'
>
> (III. ii. 46-47).

It is also possible that Macbeth doesn't tell his wife about his plan to murder Banquo and Fleance for the following reasons: (i) He wants to prove to her that he can act independently of her, thereby winning her admiration and approval, (ii), knowing the strain she is under, he feels that she might give them away (if that strain were to be increased). Whatever view we choose to take, this point in the play marks the start of Macbeth's independence from his wife and he never consults her again.

It seems highly unlikely that Lady Macbeth really is in the dark about the murder, or murders, not if that is what she really was suggesting anyway in line 38. Then there are the give-away lines 49-51, when he asks night to use its 'bloody and invisible hand' to,

> 'Cancel, and tear to pieces, that great bond
> Which keeps me pale!'

What else could Macbeth possibly be referring to but another murder? And the only possible candidates for victims are Banquo and Fleance. Lady Macbeth plays along with her husband, showing surprise at line 55 as if to indicate that she really doesn't know what he's talking about, but she does.

Lady Macbeth knows that she pushed her husband into murdering Duncan, and that now, they both regret it. With a woman's intuition, she isn't going to push him anymore; he will blame her if things go wrong. She will be more subtle this time to get her way. But her subtle hint, of course, is unnecessary; Macbeth has the stomach for murder now and he has seen to Banquo and Fleance's deaths without his wife's prompting.

Lines 47-54 are notable for the way evil becomes symbolically associated with night and darkness. This is part of the recurring imagery of the play which is dealt with in Section 6 iii. Night is falling and the forces of evil are gathering to strike once again:

> 'Come, seeling Night,
> Scarf up the tender eye of pitiful day,
> And, with thy bloody and invisible hand,
> Cancel, and tear to pieces, that great bond
> Which keeps me pale! — light thickens; and the crow
> Makes wing to the rooky wood;
> Good things of day begin to droop and drowse,
> Whiles night's black agents to their preys do rouse.'

The doubts and misgivings which characterised Macbeth's speeches before Duncan's murder now give way to a tone relishing in evil. Macbeth's identity seems to have merged with 'night's black agents'. The good, the innocent, feel sleep coming on: 'Good things of day begin to droop and drowse', but Macbeth sleeps no more, for he is no longer innocent and has become a predator of the night. The forces of goodness associated with daylight attempted to assert themselves with the arrival of Macduff at Inverness Castle in II. iii, but the powers of evil were too strong and day refused to break, the sun hiding its light in shame (II. iv. 5-10). The full force of virtue reasserting itself over evil, of daylight evaporating the darkness, is not felt until much later on in the play at V. ii.

Act Three Scene III

Later that evening at sunset, beside a road leading through a park to the castle gate, three Murderers wait for Banquo and Fleance to return from their ride. The Third Murderer says that he was sent by Macbeth to join the other two. The Second Murderer tells the First that they need not mistrust him, since he knows the details of their plan (and therefore must be telling the truth). The First Murderer tells the newcomer to join them, then delivers some moving lines of poetry describing the day's end.

They wait. Horses are heard. Banquo's voice offstage calls for a light. The Second Murderer recognises Banquo's voice. Banquo and Fleance have dismounted and are walking the last mile to the castle gate (which is what most people do). They enter, with Fleance carrying a torch. The Murderers prepare to attack. Banquo pauses for a moment, looks up at the sky and tells Fleance it will rain later that night, then the First Murderer cries out 'Let it come down', strikes out the light, while the other two assault Banquo.

Banquo dies, but Fleance escapes in the darkness. The Third Murderer is annoyed that the torch was put out, but the First Murderer believes that this was part of the plan. Realising they have failed in half of their appointed task, they leave to report to Macbeth.

Commentary

It is generally agreed that the Third Murderer (who doesn't appear in III. i) has been sent by Macbeth to ensure the other two men do not betray him, making the point that the tyrant now trusts no one. It has also been argued that the Third Murderer is to kill the other two after they have done their work, to cover Macbeth's tracks a little better. But we don't hear of their deaths after III. iv (when the First Murderer turns up at the banquet (to speak to Macbeth) so this theory can't be proven. The Second Murderer tells the First that they need not distrust the Third Murderer, who presumably they have never met before, because he knows in detail what they have been told to do and so he must have been sent by Macbeth:

> 'He needs not our mistrust, since he delivers
> Our offices, and what we have to do,
> To the direction just'
>
> (III. iii. 2-4).

These lines are sometimes read two other ways: (i) Macbeth doesn't need to mistrust us, as he has given us precise instructions (so we know what to do); (ii) There is no need for us to mistrust him (the Third Murderer) as he is bringing the details of the plan (to kill Banquo and Fleance), which Macbeth promised to give us at III. i. 127-131. Neither of these interpretations is preferred to the one given above.

Macbeth told the Murderers at III. i. 133 to 'leave no rubs, nor botches, in the work', but the job is botched (bungled). The First Murderer is responsible; he strikes out the light (line 15), enabling Fleance to make his escape in the darkness while the other two are assaulting Banquo. The Third Murderer seems to blame the First for not following the plan, while he seems confused as to what the plan was:

> *3 Murderer*
> Who did strike out the light?
>
> *I Murderer*
>   Was't not the way?
>
> (III. iii. 19)

The 'way' referred to here is the plan they all agreed upon, or were told by Macbeth, to carry out the assassinations. The First Murderer must have got it wrong — he should have attacked Fleance right away, forgetting about the light, while the other two took on the stronger Banquo.

It seems strange and inappropriate to give the First Murderer these fine lines of verse to speak:

'The west yet glimmers with some streaks of day:
Now spurs the lated traveller apace,
To gain the timely inn'

(III. iii. 5-7).

We have an impression of the Murderers as sullen, disgruntled, coarse figures; hardly the sort given to poetic expression. The lines continue, 'and near approaches/ The subject of our watch'; perhaps what Shakespeare is doing, is creating in us a heightened sense of evil preying on unsuspecting innocence by juxtaposing images of beauty and calm with images of menace and death. However, the lines also have a more practical and obvious value in that they tell us the time of day — sunset.

Banquo's remark to Fleance, 'It will be rain tonight' (line 15), is a suitable point for them to pause (i.e. stop walking across the stage), to look up at the sky, so that while their attention is elsewhere, the Murderers can take them completely by surprise. Also, the sky would be overcast, the stars hidden, reminding us of Macbeth's words in I. iv. 50-51, 'Stars, hide your fires!/ Let not light see my black and deep desires'; it is as though heaven is responding yet again to Macbeth's appeal for it to turn its pitying face away from his cruel deeds.

Act Three Scene IV

Much later on that night (and into the early hours of the next morning, see line 127), a banquet is in progress at Forres Castle. Macbeth is celebrating his ascendancy to the throne in grand style. He enters, with Lady Macbeth by his side as

Queen and tells Rosse, Lenox and the other lords to take their places at the table according to their social ranks (i.e. with the highest at the head of the table and so on). Graciously, Macbeth says he will stand for a while to mingle with his guests and play host while Lady Macbeth takes her place at the table.

The First Murderer enters and stands at the door. Macbeth looks for an empty seat, comments that both sides of the table are evenly occupied and says that he will sit in the middle. Then he spots the First Murderer; telling the others to pass round the wine, he goes to the door to speak with him. The First Murderer tells Macbeth that the blood smeared across his face is Banquo's, whose throat has been cut. Macbeth is pleased and he hopes the same was done to Fleance; but he is told that Fleance escaped. Macbeth's trepidation returns, replacing the momentary feeling of relief that came with the news of Banquo's death; now he is once again wracked by doubts and fears. The First Murderer assures Macbeth that Banquo is dead, his body lying in a ditch with twenty deep gashes in the head, the least of them a fatal wound. Macbeth draws some comfort from this, saying that Fleance has the potential to make trouble for him but is harmless at the moment. He dismisses the First Murderer, telling him they will speak again the next day.

Lady Macbeth mildly rebukes her husband for neglecting his guests, saying that what gives a feast its flavour is not mere food but the company. Lenox politely asks Macbeth to sit. Macbeth comments that they would have all the nobles in the land under one roof if Banquo were now present; he hopes Banquo's absence is caused by thoughtlessness rather than an accident. Banquo's Ghost enters and sits in Macbeth's place. Rosse blames Banquo for breaking his promise to attend the banquet; then he, too, asks Macbeth to join them at the table. Macbeth replies that the table is full. Lenox points to a seat reserved for Macbeth, but the Ghost (which only Macbeth can see) is sitting in it. Lenox points again to the seat but noticing Macbeth is upset about something, he asks what is troubling him. Macbeth points to the Ghost and demands to know which of the lords has done this. They are all bewildered. Macbeth tells the Ghost not to shake its bloody head accusingly at him. Rosse tells the lords to rise, saying Macbeth is unwell, but Lady Macbeth asks them to remain seated. She explains that her husband is often like this and has been since his youth; the fit, she adds, will soon pass and Macbeth will be offended if they take too much notice of it. Lady Macbeth tells the company to continue eating; then she turns angrily on Macbeth, asking him 'Are you a man?' (line 58). Macbeth replies that he is a man and a brave one at that, for looking at what would scare even the devil himself.

Lady Macbeth, meanwhile, believes he is hallucinating and she compares what is happening now to the dagger episode (in II. i). She tells him these fits of fear brought on by inconsequential things are better suited to old wive's tales told around winter firesides; adding contemptuously that Macbeth is only looking at a chair. Macbeth points to the Ghost, telling the lords to look at it. He commands the Ghost to speak, but it disappears. Lady Macbeth accuses her husband of speaking foolish nonsense unbecoming a man.

Macbeth recalls that in olden days when men were more barbarous, the dead stayed dead; now, he says, they rise again with twenty fatal gashes on their heads to steal their seats. Lady Macbeth draws her husband away from his morbid thoughts and back into the company; he apologises and tells them to ignore his behaviour, for he has a sickness which is nothing to those who know him. He drinks to the happiness of all present and Banquo, wishing he were there with them. As he speaks the Ghost reappears, its eyes gleaming. Macbeth tells it to go back to its grave and stay dead. Then he challenges it, saying that he wouldn't be frightened if it took any living form; it it came alive again, he would fight a duel with it and if he showed fear he could be called a baby girl. The Ghost goes.

Macbeth is calm once more and he tells his guests to remain seated. Lady Macbeth reproaches him, saying he has destroyed the mood of the feast with his behaviour. Macbeth protests, saying she is making him doubt himself. He asks, how can they behold such a sight without their cheeks turning pale, when his have turned white with fear? Rosse asks what it is they are supposed to have seen, but Lady Macbeth tells him not to make her husband worse by asking questions. She asks them all to go without observing formalities and then sees them quickly out.

Macbeth wonders why Macduff didn't come to the banquet. Lady Macbeth asks if he was invited; Macbeth answers that Macduff was not actually summoned but he knew the feast was being held. (Macbeth explains that he pays one of Macduff's servants to spy for him.)

He announces that he will visit the Witches, for he must know more and nothing must now be allowed to stand in his way. He is so steeped in blood now that there is no turning back; he has to go on in the same murderous way. There are certain deeds in his mind that must be carried out.

Lady Macbeth comforts her husband by saying he lacks sleep. He tells her they will go to bed. He says that his imagination has been deceiving him, but this is just a beginner's fear and will pass as he becomes hardened by experience, for he has only just started.

Commentary

This scene forms the centre and turning point of the play (though some editors take Fleance's escape in III. iii as the turning point), concluding its first half, which has dealt with Macbeth's rise to power. At the banquet, he will say more than enough to betray himself, and the rest of the play's action deals with the process of his downfall.

The banquet has a symbolic significance, representing two things about society: (i) human fellowship and (ii) order. Lady Macbeth makes the first point when she calls her husband away from the door, where he is talking to the First Murderer:

> 'the sauce to meat is ceremony;
> Meeting were bare without it'
>
> (III. iv. 36-37).

She is saying that what gives a feast its flavour is the company; without which the feast would be poor. We saw Macbeth alienated from the warmth of human fellowship in I. vii; the others were banqueting to honour him at Inverness Castle, while he had shut himself out away from it all by ruminating over evil, guilt and damnation in another room. In this scene, III. iv, Macbeth remains outside the circle of human fellowship; he never joins the banquet by sitting down at the table; for Banquo, who has failed to expose Macbeth as a murderous traitor during his lifetime, will do so now in death. His Ghost, perched in Macbeth's seat, reminds us of the irony of Macbeth's words at III. i. 27, 'Fail not our feast'. Banquo's reply had been, 'My lord, I will not', and he has kept his promise. Macbeth set a trap to catch Banquo, but has fallen into it himself.

Macbeth's first line in the scene is:

> 'You know your own degrees, sit down: at first and last'.

The seating of the lords at the table, according to their ranks, reflects the proper, stable, hierarchical order of the state. But Macbeth has disturbed the harmony of this order by usurping the throne; there is only an illusion for a few lines of the restoration of order following the turmoil of Duncan's death. Macbeth cannot find an empty seat at the table after line 41 (the Ghost's first appearance), suggesting his alienation from society and the company of men by his evil deeds. His behaviour breaks up the banquet, the lords leaving not in order (as they had taken their places) but randomly and unceremoniously, reflecting the chaos Macbeth has brought down upon Scotland. Lady Macbeth expresses this idea of the thin veneer of harmony and stability, shown at the beginning of the scene, being stripped away to expose the grim reality of disorder within the state:

> 'You have displaced the mirth, broke the good meeting,
> With most admired disorder'
>
> (III. iv. 109-110).

It is she who tells the lords to go at once, abandoning ceremony and formality:

> 'Stand not upon the order of your going,
> But go at once'
>
> (III. iv. 119-120).

Is Banquo's Ghost an actual ghost or an hallucination, like the airborne dagger in II. i? Critics and producers of the play seem divided on this question. Some argue that as it can only be seen by Macbeth and only appears when he is thinking about Banquo, it is, therefore, an hallucination — the product of Macbeth's imagination. But the Elizabethans and Jacobeans believed that ghosts could at times be seen by only one person, and it is perhaps a more attractive idea than the hallucination theory, firstly, because Banquo is taking revenge on Macbeth for his murder by terrifying and exposing him, and secondly, his Ghost is also fulfilling in death the moral obligation to betray Macbeth which it neglected in life.

In line 39, Lenox asks Macbeth to sit, but he doesn't respond to the question as he is thinking about Banquo, the First Murderer having left only a few lines earlier. Then, as if he fears that his thoughts can be read, he tries to cover himself by saying:

> 'Here had we now our country's honour roofed,
> Were the graced person of our Banquo present;
> Who may I rather challenge for unkindness,
> Than pity for mischance!'
>
> (III. iv. 40-43).

The Ghost enters at line 41, as though to 'challenge' in turn the hypocrisy of Macbeth's words. Rosse reminds us of Banquo's promise to attend the banquet (line 44). Macbeth's words to the Ghost, even though he appears to be talking into thin air, cannot fail to give him away:

> 'Thou canst not say I did it. Never shake
> Thy gory locks at me'
>
> (III. iv. 50-51).

There is something pathetic and absurd about Macbeth here; in trying to disclaim guilt to the Ghost, he reveals it to the lords. They know: they must surely have made the connection between Banquo's absence, Macbeth's reference to him, followed by the terror of the haunting or hallucinating, and Macbeth's guilt. It is possible though since Banquo's name is not mentioned, that they think he is being haunted by the ghost of Duncan.

Lady Macbeth, on the other hand, assumes her husband is hallucinating and, as she compares this incident with the dagger in II. i and knows nothing of the plot to murder

Banquo, must think that Macbeth has lapsed into morbid thoughts about murdering Duncan:

'This is the very painting of your fear:
This is the air-drawn dagger which, you said,
Led you to Duncan'

(III. iv. 61-63).

She rises wonderfully to the occasion, coming to her husband's rescue as she did at II. iii. 115. She instantly concocts a story about an illness Macbeth has had since youth. She knows he is going to give himself away (if he hasn't already), so she makes the familiar verbal assaults on his manhood to try to snap him out of it:

'Are you a man?'   (line 58);

'these flaws and starts
(Imposters to true fear) would well become
A woman's story at a winter's fire,
Authorised by her grandam. Shame itself!' (lines 63-66);

'What! quite unmanned in folly?'   (line 73).

The Ghost's visitation hardens Macbeth, but it would be wrong to say that the abuse from Lady Macbeth achieves this. It is more like a determination to fight back against fear, the burden of fear that he has lived with since he first met the Witches in I. iii and which he assumed he could free himself from by killing Banquo. We feel this toughening in line 70 when, having ranted at the lords because of their lack of response to the Ghost, he says, 'Why, what care I?' He knows he has given himself away but the doubts and fears have become too much for him and now he no longer cares; the effort of hiding is over for him. And although the Ghost doesn't cease to frighten him after line 70, he is prepared to stand up to it and confront it, perhaps almost disdainfully:

'If thou canst nod, speak too' (line 70). Macbeth's words in lines 78-80 now match and echo in their savagery Lady Macbeth's image of unpitying ruthlessness in I. vii 54-59 ('plucked my nipple from his boneless gums,/ And dashed the brains out'):

> 'the time has been
> That, when the brains were out, the man would die,
> And there an end'.

The continuation of these lines amounts to a murder confession from Macbeth, given now with a hardened indifference to the consequences:

> 'but now they rise again,
> With twenty mortal murders on their crowns,
> And push us from our stools. This is more strange
> Than such a murder is'
>
> (III. iv 80-83).

The Ghost re-appears at line 91, again when Macbeth is lying hypocritically about Banquo:

> 'I drink to the general joy of the whole table,
> And to our dear friend Banquo, whom we miss;
> Would he were here'
>
> (III. iv. 89-91).

But this time Macbeth challenges it (lines 99-107) and the Ghost must seem to Macbeth to have been frightened off, for his words immediately after it has gone are triumphant: 'Why, so; — being gone,/ I am a man again' (lines 107-108).

Macbeth has conquered fear. Never again in the play will we see him hesitate in his actions to keep the crown, as he hesitated in taking it; never again will conscience so trouble him. And there will be no more hallucinations, which is what

Macbeth takes the ghost to be — a hallucination brought on by a beginner's fear:

> 'My strange and self-abuse
> Is the initiate fear, that wants hard use:
> We are yet but young in deed'
>
> (III. iv. 142-144).

The demoniac Macbeth has come to terms with himself in that he now recognises fear as his greatest enemy; he has stood up to it and chased it away in this scene and, as lines 142-144 tell us, he knows it will trouble him less and less as his career of bloodshed grows and matures.

Lady Macbeth's mental resolve begins to weaken in this scene, going in the opposite direction to her husband's. At the beginning she appears subdued, asking her husband to welcome the guests on behalf of them both as he plays host. We remember her disillusionment from III. ii and this perhaps explains her mood here. When the First Murderer enters and speaks to Macbeth, she must appear cheerful to her guests to cover for her husband's neglect of them. Then, when the Ghost enters, she has two jobs to do: to make excuses for Macbeth and to try to stop him betraying himself. It is a losing battle. She keeps up the pretence of social grace to the last, bidding the lords, 'A kind good night to all' (line 121), but the strain has been too much for her. After the lords have gone, she has no strength left to protest at her husband's behaviour; her energy is spent and she is exhausted. Her reply to Macbeth's question (about the absence of Macduff at the banquet) is short and, for her, feeble: 'Did you send to him, Sir?' (line 129). All she can do is comfort her husband by telling him that he needs to sleep, but in reality it is Lady Macbeth who is in need of respite, while her husband is drawing on new reserves of strength.

We don't see Lady Macbeth again until V. i, the

sleepwalking scene, by which time it is obvious that her mental deterioration is almost complete. Her decline began in III. ii (or II. ii, if we take the fainting to be a genuine sign of strain); it continues here in III. iv, leading on to the full-blown symptoms of a nervous breakdown in V. i. The news of her death is given to Macbeth in V. v, but it is not until later that we learn that she killed herself and thus of the depths of her despair.

Line 122, 'It will have blood, they say, blood will have blood', echoes an earlier thought of Macbeth's: 'we but teach/ Bloody instructions, which, being taught, return/ To plague th' inventor' (I. vii. 8-10). Macbeth is saying that bloodshed is repaid by bloodshed. He knows that the Ghost's purpose was to force him into betraying himself, so that he might be destroyed and the revenge cycle completed, but Macbeth is no coward (see I. ii. 16-23; III. iv. 99-106; V. v. 46-52; V. viii. 27-34). (Macduff calls Macbeth a coward in V. viii. 23, but the reference is more to the sneaky attack made on his family by Macbeth's assassins, and this is not convincing evidence of cowardice.) His fears, up to Act III, have been moral and spiritual; after that he fears losing the crown, but in the physical sense, he remains a brave man throughout the play.

In the Commentary to III. ii, the point was made that the presence of the Third Murderer demonstrates Macbeth's unwillingness to trust anyone. This point is reinforced here when Macbeth tells his wife that he keeps spies in the homes of all his lords: 'There's not a one of them, but in his house/ I keep a servant fee'd' (lines 131-132). Thus, it would seem that while Macbeth now fears no man, he mistrusts every man.

Macbeth is determined to see the Witches again the following day (lines 132-135). His first meeting with them was unsought but now that he is too far down the path of evil to turn back, he willingly seeks their support to help him continue along it. He sees himself as past the point of no return on this path of bloodshed, and the following lines hint that he would like to turn back, but can't; instead he is forced to go wearily on:

> 'I am in blood
> Stepped in so far, that, should I wade no more,
> Returning were as tedious as go o'er'
>
> (III. iv. 136-138).

Act III Scene V

Hecate, the goddess of witches, meets the weird sisters on a heath and reprimands them for having dealings with Macbeth (whom she calls 'a wayward son,/ Spiteful and wrathful', lines 11-12) without informing her. She tells the Witches to meet in the morning, for Macbeth will come to them 'to know his destiny' and she will contrive spells to draw him on, spurning wisdom, fate and death, to his destruction. A song, "Come away, come away", is heard offstage; Hecate is being summoned by her attendant spirit, so she exits, followed by the Witches.

Commentary

There is general agreement among editors and critics that this scene was not written by Shakespeare. There are three reasons for this belief: (i) tetrameter (four stressed syllables a line) is used, as in the other Witch scenes, but here with a different rhythm from these other scenes; (ii) Hecate's speech does not agree with the image of Macbeth which the rest of the play has created; e.g. Macbeth is hardly 'wayward' (line 11), meaning childish and self-willed, nor is he 'Spiteful and wrathful' (line 12) at this stage, though admittedly he becomes so after IV. i; (iii) the song's title is given ("Come away, come away") but not the words. As this song appears in full in a contemporary play called *The Witch* by Thomas Middleton, it is thought that he either wrote the scene at Shakespeare's request (which seems unlikely), or, it was put into the play after Shakespeare had written *Macbeth,* probably after he had either retired to Stratford or died. This last theory seems the most likely. Perhaps a producer, recognising the popularity of the Witches in the play, got Middleton or someone else to write the extra scene, and from there it was transcribed into the First Folio.

Act Three Scene VI

Lenox, speaking to another lord, confirms that suspicions of Macbeth's guilt are widespread. With sarcasm and bitter irony he says that Duncan was pitied by Macbeth and then Duncan died; Banquo walked late and seems to have been killed by Fleance, for Fleance has run away; and everyone knows how monstrous it was for Malcolm and Donalbain to kill their own father. Macbeth was so overwhelmed with grief, Lenox adds (continuing with the sarcasm and irony), that he immediately stabbed the two delinquent grooms who were helpless with drink and fast asleep; of course, Macbeth acted properly for it would have angered any thinking and feeling person to hear them deny responsibility.

Lenox suggests that if Macbeth had Malcolm and Donalbain as prisoners in his dungeon, he would kill them (to silence them) and then pretend this was punishment for their crime; and the same goes for Fleance. Lenox says that Macduff is in disgrace for speaking too openly and missing the banquet, and asks the other lord if he knows of Macduff's whereabouts. The anonymous lord replies that Malcolm, the true heir to the throne of Scotland, is living at the English court where, despite his misfortune, he is treated with great respect by the devout English King, Edward the Confessor; Macduff has gone there also to seek aid from the

Earl of Northumberland and Siward. With their help, and
with God behind them, the lord hopes they may soon be free
again.

The news of Macduff being in England has so angered
Macbeth that he is preparing for war. Lenox asks if Macbeth
sent for Macduff and is told that Macduff flatly refused to
come, and Macbeth's messenger turned his back and hummed
as if to say, 'I'll take my time returning with such an
unwelcome reply and you'll live to regret it.' Lenox says the
messenger would be well advised to keep his distance from
Macbeth's anger. He prays that an angel might fly to the
court in England and speed their deliverance.

Commentary

The purpose of this scene is to let the audience know that
suspicions of Macbeth's guilt are now widespread among the
nobility of Scotland, the anonymous lord serving as the
representative of that class, just as the Old Man in II. iv
represented the voice of the ordinary people.

Lenox's sarcasm and irony may be for either of two
reasons: (i) he is stating the case against Macbeth obliquely to
avoid accusing him directly, for, presumably, no one can be
trusted at court now; (ii) his tone is designed to show his
anger and contempt for Macbeth, since he makes little effort
to be cautious by disguising the drift of his words and is quite
prepared to refer directly to Macbeth as a tyrant (line 22).

Until now, Macduff has been Macbeth's main accuser; it is
he who has been openly denouncing Macbeth and his 'broad
words' (open allegations) line 21, along with his failure to
attend the banquet, have placed him 'in disgrace' (line 23),
though this is clearly Macbeth's choice of words and Lenox is
continuing with his irony by repeating them.

Macbeth, the tyrant, is made to stand in contrast to 'the

most pious Edward' (the King of England), who is showing
Malcolm the hospitality due to Duncan's heir and the rightful
King of Scotland:

> 'The son of Duncan,
> From whom this tyrant holds the due of birth,
> Lives in the English court; and is received
> Of the most pious Edward with such grace,
> That the malevolence of fortune nothing
> Takes from his high respect'
>
> (III. vi. 24-29).

Two of the play's basic images — feasting and sleeping —
are used by the lord to describe the sad plight that those who
live under Macbeth's reign of terror find themselves in. The
lord looks forward to a time when,

> 'we may again
> Give to our tables meat, sleep to our nights,
> Free from our feasts and banquets bloody knives'
>
> (III. vi. 33-35).

When Shakespeare wrote this scene, it was obviously
meant to follow IV. i. At the end of III. iv, Macbeth said he
intended to visit the Witches the next day and also to send a
messenger to Macduff (to find out why Macduff failed to
attend the banquet). In lines 39-43, we learn that the
messenger has returned from Fife already and yet Macbeth
still hasn't been to see the Witches. The explanation is that
this scene was moved back from its position after IV. i to
separate the two Witch scenes when III. v was added (see
Commentary to III. v). The other point to support this is that
in IV. i we have (or Shakespeare intended us to have) a
moment of dramatic tension when Macbeth hears galloping
horses and learns that Macduff has fled to England (see IV. i.
139-142). Shakespeare would not have allowed this (Macduff's

escape from Macbeth's clutches) to be an anticlimax by telling us of Macduff's flight beforehand.

Act Four Scene I

The three Witches move around a boiling cauldron in a dark cave, chanting 'Double, double, toil and trouble' as they throw various obnoxious objects into the cauldron. They are making 'a charm of powerful trouble' (line 18) which will summon the Apparitions later in the scene. Hecate joins the three Witches. There is music and a song, "Black Spirits". The Second Witch knows, from a pricking sensation in her thumbs, that something unusual is about to happen. She says, 'Something wicked this way comes' (line 45). There is a knocking and Macbeth enters.

Disdainfully calling the Witches 'you secret, black, and midnight hags' (line 48), Macbeth demands to know what they are doing. They reply in unison, 'A deed without a name' (line 49). Macbeth again fiercely demands an answer. The First Witch asks if he would rather hear from them or their masters, and Macbeth tells her to call them.

The First Apparition, a head clad in armour, appears with a clap of thunder. Macbeth is told his thoughts are already known to it; he may listen, but not speak to it. The First Apparition tells him to beware of Macduff, and then starts to go. Macbeth thanks it for the warning, saying it has rightly guessed his fear. He wants to ask more but the Apparition will not be ordered by him and disappears.

The sound of thunder is heard again and the Second Apparition, a child covered in blood, appears. It tells Macbeth to scorn the power of men, for none born of woman can harm him, before vanishing like the First Apparition. Macbeth says that he need not fear Macduff then, but he will kill him nevertheless to be doubly sure and to give fate extra support. He adds that, with this done, he will be free from fear and able to sleep through thunder.

Thunder is heard again and the Third Apparition, a child, crowned, with a tree in his hand, faces him. It tells Macbeth to be brave, proud and fearless of those who oppose him, for he will never be vanquished till Birnam Wood comes to the hill of Dunsinane Castle. After it has gone, Macbeth exults in what he think is his invincibility, but he yearns to know one more thing — if Banquo's children will one day reign.

The Witches tell Macbeth to ask no more, but he insists. The cauldron begins to sink and trumpets sound. The Witches chant, 'Show his eyes, and grieve his heart' (line 110) and a procession of eight kings, the last holding a mirror, followed by Banquo's Ghost, enters.

Macbeth recognises something of Banquo's looks in the first three kings. As the fourth approaches, Macbeth scolds the Witches. The fifth and sixth pass, and Macbeth asks if the line will stretch forever. He looks on in horror as the seventh king passes by and then the eighth, who holds the mirror towards Macbeth, showing him many more. Macbeth notices that some of the kings reflected in the mirror wear the crown of two kingdoms (i.e. Scotland and England; see Commentary).

The blood-spattered Ghost of Banquo, which brings up the end of the procession, smiles at Macbeth and points to the kings, indicating that they are his offspring.

The First Witch asks Macbeth why he is so amazed. She says they will dance to cheer him up. They do so and then vanish, with Hecate. Macbeth, in a rage, says this hour must be forever cursed in the calendar. He calls to someone outside the cave and Lenox enters. Macbeth asks if he saw the Witches, but Lenox didn't. He curses them and all who put their trust in them. Then he says he heard horses galloping past and asks Lenox who it was. He is told that messengers have brought news that Macduff has fled to England.

Macbeth, thinking aloud to himself, says he must act instantly in future, so that his deeds keep pace with his plans. He will act on his ideas the moment they come to him, and the first idea that does cross his mind is to mount a surprise attack on Macduff's castle and kill his wife and family. He will not boast like a fool and thereby delay taking action; he will do it before his anger cools.

Commentary

All of the fragments the Witches throw into the cauldron are (or were thought to be at the time) harmful to man, for, whatever Macbeth might think at the beginning of this scene, the Witches are not on his side; they are making 'a charm of powerful trouble' (line 18) to do just that - make trouble for him. Certain of the contents are chosen for their anti-Christian symbolism, perhaps to thwart any protection from the charm Macbeth might seek later on through prayer: the 'Liver of blaspheming Jew' (line 26) is an allusion to the widespread mediaeval legend of the Jew who, because he abused Christ on the way to Calvary, was cursed by God and made to wander the earth for all eternity; the 'Nose of Turk, and Tartar's lips' (line 29) are included because both the Turks and the Tartars (Asiatic horsemen) were hostile to Christianity.

Hecate's speech between lines 39-43 and the song, "Black Spirits", were almost certainly not written by Shakespeare but were put in as an addition by the same author who wrote III. v (see Commentary to that scene).

Macbeth enters the cave and his greeting to the Witches is contemptuous and irreverent, probably reflecting the disillusionment he feels with the way the prophecies have worked for him so far:

'How now, you secret, black and midnight hags!'
(IV. i. 48).

However, Macbeth's appeal to the Witches, in lines 50-61, has a tone of desperation about it, as though he is placing the same curse on virtue, harmony, and Christianity as the Witches themselves and would join them in the havoc they wreak. But he is mistaken in thinking they are on his side, for they remain hostile and determined to confound him. We feel his attempt to join them, to be familiar with them, in the chummy informality of the words in line 63: 'Call 'em; let me see 'em'.

When the Apparitions are conjured up, they hold Macbeth at a distance; he can only listen to them, but not question them; they know his thoughts, but he isn't given access to theirs, and so he is being used, for they only tell him what they want him to know and that is just enough to mislead him. The Apparitions are not serving Macbeth's interests by accurately revealing the future to him; they are serving the Witches' interests by tricking him. Macbeth interprets the Apparitions wrongly — seeing only what he wants to see — failing to understand the way their symbolism points to his downfall.

The first Apparition, the armed head, which tells him to beware of Macduff, he probably takes to be Macduff, but the image represents his own head which is severed from his body by Macduff in Act V. There is macabre irony in the way Macbeth thanks the First Apparition at line 73, when we consider what it is that Macbeth has been looking at — his own decapitated head. The stage directions indicating the Apparitions' descent tell us that they exit (and probably enter) through the stage's trap-door, the suggestion being that they, the Witches' masters, are rising from and returning to the burning bowels of hell.

The Second Apparition, the bloody child, which tells him 'to scorn/ The power of man, for none of woman born/ Shall harm Macbeth' (lines 79-81), again deceives him, for the infant, which seems so helpless, stands for Macduff at the time of his birth — not 'of woman born' but 'from his mother's womb/ Untimely ripped' (V. viii. 15-16).

The Third Apparition, a child crowned, with a tree in his hand, is recognised by Macbeth as 'the issue of a king' (line 87); perhaps he hopes the vision represents his own son. The child tells him that 'Macbeth shall never vanquished be, until/ Great Birnam wood to high Dunsinane hill/ Shall come against him' (lines 92-94); but the child is Malcolm, wearing the crown of Scotland and holding in his hand a branch from Birnam wood signifying how this seemingly impossible feat will be accomplished and the prophecy fulfilled (see V. iv. 4-7, and V. v. 33-46).

After the Third Apparition has gone, Macbeth feels re-assured that he will live a full lifespan and die of old age:

> 'our high-placed Macbeth
> Shall live the lease of nature, pay his breath
> To time and mortal custom'
>
> (IV. i. 98-100).

He has, of course, been deceived throughout and lulled into a false sense of security, for the Witches have juggled with words ('these juggling fiends', V. viii. 19) and he has placed a construction on what he has seen and heard that best suits his purposes. He has only heard what he wanted to hear; he has heard but not properly understood.

Although Macbeth was not allowed to question the Apparitions, he never doubted them or considered the possibility that there might be an alternative interpretation to what he saw or heard than the one they placed invitingly in front of him. He knows they are evil but he assumes that as

he is evil too, they are in league with him and accessories to
his crimes; whereas the truth is that he is a victim of their
machinations.

Macbeth already knows what the Witches prophesied for
Banquo, for it was told within his hearing in I. iii. The future
the Witches foretell is fixed and unalterable. So Macbeth's
question in lines 100-103,

> 'Yet my heart
> Throbs to know one thing: tell me (if your art
> Can tell so much), shall Banquo's issue ever
> Reign in this kingdom?'

(for which he already has an answer: 'Lesser than Macbeth,
and greater' ... 'Thou shalt get kings, though thou be none',
I. iii. 65 and 67) can only be interpreted as an attempt by
Macbeth to get the Witches to do the impossible — change
their prophecy and therefore change the course of fate.

He is told: 'Seek to know no more' (line 103), but this
response angers Macbeth and he threatens to curse the
Witches if they deny him a reply:

> 'I will be satisfied: deny me this,
> And an eternal curse fall on you!'

(IV. i. 104-105).

Earlier on we saw Macbeth adopting an almost patronising
tone of familiarity (line 63); now he thinks he can bully the
Witches into telling him what he wants to know. Macbeth
wrongly assumes that he is in control; but he is not, the
Witches are and, like the Apparitions earlier on in the scene
(see line 75), they are unwilling to be ordered about.

As the Witches can tell what the future holds, they knew
Macbeth would ask this question, so they have prepared a
charm in advance to summon the show of eight kings,
followed by Banquo's Ghost. They pretend a reluctance to

answer his question (line 103), then appear to give in to him so they can watch him being punished for his arrogance and impertinence by the anguish he is put through. They all chant in unison: 'Show his eyes, and grieve his heart' (line 110).

The royal pageant of kings and Banquo's Ghost prove to Macbeth, firstly, that fate cannot be altered and, secondly, that all his bloody deeds will prove futile. Banquo's Ghost smiles at Macbeth and points to his line of descendants, exulting in Macbeth's agony and his own triumph. He is now 'lesser than Macbeth' (I. iii. 65) in that he is dead and Macbeth is King, but he is 'greater' because he will be the ancestor of a line of kings which will 'stretch out to th' crack of doom' (line 117).

At the time *Macbeth* was written, 1606, James I (formerly James VI of Scotland) was the new King of England. James was a descendant of Banquo's, and so Shakespeare was flattering his King by suggesting that his line, the House of Stuart, which had reigned in Scotland since 1371 and was now reigning in England as well, would hold the throne forever. In fact, the House of Stuart lasted as England and Scotland's royal family until 1688. The 'two-fold balls' (line 121) point to the union of England and Scotland under the one crown of James I and the 'treble sceptres' probably stand for the union of England, Scotland and Ireland (something James I tried to force on a very unwilling Ireland after he came to the throne in 1603).

When the pageant is over and Banquo's Ghost gone, the Witches are delighted with the result of their labours. They cavort gleefully at line 132, knowing they have brought Macbeth to the edge of despair. The First Witch asks sarcastically: 'but why/ Stands Macbeth thus amazèdly?' (lines 125-126); she is implying that Macbeth has only got what he asked for and, with still more sarcasm, adds that Macbeth has now been repaid for his contemptuous treatment of them: 'this great king may kindly say,/ Our duties did his welcome pay' (lines 131-132). The Witches vanish, leaving Macbeth to curse them and 'all those that trust them' (line 139). Thereby, ironically, cursing himself.

He then summons Lenox into the cave and is given the news that Macduff has escaped to England, confirming the First Apparition's warning — that Macduff is a threat to Macbeth.

In his speech in lines 144-156, we see Macbeth abandoning any sensitivity and feeling left in him. From this point on in the play he is a hardened man, no longer held back by doubts, fear, or moral scruples. He says he will convert every cruel thought into instant action:

'The very firstlings of my heart shall be
The firstlings of my hand'

(IV. i. 147-148).

His decision to take Macduff's castle and slay his family shows Macbeth to have become a barbaric tyrant. Although he cannot strike against Macduff himself, he is determined to fulfil the promise he made to himself in lines 147-148 and so will take revenge by killing Macduff's family. His own sons can never be kings, so he intends to destroy the children of his enemy out of pure, malicious spite.

Taking this last point, we can see that it is Banquo (as much as Macduff) that Macbeth is lashing out at in his attack on Fife Castle. The Witches' prophecy for Banquo, confirmed in this scene by the royal pageant and Banquo's Ghost, has told Macbeth that his own offspring will never benefit by his reign. But Banquo is dead and Fleance is out of reach. So Macbeth directs his vengeance against Macduff, not just because he is a threat, but also because he is jealous of Macduff for having some promise for the future in his family line; hence Macbeth will get even by sending his men to Macduff's castle to 'give to th' edge o' th' sword/ His wife, his babes, and all unfortunate souls/ That trace him in his line' (lines 150-152). Macbeth, like so many tyrants, is taking his personal frustrations and disappointments and expressing them in mass murder against those who might succeed where he has failed.

The news of Macduff's escape to England comes as an anticlimax in this scene. We already know about it because we were told in III. vi. This was not Shakespeare's intention. It was brought about when III. v was added by someone other than Shakespeare and III. vi and IV. i were reversed in their order to separate the two Witch scenes (see Commentaries to III. v and III. vi).

It was stated in the Commentary to I. i that the Witches don't make Macbeth do anything; that he is a free moral agent confronted from first to last with a choice between good and evil. There is no harm in repeating those points here. Macbeth is under no spell compelling him to commit his crimes, and it is worthwhile remembering that a criminal is what Macbeth is. The Witches tempt Macbeth throughout the play because they know what his ambitious dreams are. They tell him that he will become King, but they don't tell him to use evil means to get it. Macbeth never blames the Witches for tempting him to murder Duncan, for the very obvious reason that they never made the suggestion in the first place. What Macbeth does blame the Witches for is juggling with words and lulling him into a false sense of security. We see this in V. viii. 19-22:

> 'And be these juggling fiends no more believed,
> That palter with us in a double sense,
> That keep the word of promise to our ear,
> And break it to our hope'.

Macbeth probably had the germ of the idea of murdering

Duncan planted in his mind even before he met the Witches in I. iii; all the Witches have done is water the seed and nurture his ambitions. Macbeth murders Duncan out of ambition; the grooms out of fear of the discovery of his crime; Banquo out of fear of the Witches' prophecy regarding Banquo's descendants, and because Banquo's 'royalty of nature', the 'dauntless temper of his mind' and his wisdom (III. i. 49-52) are a reminder to Macbeth of his own evil nature ('under him/ My genius is rebuked', III. i. 54-55); and Macduff's family, as we saw from the previous paragraphs, out of revenge, frustration, and spite.

Act Four Scene II

In a room in Macduff's castle in Fife, Lady Macduff complains to Rosse that her husband's flight to England was motivated by fear rather than wisdom. She says that her husband has acted unnaturally, for even the wren, the smallest of birds, will fight for her young ones in the nest against the owl. Rosse defends Macduff, saying he is noble, wise, of sound judgement, and well understands the troubles that surround them. He is scared to speak too openly but he says that times are cruel when people are made traitors without knowing why. Rosse continues, saying fear breeds rumours, though what they fear is uncertain; they are tossed this way and that, as if on a stormy sea. He is about to go, but he assures Lady Macduff he will return soon. His parting words of comfort are that if things are as bad as they can be, they will either cease or get better. Rosse blesses Lady Macduff's son, but she comments bitterly that the boy is without a father. Rosse leaves.

Lady Macduff tells her son in a teasing tone that his father is dead and she asks him how he will live. He replies that he will live as birds do, on anything he can find. She asks if he would be frightened of traps set for birds, but he asks in return why he should be, for traps are not set for poor birds (i.e. only for rich ones).

The boy insists his father isn't dead, whatever his mother claims, while Lady Macduff in turn insists he is, and again asks what he will do for a father. They continue to banter. The boy responds to his mother's question by asking what she will do for a husband; she says she can buy twenty at any market, and his retort is that she can buy them to sell them again. Then the boy asks if his father was a traitor. Lady Macduff, still teasing her son, says he was. He asks what a traitor is and is told that it is a person who swears and lies; she adds that everyone who swears and lies is a traitor and must be hanged. The boy asks who must hang them; she replies, the honest men, but the boy thinks the liars and swearers are fools for there are enough of them to beat the honest men and hang them. Lady Macduff laughs at her son's clever reply. Then he adds another witty observation: that if she didn't weep, he'd know he would soon be getting a new father.

A Messenger enters and tells Lady Macduff that danger is close at hand and she should flee with her children. He is sorry for frightening her but says that not to do so would be a greater cruelty, and cruelty is near at hand. The Messenger leaves. Lady Macduff asks where she can run to; she has done no one harm, but then she remembers that she is in a world where to hurt others is considered worthy and to do good is dangerous folly.

The Murderers enter and one of them asks where Macduff is. Lady Macduff scornfully replies that she hopes he is in no place so unholy that a man of his sort might be there to find him. The same Murderer accuses Macduff of being a traitor; the boy defends his father and is stabbed to death. Lady

Macduff runs off screaming, pursued by the Murderers. She is killed offstage.

Commentary

Lady Macduff's bitterness towards her husband is understandable, for *we* know why he has fled to England (see III. vi. 24-37) but *she* does not. She tells Rosse that Macduff's behaviour is folly, for, though he is innocent of any act of treason against the King, running away out of fear makes him appear to be a traitor:

'His flight was madness: when our actions do not,
Our fears do make us traitors'

(IV. ii. 3-4).

Rosse, arguing in defence of Macduff, suggests that his flight may have been motivated by wisdom rather than fear (lines 4-5), but we agree with Lady Macduff when she scorns this idea:

'Wisdom! to leave his wife, to leave his babes,
His mansion, and his titles, in a place
From whence himself does fly?'

(IV. ii. 6-8).

She feels helpless and vulnerable, and this accounts for her bitterness. We know from what happens later in this scene and in IV. iii that she is exaggerating when she adds, 'He loves us not' (line 8). But Macduff has acted irresponsibly in assuming that Macbeth is not so brutal as to take revenge against his innocent family. We, on the other hand, know he is from what happened in IV. i, and recognise how rash Macduff is to rely on a tyrant's sense of fair play.

By abandoning his family, Macduff has done something

unnatural, and Lady Macduff points this out to Rosse in a touching image:

'He wants the natural touch; for the poor wren,
The most diminutive of birds, will fight,
Her young ones in her nest, against the owl'

(IV. ii. 9-11).

But once more Rosse comes to Macduff's defence, assuring her that, 'He is noble, wise, judicious, and best knows/ The fits o' th' season' (lines 16-17). Then, speaking in fits and starts, which indicate how troubled he really is by Lady Macduff's helpless situation, he gives a graphic account of the times they are living in, when a man can be branded a traitor without good reason and rumours breed fear, though even what is to be feared is uncertain:

'But cruel are the times, when we are traitors,
And do not know ourselves; when we hold rumour
From what we fear, yet know not what we fear,
But float upon a wild and violent sea
Each way, and move — '

(IV. ii. 18-22).

It is his state of anxiety that makes Rosse break off in mid-sentence (line 22), 'and move — '. He starts comparing the troubled times to being tossed about on a violent sea, but the image is not completed. It is possible that, as well as fearing for Lady Macduff's safety, he feels guilty about not staying by her side, so he breaks off abruptly and takes his leave. What he actually says is that if he stays any longer, he won't be able to hide his feelings, to his disgrace and Lady Macduff's embarrassment:

'I am so much a fool, should I stay longer,
It would be my disgrace and your discomfort:

I take my leave at once'

(IV. ii. 28-30).

Left on their own after Rosse has gone, the full extent of Lady Macduff's and her son's vulnerability is emphasised. Their banter gives expression to Lady Macduff's bitterness and sense of helplessness, though we, like her son, should take nothing she says about her husband seriously. His witty responses to her remarks are cheerful and charming (in a precocious way) and they contribute to the main purpose of this good-humoured interlude, which is to relax the mood slightly so that the tension is more dramatic when the Messenger enters at line 61. However, we never relax completely during this interlude and feel an undercurrent of uneasiness despite the good humour.

When the Messenger enters, bringing news of the Murderers' approach, we feel a sense of horror at the intrusion into this intimate family tableau by Macbeth and his evil influence. Lady Macduff pleads innocence, but Macbeth's crimes are against innocence, and so she has no defence. She remembers that she is living in a world where values have become inverted; where to harm others is considered praiseworthy, and to do good is dangerous:

'I have done no harm. But I remember now
I am in this earthly world, where to do harm
Is often laudable, to do good sometime
Accounted dangerous folly'

(IV. ii. 71-74).

When the Murderers enter and ask Lady Macduff where her husband is, her reply indicates her true feelings about Macduff:

'I hope, in no place so unsanctified,
Where such as thou may'st find him'

(IV. ii. 78-79).

In other words, she knows her husband is too decent a man to ever be in the kind of unholy place which the likes of the Murderer would visit. And when the First Murderer calls Macduff a traitor, the boy leaps to his father's defence, 'Thou liest, thou shag-eared villain!' (line 80), sadly recalling the innocent, good-humoured chatter about traitors earlier on in the scene (lines 45-56).

Macbeth's crimes are perversely associated with images of childhood and fertility, emphasising their unnaturalness. In IV. i, Macbeth described his thoughts of murder and murder itself in these terms: 'The very firstlings of my heart shall be/ The firstlings of my hand', IV. i. 147-148 ('firstlings' suggesting 'first-born children'); here, in IV. ii, as the Murderers plunge their daggers into Macduff's son, the First Murderer uses images of youth and fertility as terms of abuse: 'What, you egg!/ Young fry of treachery!' (lines 80-81).

Act Four Scene III

The scene shifts to England, in a room in the palace of King Edward the Confessor. Malcolm enters with Macduff. Malcolm suggests they find a shady spot and there weep away their sadness, but Macduff says it would be better for them to take up arms in defence of their homeland. Every new day, Macduff says, new widows grieve, new orphans cry, new sorrows offend heaven, so that it groans in sympathy with Scotland and lets out similar cries of sorrow. Malcolm replies that he is prepared to mourn but he is uncertain of the truth. What wrongs he can redress, he will do so when the time is right. What Macduff has said might well be true, but Malcolm adds that this tyrant, Macbeth, was once thought to be honest. Macduff, he points out, once loved Macbeth and, as Macduff has not yet been made to suffer by Macbeth, he might be trying to do himself some good by betraying Malcolm to him — like appeasing an angry god by sacrificing an innocent lamb to it. Macduff denies he is a traitor, but Malcolm points out that Macbeth *is,* and even a good and honest man may yield to the pressure of a royal command. He asks Macduff's pardon, but adds that his thoughts won't make Macduff genuine. He realises that loyalty still exists among men even when others are disloyal, and worries all the more about how to differentiate between them since wickedness always tries to look like virtue, whereas virtue cannot change its appearance in spite of this.

Macduff says that he has lost hope, and Malcolm replies that this could be one reason why he is suspicious of him. He asks why Macduff left his wife and child exposed to danger; then he says that he doesn't want to cast dishonour on Macduff by his suspicions, for Macduff may well be honourable, whatever doubts he has. Macduff is overwhelmed with grief for his country and, frustrated by Malcolm's words, he bids him farewell, saying that he refuses to be called a villain and wouldn't be one even if the prize were Scotland and the rich countries of the East. Malcolm tells him not to take offence, for he doesn't totally distrust him. He knows Scotland's sorry plight, but thinks there are many who would fight in his cause to save her. He adds that the English King has offered several thousand men, but once the tyrant, Macbeth, is overthrown, his poor country will suffer even more under its new King. Macduff asks who the new King will be, and Malcolm replies that he is referring to himself. He says that he is so steeped in vices that Macbeth will seem as pure as snow in comparison with him; Macbeth will seem like a lamb next to his infinite evil.

Macduff protests, saying that nowhere in hell could there be found a devil more steeped in evil than Macbeth. Malcolm grants that Macbeth is full of vices, but he says that there is no limit to his own lust; there are not enough women to satisfy his desires; it is better that Macbeth should reign, he adds, than a man like himself. Macduff says that an unrestrained sexual appetite has caused the downfall of many kings, but he points out that Malcolm can indulge himself in sexual pleasures secretly without seeming unchaste; there are so many willing women that they will far exceed his appetite. Malcolm says that as well as lustful, he is also insatiably greedy; he would execute his subjects for their possessions, and the more he had, the more he'd want; he would invent quarrels against the good and loyal to destroy them for their wealth. Macduff replies that Scotland is rich enough to satisfy Malcolm's needs and that all the faults Malcolm is admitting to are tolerable so long as they are balanced by other virtues.

In reply, Malcolm says he has no virtues whatsoever that would become a king; he only knows criminal behaviour, and if he came to power, tolerance would be sent to hell, and peace and unity on earth would be destroyed. He asks if such a man as himself is fit to govern. Macduff replies that he isn't even fit to live. He reminds Malcolm that his father was a saintly king and his mother deeply religious. He bids Malcolm farewell, saying that the evils Malcolm has told against himself will stop him, Macduff, from ever returning to Scotland.

Macduff is in agony, seeing no hope left for his country, but then Malcolm admits that he has been putting Macduff to the test and that the despair Macduff has expressed has wiped away his suspicions and satisfied him that Macduff is both truthful and honourable. Malcolm says that Macbeth has used similar tricks to draw him into his power; so wisdom forbids him to be persuaded of the virtue of others too easily. He promises to be guided by Macduff, and renounces the stains on his character which he said he had. Malcolm says he is a virgin; that he's never broken his word and barely wants what belongs to him already without ever coveting what belongs to others. He announces that Old Siward with ten thousand soldiers was about to set off for Scotland when Macduff arrived; now they will go together, and he hopes the success of their venture matches the justice of their cause. Macduff is struck dumb by what he has just heard, finding it hard to reconcile what Malcolm said earlier about himself with what he is saying now.

A Doctor enters and we are told that the King is coming out and that a crowd of sick people, with an illness which defies medicine, are waiting to seek his cure. The King is so holy that those he touches soon recover. The Doctor goes. Malcolm explains that the disease is called the King's evil and that King Edward cures people by hanging a gold coin around their necks while he is praying. As well as this remarkable skill of healing, he also has the divine gift of prophecy. Malcolm says that Edward's reign is blessed.

Rosse enters. They greet each other and Macduff asks if Scotland is just the same. Rosse replies that Scotland hardly knows itself; it is no longer their motherland, but more like their grave. Only the ignorant smile; sighs, groans and shrieks go unheeded. Violence and sorrow are everyday occurrences and nobody bothers to ask who has died when the church-bells toll. Good men live shorter lives than the flowers they wear in their caps, dying before their time. Rosse says that news an hour old is stale, for new miseries happen every minute.

Macduff then asks how his wife is; Rosse replies, 'Why, well' (line 177), and he gives much the same answer when Macduff asks after his children. Macduff asks if the tyrant has left his family in peace and Rosse replies evasively that they were all at peace when he left them. Macduff presses for more news. Rosse says that many men are up in arms against

Macbeth, and Macbeth's forces are on the march. He asks for Malcolm's help, saying that his appearance in Scotland would guarantee the raising of an army. Malcolm tells Rosse to take comfort, for they are about to leave for Scotland with Old Siward and ten thousand men.

Rosse now turns to Macduff and says that he has no words of comfort to offer him. Macduff seems to guess what is coming, and then he is told that his castle has been taken and his wife and children savagely slaughtered. Malcolm tells Macduff not to hide his grief, for grief that is held in breaks the heart. Macduff asks if his children were killed as well, and Rosse tells him that all who could be found, his wife, children, servants, were put to the sword. Macduff blames himself for being away from home, then asks after his wife, as though in a desperate hope that he has misheard, but is given the same reply.

Malcolm promises Macduff revenge, but Macduff says that Macbeth has no children. When Malcolm tells him to face it like a man, Macduff replies that he will, but he must also feel like a man; he cannot easily forget what was so precious to him. He blames heaven for not defending them; then blames himself, saying they died for his sins and not their own. Malcolm tells him to turn his grief into anger, and to let this sad news sharpen his sword. Macduff says that he could weep like a woman, but promises that once he and Macbeth are face to face, there will be no escape for Macbeth. Malcolm welcomes the manliness of Macduff's words. He suggests they take their leave of the King and set out for Scotland right away. Macbeth, he continues, is ready for toppling and heaven will help them in this. He asks the others to take comfort from this saying: It's a long night that has no dawn.

Commentary

Malcolm's expression of despair at the beginning of the

scene, 'Let us seek out some desolate shade, and there/ Weep
our sad bosoms empty' (lines 1-2) sounds weak and ineffectual coming from a man who is to become the rightful King
of Scotland. We know very little about Malcolm, and his
words here disappoint us as much as they disappoint Macduff
(who urges action rather than sentiment in his reply: 'Let us
rather/ Hold fast the mortal sword, and like good men/
Bestride our down-fall birthdom', lines 2-4). But Malcolm's
words are part of the pretence to deceive and test Macduff.
Later on, in lines 131-135, when Malcolm reveals his true self
to Macduff, we learn that he is far from weak and ineffectual, and that he has already made arrangements for
Macbeth's overthrow and Scotland's relief from this tyrant:

> 'What I am truly
> Is thine, and my poor country's, to command:
> Whither, indeed, before thy here-approach,
> Old Siward, with ten thousand warlike men,
> Already at a point, was setting forth.'

This sounds more worthy of Scotland's future King, as do
his words at the end of the scene when he tells Macduff not to
hide his grief, for it will break his heart — 'Give sorrow
words; the grief that does not speak/ Whispers the o'er-
fraught heart' (lines 209-210) — and, a little later on, to
convert his grief into anger so that he may take revenge
against Macbeth for his family's death:

> 'Be this the whetstone of your sword: let grief
> Convert to anger; blunt not the heart, enrage it'
> (IV. iii. 228-229).

Up until this scene, we have had two fairly general accounts
of the state of fear which exists in Macbeth's Scotland; that
given by the anonymous Lord in III. vi. 33-37, and Rosse in
IV. ii. 18-22, and we have seen the atrocity committed against

Macduff's family in IV. ii. Now, Macduff tells us that terror, grief, and slaughter are widespread: 'Each new morn,/ New widows howl, new orphans cry; new sorrows/ Strike heaven on the face' (lines 4-6) and, when Rosse arrives, he paints an even grimmer picture of the living hell Scotland has become:

> 'It cannot
> Be called our mother, but our grave; where nothing,
> But who knows nothing, is once seen to smile;
> Where sighs, and groans, and shrieks that rend the air
> Are made, not marked; where violent sorrow seems
> A modern ecstasy: the dead man's knell
> Is there scarce asked for who; and good men's lives
> Expire before the flowers in their caps,
> Dying or ere they sicken'
>
> (IV. iii. 165-173).

In III. vi and IV. ii, we may have thought that Macbeth's reign of terror is felt only by the nobility of Scotland but the accounts given by Macduff and Rosse in this scene suggest that the violence is escalating and that it is directed at the nation's population at large. Rosse seems to imply that anyone found to be virtuous is put to the sword.

As was said earlier, we don't know much about Malcolm, except that in II. iii, after his father was found murdered, he could exercise control over his emotions and think coolly and clearly in a crisis. We need to know much more about him to judge whether he has the qualities of a good King. He is young (line 14), which suggests that he might not be wise. His father, Duncan, spoke wisely about not trusting people ('There's no art/ To find the mind's construction in the face', I. iv. 11-12), even while trusting others too easily — the former Thane of Cawdor and Macbeth being the obvious examples. Malcolm, on the other hand, is much more cautious. He makes a very good case for not trusting Macduff:

(i) Macbeth 'Was once thought honest' (line 13), therefore he knows better than to trust appearances; (ii) Macduff once loved Macbeth and, as Macduff has not yet suffered at the tyrant's hands, there is the possibility that Macduff might be trying to do himself some good by betraying him (Malcolm) to Macbeth, like sacrificing an innocent lamb to appease an angry god:

> 'you have loved him well;
> He hath not touched you yet. I am young; but something
> You may deserve of him through me, and wisdom
> To offer up a weak, poor, innocent lamb,
> T' appease an angry god'
>
> (IV. iii. 13-17);

(iii) wanting a person to be virtuous won't make him so, and all wickedness tries to look like virtue, so Macduff might be a devil in disguise:

> 'That which you are, my thoughts cannot transpose:
> Angels are bright still, though the brightest fell:
> Though all things foul would wear the brows of grace,
> Yet grace must still look so'
>
> (IV. iii. 21-24);

(iv) finally, Malcolm is suspicious of Macduff because Macduff has left his wife and children unprotected in Scotland, which suggests the possibility of Macduff being in league with Macbeth (for if he were, he would not fear for his family's safety):

> 'Why in that rawness left you wife and child...?'
>
> (IV. iii. 26).

Malcolm's exaggerated claims to vice are to trick Macduff and expose any evil intentions he may have. The device is rather too obvious for us to be taken in by it, although it succeeds in fooling Macduff. But it does serve three purposes: it allows a discussion of the wicked temptations tyrants succumb to; contrasts the qualities of a tyrant with those of a good king; and allows Macduff's virtue to be proved both to Malcolm and to ourselves. Macbeth is:

> 'bloody,
> Luxurious, avaricious, false, deceitful,
> Sudden, malicious, smacking of every sin
> That has a name'

(IV. iii. 57-60).

But, acting the part of the prospective tyrant himself, Malcolm claims that he would be no better then Macbeth:

> 'the king-becoming graces,
> As justice, verity, temperance, stableness,
> Bounty, perseverance, mercy, lowliness,
> Devotion, patience, courage, fortitude,
> I have no relish of them'

(IV. iii. 91-95).

In these two quotations, the negative characteristics of an evil monarch are juxtaposed with the fine qualities of a virtuous one. When Malcolm reveals his true self after line 114, we must assume that these 'king-becoming graces' which he claims he doesn't have for the purposes of deceiving Macduff, actually do belong to him; that he is the true son of his saintly father and pious mother (lines 108-111); and that he will make Scotland a fine King. But before this, while the deception is still in force, Malcolm says that he is insatiably lustful; that there would not be enough women in Scotland to appease his sexual desires, and none would be allowed to refuse him:

> 'your wives, your daughters,
> Your matrons and your maids, could not fill up

The cistern of my lust; and my desire
All continent impediments would o'erbear
That did oppose my will'

(IV. iii. 61-65).

So we add rape and licentiousness to the list of the would-be
tyrant's failings. Macduff's response is interesting; he seems
to feel that the King has a right to a certain sexual licence
(although he warns that 'Boundless intemperance' has been
the 'fall of many kings' in lines 66-69), and goes on to tell
Malcolm:

'But fear not yet
To take upon you what is yours; you may
Convey your pleasures in a spacious plenty,
And yet seem cold — the time you may so hoodwink:
We have willing dames enough; there cannot be
That vulture in you, to devour so many
As will to greatness dedicate themselves'

(IV. iii. 69-75).

Macduff is telling Malcolm not to be frightened of taking
what belongs to him (i.e. his female subjects); Malcolm can
gratify his sexual urges in secret and still seem chaste to the
rest of the world, and there would be more than enough
women attracted by Malcolm's greatness to satisfy his sexual
urges.

If Macduff doesn't take the sin of lust too seriously in a
king, he is more worried by Malcolm's claim to 'A staunchless
avarice', line 78, (an insatiable greed). Malcolm says that,
were he King, he would execute his nobles for their lands,
desire this man's jewels and that man's house, and invent
unjust quarrels against the good and loyal to destroy them for
their wealth. However, even greed can be tolerated in a king,
Macduff, says, as long as Malcolm possesses other virtues

that outweigh these faults. But Malcolm denies having any of
the virtues of the ideal king (lines 91-94), instead, he would
reign as a criminal and,

> 'Pour the sweet milk of concord into hell,
> Uproar the universal peace, confound
> All unity on earth'

(IV. iii. 98-100).

There are echoes of Lady Macbeth here: 'too full o' the milk
of human kindness' (I. v. 15).

By line 100, Malcolm has convinced Macduff that he has
no redeeming qualities to offset his self-confessed vices. Now
Macduff believes Malcolm's earlier assertion that should he
become King, Scotland 'Shall have more vices than it had
before,/ More suffer, and more sundry ways than ever' (lines
47-48). Macduff, however much he earnestly hoped that
Malcolm would prove worthy of the crown, laments, his hopes
dashed, and he must for a moment believe the point made by
Malcolm, at the start of the deception, that he would be a
worse king than Macbeth:

> 'It is myself, I mean; in whom I know
> All the particulars of vice so grafted,
> That, when they shall be opened, black Macbeth
> Will seem as pure as snow; and the poor state
> Esteem him as a lamb, being compared
> With my confineless harms'

(IV. iii. 50-55).

At this early stage, Macduff couldn't imagine a man more
capable of evil than Macbeth: 'Not in the legions/ Of horrid
hell can come a devil more damned/ In evils, to top Macbeth'
(IV. iii. 55-57). (Notice how Macbeth is compared to Satan,
both here and in line 22. The image of a lamb is used in
lines 16 and 54 to symbolise virtue; the lamb image suggests

Christ; but Malcolm, despite his real virtue, never achieves a Christ-like stature in this scene or in the rest of the play.)

After his admission of insatiable lust and cruel greed, his claim to having none of the 'king-becoming graces' (line 91), Malcolm asks Macduff if he is fit to govern (line 101). This is Macduff's real test. He must choose between good and evil. If he chooses evil, if he accepts temptation, everything is to his apparent benefit: he will enjoy a privileged position under his new King, be reunited with his family, and reap the rewards of villainy. If he chooses virtue, he loses his family and everything he possesses, apart from his honour, for he will be banished from Scotland. Macduff doesn't hesitate: he chooses virtue and accepts banishment:

> 'Fit to govern?
> No, not to live'
>
> (IV. iii. 102-103);

> 'These evils thou repeat'st upon thyself
> Hath banished me from Scotland. — O my breast,
> Thy hope ends here!'
>
> (IV. iii. 112-114).

Macduff has proved his virtue, not just to Malcolm but to the audience, which is important because at the end of the play, when Macduff kills Macbeth in V. viii, virtue must be seen to triumph over evil, for this is the true nature of Shakespearean tragedy. Only then can catharsis be achieved. (*Catharsis* is a word which comes to us from Aristotle, a Greek philosopher, who believed that the function of tragedy is to purge the feelings through the arousing of pity and terror. We may have certain feelings of pity and admiration for Macbeth as the play progresses, but at the end of it we think: 'This is how it had to work out. Macbeth had to die like this. Nobody could do anything to prevent it. Because of a flaw in Macbeth's character, a flaw he couldn't control, all this tragic upheaval had to happen.' The pity and terror are purged out of our systems, to be replaced by a mood of resignation, and an acceptance that good will always triumph over evil in the end.)

Once Macduff has shown a readiness to reject evil, Malcolm explains why he thought it necessary to test Macduff's good faith by pretending to be evil:

> 'Devilish Macbeth
> By many of these trains hath sought to win me
> Into his power, and modest wisdom plucks me
> From over-credulous haste'

(IV. iii. 117-120).

We are to understand from this that Macbeth has tried to lure Malcolm into his power, by sending messengers to him in England falsely declaring love and friendship, in the hope of getting Malcolm to return to Scotland where, without doubt, he would find himself in Macbeth's dungeons (we recall Lenox's words at III. vi. 18-20: 'had he Duncan's sons under his key/ [As, an't please Heaven, he shall not], they should find/ What 't were to kill a father'. Lenox is saying that Macbeth would throw Malcolm and Donalbain behind bars under the pretence of punishing them for murdering their father).

Malcolm now shows his true virtue by asking God to exercise control over the relationship between himself and Macduff, and by renouncing the sins of lust, avarice and dishonesty that he earlier pretended to possess:

> 'I am yet
> Unknown to woman; never was forsworn;
> Scarcely have coveted what was mine own;
> At no time broke my faith: would not betray

The devil to his fellow; and delight
No less in truth than life: my first false speaking
Was this upon myself'

(IV. iii. 125-131).

Macduff makes no response; there is no shaking of hands, no expression of relief from him — just silence. Malcolm asks, 'Why are you silent?' (line 137); Macduff replies:

'Such welcome and unwelcome things at once,
'T is hard to reconcile'

(IV. iii. 138-139).

We may assume that Macduff is stunned into silence by Malcolm's revelation of his 'true self', or could it be that now Macduff doesn't know what to believe and his silence indicates confusion, a part of him feeling that he has been drawn into Malcolm's power by false declarations of virtue (as Macbeth has tried to lure Malcolm by false declarations of love)? Macduff, after all, has no more good reason to trust Malcolm, than Malcolm had to trust him at the beginning of the scene.

Earlier on, in lines 91-94, we had the 'king-becoming graces' listed. Now, with the entrance of the Doctor, we are introduced to an ideal King, Edward the Confessor (who lived between 1002-1066 and was King of England from 1042-1066). Edward, because he is blessed by God, has the power of healing. The ills that have beset Scotland under Macbeth are frequently referred to in terms of physical injury or sickness, e.g.:

'each new day a gash
Is added to her wounds'

(IV. iii. 40-41).

The suggestion arising from this little episode is that only a

King blessed by God, i.e. Malcolm, can heal Scotland (see also Section 6 iii, 'The Recurrent Imagery of *Macbeth*').

Rosse enters and gives his grim news of Scotland (lines 164-173). When asked what the latest sorrow is, he replies that now, news of calamities just one hour old is old news, for new sorrows occur by the minute:

> *Malcolm*
>   What's the newest grief?
>
> *Rosse*
> That of an hour's age doth hiss the speaker;
> Each minute teems a new one.
>   (IV. iii. 174-176).

Rosse is reluctant to tell Macduff about the death of his family and he stalls as long as he can, from line 176, when Macduff asks about his wife, until lines 204-205, by which time Macduff has sensed that Rosse is being evasive and guessed what is being concealed from him. The news comes in a sudden rush from Rosse, for he knows there is no way to cushion the cruel blow than to deliver it quickly, at least putting Macduff out of the misery of uncertainty:

> 'Your castle is surprised; your wife and babes
> Savagely slaughtered'.

Macduff's expressions of grief after finding Duncan's murdered body in II. iii had been loud and eloquent, but now he is silent, holding his sorrow inside himself. Malcolm wisely tells him to let it out, for grief bottled up inside will break the heart:

> 'What, man! ne'er pull your hat upon your brows:
> Give sorrow words; the grief that does not speak
> Whispers the o'er-fraught heart, and bids it break'
>   (IV. iii. 208-210).

Macduff's repeated questioning of Rosse (lines 211-219) shows his state of shock. He is tormented by the thought that he was not at home when it happened (line 212), and that they died, not for their own sins, but because of his:

> 'Sinful Macduff!
> They were all struck for thee. Naught that I am,
> Not for their own demerits, but for mine
> Fell slaughter on their souls'
>
> (IV. iii. 224-227).

Three explanations have been given for Macduff's remark, 'He has no children' (line 216): (i) 'He' refers to Malcolm, who, if he had children of his own, would not suggest that Macduff 'Be comforted' and would know that revenge is no cure for Macduff's grief; (ii) 'He' refers to Macbeth, who could never have brought himself to kill another's children if he had had any of his own; (iii) Macduff is saying that Macbeth has no children, so he cannot take an eye-for-an-eye revenge on him. The third explanation is favoured here. Shakespeare can be inconsistent about details when it suits his dramatic purposes and, whereas Macbeth has referred to his children elsewhere in the play, e.g. III. i. 63 (and, of course, Lady Macbeth at I. vii. 54-59), he wants him to be childless here, probably because they would be difficult loose ends for Shakespeare to tie up at this stage of the play, just as we are about to enter the quickened pace of Act V. Perhaps Shakespeare hoped his audience wouldn't notice the inconsistency.

One of the most important purposes of this scene is to establish that Malcolm is a worthy future King. As was said earlier, II. iii proved that he is in control of his emotions and can think quickly: he knew that tears shed for his dead father at the time might be construed as hypocritical and the best course of action was for Donalbain and himself to flee Scotland:

'To show an unfelt sorrow is an office
Which the false man does easy'

(II. iii. 134-135).

Malcolm also knew that he and his brother were at risk:

'This murderous shaft that's shot
Hath not yet lighted, and our safest way
Is to avoid the aim: therefore, to horse,
And let us not be dainty of leave-taking,
But shift away'

(II. iii. 139-143).

(It is also possible to argue that Malcolm and Donalbain's refusal to grieve in II. iii shows insensitivity, and that by running away, thereby drawing suspicion upon themselves, they were being recklessly immature; although it doesn't seem likely that Shakespeare would have wanted us to draw either of these conclusions.)

If we take a positive (rather than a cynical) view of Malcolm, by the end of IV. iii we can say he is virtuous, wise, has a healthy scepticism (which distinguishes him from his father) and that he is a man of action. These are certainly 'king-becoming graces'.

Act Five Scene I

Macbeth and his wife are now in Dunsinane Castle. It is night. A Doctor of Medicine enters with a Waiting-Gentlewoman (a woman of noble birth who attends to Lady Macbeth). The Gentlewoman has told the Doctor about Lady Macbeth's sleepwalking; he has stayed awake for two nights to see things for himself, but nothing has happened yet to confirm the Gentlewoman's report. The Gentlewoman says that since Macbeth marched out with his army, she has seen

Lady Macbeth rise from her bed, throw on a nightgown, unlock her cupboard and take out paper, write on it, read it, then seal it, and return to bed again; all this while Lady Macbeth is fast asleep. The Doctor finds this most unnatural: to be deep in sleep, yet behave as if she is awake. The Doctor asks what Lady Macbeth has said while she is sleepwalking, but the Gentlewoman refuses to tell him.

Lady Macbeth enters, carrying a candle. She is fast asleep. The Doctor and Gentlewoman hide and observe her. The Doctor asks where Lady Macbeth got the candle from and is told that she has ordered a light to be placed by her bedside at all times throughout the night. The Doctor notices that Lady Macbeth's eyes are open, but the Gentlewoman says that they see nothing.

Lady Macbeth rubs her hands, as though washing them and the Gentlewoman says that she has seen her do this for up to a quarter of an hour. Then Lady Macbeth speaks: 'Yet here's a spot' (line 25), and the Doctor says he will write her words down to help him remember them. 'Out, damned spot!' says Lady Macbeth (line 28). Then, remembering the bell she struck as a signal on the night of Duncan's murder (see II. i. 61), she counts, 'One, two', and says that now is the time to do it. Lady Macbeth thinks about the darkness of hell for a moment, then her thoughts return to the night of the murder; she scolds her husband for being frightened, and says they have nothing to fear, for no one can challenge their authority. She pauses, her thoughts wandering; then she recalls Duncan's murdered body and wonders at the amount of blood that flowed from him.

The Doctor shows surprise at what he is hearing, as Lady Macbeth, in a rambling way, reveals the secret of Duncan's murder. Her thoughts now turn to Macduff and she chants: 'The Thane of Fife had a wife: where is she now?' (lines 34). She rubs her hands again, trying to clean the imaginary blood

from them. Then, as if they are still at the banquet and
Macbeth is seeing Banquo's Ghost, she tells her husband to
control himself, saying he is spoiling everything with his show
of fear.

The Doctor tells the Gentlewoman that she has heard
things she is not meant to hear. She replies that Lady
Macbeth has spoken things she shouldn't. Lady Macbeth
smells her hand and says that all the perfumes of Arabia
couldn't make it smell sweet again. The Doctor observes that
Lady Macbeth is deeply troubled. The Gentlewoman is glad
that her heart is not so heavily burdened as Lady Macbeth's
and would not change places with her, despite her queenly
rank. The Doctor says the disease is beyond his skill, but that
he has known people who walked in their sleep but still died
holily in their beds.

Continuing to relive the past, Lady Macbeth tells her
husband to put his night-gown on and not to look so pale; she
adds that Banquo is dead and buried and cannot leave his
grave. Meanwhile, the Doctor realises how bad the things are
that he is hearing. Lady Macbeth calls her husband to bed,
saying there's a knocking at the gate (i.e. Macduff and Lenox
at the end of II. ii and the beginning of II. iii) and here she
repeats what she said in III. ii — that what is done cannot be
undone. Lady Macbeth exits, to go to bed, as she always does
at this point, so the Gentlewoman tells the Doctor.

This scene has so far been entirely in prose, but now the
Doctor brings it to a close in verse, saying that terrible
rumours are circulating and if these are true, then it's not
surprising that such unnatural behaviour should result. He
continues, saying that those with disturbed minds (such as
Lady Macbeth) confide their secrets to their deaf pillows; he
knows that Lady Macbeth needs a priest more than a physician. He asks God's forgiveness for all of them and tells the
Gentlewoman to look after her and to take all harmful things

away from her. He bids the Gentlewoman goodnight and says that Lady Macbeth has confused his mind and amazed his eyes: what thoughts he has, he dare not express.

Commentary

If Macbeth's heart has hardened in the second half of the play (from IV. i onwards), the opposite has happened to Lady Macbeth. Her callousness, her ruthless firmness of purpose, so obvious in the first two acts, began to give way soon after (possibly even in Act II itself) to be replaced by a gradual nervous decline, leading to her suicide in V. v. Opinions differ as to where the strain first begins to appear in her: some critics trace her loss of nerve to as early on as II. ii, when she couldn't bring herself to murder Duncan because he resembled her father as he lay sleeping:

> 'Had he not resembled
> My father as he slept, I had done 't'
>
> (II. ii. 12-13).

Others give the start of her decline as II. iii. 115, when she faints, shortly after Duncan's body has been discovered. Without question, Lady Macbeth's disillusionment is obvious at the beginning of III. ii, and there are clear signs of strain and nervous exhaustion at the end of the banquet scene (III. iv). In this scene, V. i, the last time we see Lady Macbeth on stage, she is on the verge of, or actually suffering from, a nervous breakdown; her suicide is anticipated by the Doctor's remark at line 64, when he tells the Gentlewoman: 'Remove from her the means of all annoyance' (i.e. 'Take all harmful things away from her').

The scene is written in prose, except for the last nine lines, not because the Doctor and Waiting-Gentlewoman are lowly characters (they are not), nor because of any lack of emotional intensity, emotion being associated with verse, but because the mental meanderings of Lady Macbeth are best suited to the medium of prose.

Macbeth 'hath murdered sleep' (II. ii. 41) and now Lady Macbeth, who had scorned the fears generated by her husband's imagination (see, for example, II. ii. 49-54 and III. iv. 60-68) is now tormented in her sleep by her own imaginings. Lady Macbeth's soul is sick of evil; earlier she had summoned darkness (symbolically associated with evil; see I. v. 48-52); now she must sleep with a candle always by her side, its light (light being associated with virtue) comforting her:

'She has light by her continually; 't is her command'
(V. i. 18-19).

The Gentlewoman (in lines 3-6) describes Lady Macbeth writing in her sleep. It is interesting to speculate just what she is writing and to whom. Some critics suggest she is writing to Macbeth, trying to regain control of him, a control she has lost for he no longer consults her. Possibly she is writing or preparing a suicide note, confessing her crimes.

Just as Macbeth's inability to control his imagination during the banquet scene revealed his guilt there (if Banquo's Ghost was an hallucination), so Lady Macbeth's imagination, or her subconscious revealing itself through her dreams, gives her away in this scene. The Gentlewoman's refusal to tell the Doctor what she has heard Lady Macbeth say (lines 11-14) is understandable, considering the type of regime she is living under in Macbeth's Scotland: if she did tell the Doctor what she has heard and he then decided to break that confidence by telling Macbeth, she would almost certainly be put to death for knowing too much (but then the Doctor would probably meet the same fate, so he would be unlikely to reveal anything). Lady Macbeth's attempts to wash away imaginary blood from her hands suggest two emotions —

guilt and fear; guilt for her crimes and fear of discovery. But in lines 30-31 she quite rightly points out, 'What need we fear who knows it, when none can call our power to account?' So, if she has no reason to fear retribution on earth, perhaps she fears for her soul in the next life. Immediately before this (line 29) she makes her only religious statement of the play, 'Hell is murky', which does rather support this idea of her new-found fear of damnation. Alternatively, her fear of discovery belongs to the period she is reliving in her dreams — the time of Duncan's murder or not long after — before Macbeth consolidated his power with Banquo's murder. If this is the case, it might suggest that even then, in spite of herself, Lady Macbeth was not quite so tough and self-contained as she appeared and that she did have other dimensions to her personality — just as we would expect of one of Shakespeare's characters.

Now, for the first time in the play, the audience gets the impression that a terrible guilt is gnawing away at Lady Macbeth's soul, even though there is very little hard evidence to indicate this — except perhaps when her thoughts turn to Lady Macduff. A powerful surge of sadness is felt in the little doggerel: 'The Thane of Fife had a wife: where is she now?' (line 34). This is the only expression of remorse for another character Lady Macbeth gives in the play. (At this point it might be worth considering once again to whom Lady Macbeth writes in her dream-state. If, as it seems here, she is haunted most by the murder of Lady Macduff, it is possible that these letters are to Lady Macduff — either in warning, or asking for forgiveness. If she is the recipient, the fact that she is already dead merely helps to emphasise Lady Macbeth's confused mental state.)

Lady Macbeth's comment about Duncan, 'Yet who would have thought the old man to have had so much blood in him?' (lines 31-32) can be seen as being characteristic of her callous nature. She makes no expression of regret or sorrow, and shows little respect for Duncan, referring to him as 'the old man'. However, the inappropriateness of her remark can also be taken as a sign of her madness. To focus on the amount of blood, rather than the terrible deeds which have taken place, seems wholly unnatural — the response of someone not quite sane. Perhaps in spite of her frequently avowed hardness and determination, the actual sight of Duncan's blood-soaked corpse was just too much and it has pushed her over the edge into madness.

Lady Macbeth's thoughts are wandering from one period in the past to another, so she speaks in fits and starts, indicated by the hyphens between lines 28-35. Her remark in lines 28-29 has led to a difference of opinion among critics: 'One; two; why, then 't is time to do 't.' Some think she is referring to the bell she struck as a signal to Macbeth that all was ready for the murder (II. i. 61); others think she is dreaming of the clock that struck two in the morning when Duncan was slain.

Just as Macbeth had known that all the water in the oceans could never wash away the blood from his hands (i.e. he could never be free of his guilt):

'Will all great Neptune's ocean wash this blood
Clean from my hand? No'

(II. ii. 59-60),

so Lady Macbeth, who scoffed at her husband's qualms, saying, 'A little water clears us of this deed' (II. ii 66), now echoes his guilty fears:

'Here's the smell of the blood still: all the perfumes of Arabia will not sweeten this little hand'

(V. i. 40-41).

In his guilt, Macbeth was obsessed with the sight of Duncan's blood. It is the *smell* of Duncan's blood that torments Lady Macbeth. Perhaps this is a more feminine reaction, and perhaps Lady Macbeth managed to suppress her abhorrence of blood to gain the crown, but this suppressed fear is now revealing itself and tormenting her.

Because she is dreaming, Lady Macbeth's thoughts roam, one murder seeming to merge with another in her mind, as for example in lines 49-51:

'Wash your hands, put on your night-gown; look not so pale. — I tell you yet again, Banquo's buried: he cannot come out on 's grave.'

In line 49, she is reliving events just after Duncan's murder in II. ii, when the subject of conversation had been the blood on Macbeth's hands, and she told him to put on his night-gown and 'Be not lost/ So poorly in your thoughts' (II. ii. 70-71). Then, as there is nothing like lines 50-51 in the banquet scene, her thoughts must have shifted to the nightmares Macbeth suffered ('these terrible dreams/ That shake us nightly', III. ii. 18-19) which were brought on by his fear of Banquo. Probably, in lines 50-51, Lady Macbeth is talking to her husband in her imagination as though he has just woken up in bed after a bad dream. Then in line 54, 'To bed, to bed: there's knocking at the gate', her thoughts jump back to the end of II. ii again, to the time when Macduff was beating on the gate to rouse the Porter.

Compare lines 55-56, 'What's done cannot be undone' with III. ii. 11-12:

'Things without all remedy
Should be without regard: what's done is done.'

In III. ii, Lady Macbeth still had some reserves of mental strength left, although these were rapidly depleting, and she is saying, in what seems to be a resigned and stoical manner, that there is no point in worrying about something that cannot be changed, in this case, of course, Duncan's murder. Whereas by V. i. 55-56, there is a tone of despair in her words, as though she recognises there is no hope left for the future. Lady Macbeth has discovered that 'Things without all remedy' cannot always be 'without regard', or, to repeat Macbeth's words in I. vii. 11-12, Lady Macbeth is finding that natural justice 'Commends th' ingredients of our poisoned chalice/ To our own lips'.

The unnaturalness of Lady Macbeth's crimes is matched by the unnaturalness of their effect on her mind, which is what the Doctor means in lines 59-60:

> 'Unnatural deeds
> Do breed unnatural troubles.'

Malcolm had warned Macduff that hiding his grief, locking it within himself, would break his heart (IV. iii. 209-210). Here we see how Lady Macbeth's need to hide her guilt and fear has eaten away at her mental equilibrium:

> 'infected minds
> To their deaf pillows will discharge their secrets'
> (V. i. 60-61).

Her mind has turned in upon itself and fed upon itself, leading to this state of near mental collapse. The Doctor is correct in saying that Lady Macbeth needs a priest more than a doctor ('More needs she the divine than the physician', line 62) for a doctor cannot heal a conscience. Lady Macbeth is now trapped in a nightmare world of blood and guilt; she is probably going slowly insane, and her only escape is death.

Where is Macbeth in the meanwhile? The Gentlewoman told us in line 3 that, 'his majesty went into the field'. Dunsinane Castle is not yet under siege by the advancing forces from England; so Macbeth has marched out with his army to put down the rebellions already occurring in Scotland. In IV. iii. 182-185, Rosse mentioned the 'many worthy fellows that were out' (i.e. good men who have risen in rebellion against Macbeth) and he also mentioned seeing 'the tyrant's power afoot'.

Act Five Scene II

In the countryside near Dunsinane Castle, Menteth, Cathness, Angus, Lenox and soldiers enter. Menteth says that the English army, led by Malcolm, Siward and Macduff, is nearby. They burn for revenge. Their just cause for going to war would stir even the dead to grim and bloody battle. Angus says they will meet them near Birnam wood. Cathness asks if Donalbain is with his brother, but Lenox says he is not.

Menteth asks what the tyrant Macbeth is doing and Cathness replies that Macbeth is fortifying Dunsinane Castle. He adds that some people say Macbeth is mad, while those who hate him less call it valiant fury; but one thing is certain, that his evil ambitions have made him lose control of himself. Angus says Macbeth now feels the consequences of his secret murders and that every minute, revolts revenge his crimes. Those he commands obey him out of duty, not love. Now he feels his royal title fits him badly, like a dwarf-sized thief wearing a giant's robe. Menteth asks who can blame Macbeth's nerves for being shaken, when he is ashamed of everything about himself?

Cathness tells them to march on to where they are really needed, to where Malcolm — the one man who can cure Scotland's illness — is. With Malcolm, he says, they will shed every drop of their blood to cleanse their land of its sickness. Lenox says they will shed as much blood as is needed to water the flower of true kingship (Malcolm) and drown the weeds (Macbeth).

Commentary

The dark clouds are parting and the sun peeps through at last. Apart from IV. iii and for a brief spell in I. vi, we have been in darkness until now, but this scene sees daylight (symbolically associated with the forces of virtue) returning. The drums and colours tell us this is an army marching to battle; these are the Scottish forces, who will later meet up with the English army, led by Malcolm, Macduff and Siward, at Birnam wood. The union of the two armies is the closing of the two parts of the snake which Macbeth said had been 'scotched' but not killed (see III. ii. 13-14).

Lady Macbeth's guilty conscience led to a loss of control of herself in the previous scene; for the same reason, Macbeth has lost his self-control in this scene, but their symptoms are different: Lady Macbeth has drawn in upon herself, her guilt-stricken conscience making her brood; while Macbeth, who locked his doubts and fears away within himself for so long in the earlier scenes, has now released their energies in a flurry of agitated activity as he fortifies Dunsinane:

'Some say he's mad; others, that lesser hate him,
Do call it valiant fury; but, for certain,
He cannot buckle his distempered cause
Within the belt of rule'

(V. ii. 13-16).

Notice the way Macbeth's cause here is compared to an illness, 'distempered cause'; 'distempered' means 'diseased' or 'sick'. The comparison of evil with sickness has been made throughout the play and it forms part of the play's recurrent imagery (see Section 6 iii, 'The Recurrent Imagery of *Macbeth*'). The image gets picked up again later in the scene when Malcolm is compared to a doctor who will cure or purge Scotland of its illness:

> 'Meet we the medicine of the sickly weal;
> And with him pour we, in our country's purge,
> Each drop of us'
>
> (V. ii. 27-29).

Macbeth simply cannot live with himself any longer: 'all that is within him does condemn/ Itself for being there' (lines 24-25). Two other recurrent images — those of blood and clothing — are used to develop this point. Guilt is associated in the play with blood that sticks to the hands and cannot be washed off; we came across this idea with Macbeth in II. ii and Lady Macbeth in V. i; now the image appears here, when Angus says:

> 'Now does he feel
> His secret murders sticking on his hands'
>
> (V. ii. 16-17).

The clothing imagery is used twice in this scene. In lines 15-16, Macbeth's ambitions are said to be so wild and out of control that he is compared to a fat man who has a stomach too big for his belt. In contrast, lines 20-22 compare Macbeth's inadequacy as a King and the dishonest means he used to seize the royal title to a dwarfish thief wearing the stolen clothes of a giant:

> 'now does he feel his title
> Hang loose about him, like a giant's robe
> Upon a dwarfish thief.'

Another image used in this scene is of plants and natural growth. Malcolm is compared to a 'sovereign flower' and Macbeth to 'weeds' (line 30). The adjective 'sovereign' suggests the idea of royalty, for it means supreme in power (we talk, for example, about 'our sovereign lord, the King'); it also suggests the idea of a plant with a powerful medicinal value, thus continuing the image of sickness and healing.

Finally, notice how Shakespeare prepares us for the desertion of Macbeth's forces, mentioned in the first line of V. iii, when Angus tells us:

'Those he commands move only in command,
Nothing in love'

(V. ii. 19-20).

Act Five Scene III

In a room in Dunsinane Castle Macbeth enters with a Doctor and Attendants. He has received news that his soldiers are deserting him and, angrily, he tells an attendant that he wants to hear no more such reports. He says those who are betraying him can all run away, for he has nothing to fear till Birnam wood moves up to Dunsinane. Malcolm he dismisses as a boy, and a boy born of a woman; the spirits that can see into a man's future have told Macbeth that no man born of a woman shall ever have power over him. He tells his false thanes to run away and join the soft English, for his mind and courage will never give in to doubt or fear.

A servant enters looking pale with fear and Macbeth scolds him as he tries to speak. All he manages to say before Macbeth throws him out in a rage is that ten thousand soldiers are approaching. Macbeth calls for Seyton, a more trusted servant. Dejectedly, Macbeth says that he is sick at heart. This is the conflict which will bring him happiness forever or else unseat him from the throne. He says that he has reached the autumn of his life, and what should accompany old age — honour, love, obedience, large numbers of friends — he cannot hope to have; in their place he will have curses, not spoken loudly, but deeply felt, and his poor heart would gladly reject them but would not dare (because any support now, whether heartfelt or merely given out of fear, is necessary to him).

Macbeth calls for Seyton again; he enters and Macbeth asks what the latest news is and Seyton confirms that all the earlier reports are true. Macbeth pledges to fight until the flesh is hacked from his bones and calls for his armour. Although Seyton advises him that it is still too early for this, Macbeth says he will put it on nevertheless. He orders more scouts to be sent out to scour the surrounding countryside and to hang those who talk of fear. He calls for his armour again; then, turning to the Doctor, he asks after Lady Macbeth.

The Doctor reports that Lady Macbeth is not really sick but troubled by hallucinations which prevent her from sleeping. Macbeth asks if a diseased mind can be cured, if sorrow can be plucked from where it has taken root in the memory; he asks, again despondently, if the troubles written on the brain can be erased and whether the Doctor, by administering some drugs, can dispel what chokes the breast and weighs the heart down. The Doctor replies that in these cases the patient must find his own cure. Macbeth replies angrily that medicine should be thrown to the dogs, for it is of no use to him.

Telling Seyton to help him put his armour on, Macbeth then asks for his lance. Seyton fumbles, trying to fit the pieces of armour as Macbeth paces the stage. Then Macbeth tells the Doctor that if he could diagnose the sickness afflicting Scotland and return the nation to health, he would applaud him over and over again. Impatiently, Macbeth tells Seyton to pull off a piece of armour that is not fitting well. Turning back to the Doctor, Macbeth asks what drug could flush the English soldiers out of Scotland. He asks if the Doctor knows about the English forces. The Doctor replies that his Majesty's preparations at Dunsinane (against attack) have brought them to his notice. Impatiently refusing more attempts by Seyton to help him put his armour on, Macbeth tells Seyton to follow him with it. Macbeth exits saying that he won't be afraid of death and disaster till Birnam forest comes to Dunsinane.

The Doctor, meanwhile, wishes he were far from Dunsinane, saying that if he were, money wouldn't tempt him back again.

Commentary

We were prepared for Macbeth's loss of self-control in the previous scene (see V. ii. 13-16); instead, now we see three main emotions apparently dominating him: 'valiant fury' (V. ii. 14) when he thinks about his enemies; disgust and contempt when he thinks about those around him who are deserting him or showing fear; and despair when he thinks about his own life. But the 'valiant fury' seems slightly false and more like bravado, for, with his soldiers deserting him and his experience as a general telling him that he cannot win, his only source of courage is the Apparitions' promises. His need to repeat these promises twice, combined with his badly tattered nerves, may indicate a growing mistrust of them:

'Till Birnam wood remove to Dunsinane
I cannot taint with fear. What's the boy Malcolm?
Was he not born of woman? The spirits that know
All mortal consequence have pronounced me thus:
"Fear not, Macbeth; no man that's born of woman
Shall e'er have power upon thee"'

(lines 2-7).

'I will not be afraid of death and bane
Till Birnam forest come to Dunsinane'

(lines 59-60).

Then the need to repeat the assertion that he 'cannot taint with fear' (lines 2-7, 9-10, 59-60) is surely an expression of fear and there is something artificial about his words in lines 9-10: 'The mind I sway by, and the heart I bear,/ Shall never sag with doubt, nor shake with fear'. It is a fear that Macbeth is trying to hide from himself and others by frenetic activity: he asks for news (line 30) when he has already said that he wants 'no more reports' (line 1) and he has driven away the servant who came to tell him about the English army's approach; he calls for his armour before it's needed (line 33), then can't keep still long enough for Seyton to fit it, and Seyton is told to 'Bring it after me' (line 58) as Macbeth leaves the stage.

Macbeth is not in control of himself. His order to 'Hang those that talk of fear' (line 36) contradicts the sentiment of indifference he expressed for those who are abandoning him (lines 1 and 7-8), for if he doesn't care that he is becoming increasingly isolated, why bother hanging those who are spreading fear? The answer must be that, despite his outward appearance of 'valiant fury' and the faith he places in the Apparitions' promises, he is actually scared and uncertain. Macbeth is now isolated from his wife as well as his thanes, for he only mentions her (and then as 'your patient' to the Doctor, as though she is no longer really important to him) towards the second half of the scene. (But more will be said about this later in the section.)

Lines 7-8 show Macbeth's disgust at his hardy Scottish soldiers who are abandoning him to join 'the English epicures' (an 'epicure' is a person who lives for life's more sensual pleasures, such as eating and drinking). At this time, and perhaps until today, the Scots considered themselves a sturdier, tougher race than the English. The phrase 'English epicures' disdainfully suggests that the English are a soft, pleasure-seeking people.

A good deal of Macbeth's disgust is, of course, anger, frustration and fear in another guise. His abusive and contemptuous treatment of the servant, who is only doing his job by reporting what he has seen (lines 11-19), suggests this. Macbeth is taking out his anger, frustration and fear on the servant, using him as a sort of lightning-conductor to release the electrical energy of his feelings. The servant seems to be more frightened of Macbeth than the English army, and this is the more likely reason why he is pale in the face ('cream-faced', line 11). Notice that Macbeth also shows contempt for the Doctor in line 47, not so much because the Doctor cannot cure Lady Macbeth, but because of the feelings bottled up inside him.

It is sadly ironic that Macbeth is trying so desperately to preserve a life which he knows is no longer worth living. He admits that he has lived long enough (although he is not an old man) and when he thinks of how old age should be and compares it with what he knows he will have if he survives, his despair is very obvious:

'I have lived long enough: my way of life
Is fall'n into the sere, the yellow leaf;
And that which should accompany old age,
As honour, love, obedience, troops of friends,
I must not look to have; but, in their stead,
Curses, not loud but deep, mouth-honour, breath,
Which the poor heart would fain deny, and dare not'
(V. iii. 22-28).

No doubt Macbeth is comparing himself with Duncan, who did have 'honour, love, obedience, troops of friends'; all

Macbeth will have if he survives to be an old man are syco-
phants paying lip-service to him out of fear and cursing him
behind his back. Macbeth was once honoured by his King
and had 'Golden opinions from all sorts of people' (I. vii.
33); now the only honour he can ever enjoy, if he survives, is
'mouth-honour', a respect not earned but given out of fear,
and which he would have to accept even though his heart tells
him to reject it for its falsehood, because any support,
whether honourable or not, would be necessary for his survival. Even though Macbeth recognises that life isn't worth
living any more, that the future holds nothing worth having
for him, and that honour, for which he once lived, is dead, it is
the most basic animal instinct of survival at all costs which
keeps him going. There is no hope left: a lesser man might
contemplate suicide at this stage — an option Macbeth rejects
(V. viii. 1-3). He has already made up his mind to fight to the
death, to preserve at least some semblance of honour:

> 'I'll fight, till from my bones my flesh be hacked'
> (V. iii. 32).

Just for a moment, our respect for Macbeth returns. It is a
promise worthy of the Macbeth whom Rosse once called
'Bellona's bridegroom' (I. ii. 56); it is a promise he fulfills in
V. viii.

At line 37, Macbeth's attention suddenly switches from the
enemy to his wife. Lady Macbeth's guilty conscience will not
let her sleep:

> 'she is troubled with thick-coming fancies,
> That keep her from her rest'
> (V. iii. 38-39).

We observed some of these 'thick-coming fancies' (her
distracted, irrational behaviour) in V. i. When Macbeth asks
the Doctor in lines 40-45,

'Canst thou not minister to a mind diseased,
Pluck from the memory a rooted sorrow,
Raze out the written troubles of the brain,
And with some sweet, oblivious antidote
Cleanse the stuffed bosom of that perilous stuff
Which weighs upon the heart?'

he seems to be thinking of himself, as much as his wife. The 'sweet, oblivious antidote' Macbeth has chosen is to lose himself in the business of preparing for battle; it is this flurry of activity which takes his thoughts away from the 'rooted sorrow' of memory and 'the written troubles of the brain'. The Doctor's reply, 'Therein the patient/ Must minister to himself', lines 45-46, (with the masculine 'himself' rather than the feminine 'herself') suggests that he knows Macbeth is dwelling on his own troubles rather more than his wife's.

The only cure for this particular sickness of the soul is death, which Lady Macbeth finds at her own hands in V. v (although only her death is reported here; the announcement of her death as suicide comes in V. ix. 36-37) and which Macbeth soon seems to invite by leaving his castle to do hand-to-hand combat with numerically superior forces (V. v).

Macbeth's suggestion to the Doctor that he, 'cast/ The water of my land, find her disease,/ And purge it to a sound and pristine health' (lines 50-52), draws the comparison between the sickness of the body and the sickness of the state. Lady Macbeth is sick because of the evil she has done; Scotland is sick because Macbeth is an evil King. Malcolm is the doctor who will cure Scotland (see V. ii. 27); he is the one who will 'purge it to a sound and pristine health' (line 52). Macbeth may ask what the sickness of his nation is; the Doctor's reply no doubt, if he could speak freely, would be "You".

Act Five Scene IV

In the countryside near Dunsinane, within sight of Birnam wood, Malcolm enters with old Siward and his son, Macduff, Menteth, Cathness, Angus, Lenox and Rosse. There are flags flying and soldiers marching to the beat of a drum. They stop and Malcolm looks forward to a time when people may sleep safely in their beds. Siward asks the name of the wood that stands nearby; Menteth tells him it is the wood of Birnam. Malcolm orders that every soldier should cut down a branch and carry it in front of him to conceal the size of their army from Macbeth. Siward says that Macbeth is confident and has settled in Dunsinane ready to repel them if they besiege the castle. Malcolm says this is Macbeth's only hope, for whenever they've had the chance to escape, men of all ranks have deserted him; only conscripted wretches serve him, and they have lost heart in their cause. Macduff says they should pass judgement (i.e. on Macbeth's soldiers' willingness to fight) only after the battle; in the meantime he suggests they plan their battle strategy carefully. Siward says that the outcome of the conflict will soon be known; guessing at it is pointless. Some issues, he says, can only be settled by battle. He tells them all to march off to war.

Commentary

The Scottish forces loyal to Malcolm have met up with the English army near Birnam wood, as Angus said they would in V. ii. 5-6. Their coming together and the mention in lines 11-12 of soldiers of all ranks deserting Macbeth, emphasise his increasing isolation. However, the main purpose of this scene is to contrast the orderliness and high morale of the advancing forces with the chaotic situation within Dunsinane Castle, where Macbeth is left with 'constrainèd things,/ Whose hearts are absent' (lines 13-14).

Malcolm's remark, 'I hope the days are near at hand,/ That chambers will be safe' (lines 1-2), seems to be a reference to Duncan's murder. Malcolm means that he is looking forward to a time when they can all sleep safely in their beds without fear of being murdered.

In the previous act Macbeth drew strength from the Third Apparition's promise that:

> 'Macbeth shall never vanquished be, until
> Great Birnam wood to high Dunsinane hill
> Shall come against him'
>
> (IV. i. 92-94).

Now, as Malcolm orders his soldiers to cut down branches and carry them as camouflage to conceal the size of their army (lines 4-7), we see how Macbeth has been tricked by these supernatural creatures in whom he has placed such great faith, and how this seemingly impossible phenomenon, a forest moving up a hill, will be accomplished.

Macbeth contemptuously dismissed Malcolm as a 'boy' in the previous scene (V. iii. 3), the inference being that as he is young and inexperienced, Malcolm would be no match as a general against himself, a much more experienced warrior. IV. iii proved Malcolm to be cautious, wise and virtuous, but there is a moment here in V. iv when the boy in him shows a little. He appears to be prejudging the outcome of the battle, being a bit too optimistic about victory. Referring to Macbeth's forces, he says:

> 'And none serve with him but constrainèd things,
> Whose hearts are absent too'
>
> (V. iv. 13-14).

Macduff mildly rebukes Malcolm, saying they should pass judgement (on just how well and willingly Macbeth's soldiers can fight) after the battle. The information they have on what is going on inside Dunsinane Castle is, after all, based on hearsay, and for this reason it is unreliable. Macduff says that rather than prejudge events, they should concentrate on planning their battle strategy carefully:

> 'Let our just censures
> Attend the true event, and put we on
> Industrious soldiership'

(V. iv. 14-16).

Act Five Scene V

Inside Dunsinane Castle Macbeth orders banners to be hung on the outer walls (to signal to the enemy that he is ready to fight). The cry from those around him is still 'They're coming!', but Macbeth says that his castle is so strong that a siege is laughable; the enemy can stay outside the castle walls until they are eaten up by famine and the plague. If they hadn't been reinforced by deserters, Macbeth says they could have met them boldly, face to face and driven them back to where they came from.

Suddenly, the cries of women are heard offstage. Macbeth asks what it is. Seyton goes off to investigate, while Macbeth is thrown into gloomy reflections. He has almost forgotten the taste of fear. There was a time when a shriek in the night would have turned him cold, and on hearing a tale of horror his hair would stand on end as if alive. He has now had his fill of horror; it is now so familiar in his murderous thoughts that it can no longer frighten him.

Seyton re-enters and announces that Lady Macbeth is dead. Macbeth says that it had to happen sometime. He comments that the inexorable passage of time inevitably leads us to our graves and that life is like a candle which quickly goes out. He compares life to a moving shadow, or a wretched actor who struts and rants for a short time upon the stage, and then is heard of no more: it is a tale told by a fool, full of noise and passion, meaning nothing.

A Messenger enters. He hardly knows how to report what he has seen; but, as he stood on watch, he looked towards Birnam and the wood seemed to be moving. Macbeth scolds him, calling him a liar and a slave. The Messenger says that he will accept the consequences of Macbeth's wrath if he is wrong; however he insists that the wood can be seen moving not three miles away. Macbeth tells the Messenger that if he is lying, he will hang alive on the nearest tree until he dies of starvation. To himself, Macbeth admits that if the Messenger's report is true, he doesn't care if the same is done to him.

Macbeth says he is losing confidence and beginning to fear the evasive words of the devil, whose lies sound like the truth: 'Fear not till Birnam wood comes to Dunsinane'. And now a wood is coming to Dunsinane. He calls his soldiers to arms, telling them to leave the castle and sally forth into the field. If what the Messenger says is true, they can neither run away nor stay within the castle. The sun, life's light, begins to weary Macbeth. He wishes the world were destroyed. Ordering the alarm bell to be sounded, he yells, 'Let the winds blow! Come ruin! At least we'll die fighting.'

Commentary

Macbeth's order to 'Hang out our banners on the outward walls' (line 1) is a direct challenge to the advancing forces; he sounds as though he feels confident and safe within his castle, which he says can withstand a siege:

> 'Our castle's strength
> Will laugh a siege to scorn'
>
> (V. v. 2-3).

He contemptuously dismisses the fears of his soldiers, who

cry 'They come!' (line 2). Macbeth sees the enemy as the losers in this conflict:

> 'here let them lie,
>   Till famine and the ague eat them up'
>
> (V. v. 3-4).

But as an experienced general, Macbeth must also know that, locked within his castle, with limited reserves of food and water, famine and sickness are more likely to eat him up first. Once again then, the 'valiant fury' is bravado, a brave display of confidence to lift his own spirits and those of his soldiers. The 'sweet, oblivious antidote' (V. iii. 43) which keeps him from complete despair is this furious activity and the Apparitions' promises.

The *cry within, of women* (line 7) indicates that Lady Macbeth has died. The sound of the cry sends Macbeth's mood swaying from 'valiant fury' to disillusionment and melancholy. He reflects that he has 'supped full with horrors' (line 13) and he knows that his soul has taken flight downwards towards the pit of hell; where honour, pity, and fear once dwelt within him, there now exist only 'slaughterous thoughts' (line 14).

The news of Lady Macbeth's death throws Macbeth further into a mood of despair and he contemplates the futility and meaninglessness of life. Lines 17-18, 'She should have died hereafter:/ There would have been a time for such a word', are ambiguous. However, they should not be read flatly and unemotionally. Literally they mean, 'She had to die sometime. It had to happen.' But this rather bald statement does disservice to Macbeth, whose heart has not hardened towards his wife even though his mind is occupied with other matters. A better reading, incorporating deeper emotion from Macbeth, is 'She should have died at a more peaceful moment. Had she lived longer, there would have been a better time for me to grieve'. As Macbeth hasn't got time to indulge in the luxury of grief, he postpones it, and his reflections on his wife's death become a more general statement of life's futility.

Macbeth accepts the news of his wife's death calmly but, in contrast, he reacts violently towards the Messenger who tells him that he has seen 'a moving grove' (line 38). Remember that the Messenger does not say that Malcolm's army is advancing, but Birnam wood. Macbeth's response is not anger at the thought of an approaching battle, but anger at the realisation that the Witches have tricked him:

> 'I pull in resolution, and begin
> To doubt th' equivocation of the fiend,
> That lies like truth'

> (V. v. 42-44).

His words, 'the fiend,/ That lies like truth' aptly describe how the Witches have duped Macbeth with their promises. They knew that their promises would be accepted literally by Macbeth, and would give him a false sense of security. He had taken the Third Apparition's prediction (IV. i. 92-94) to mean, 'Just as Birnam wood can never move up to Dunsinane hill, so you can never be vanquished'. But what the Apparition was actually saying was, 'Birnam wood will come to Dunsinane hill and then Macbeth will be vanquished'. Macbeth's security has depended so much on the Apparition's promise, but now that he can no longer hold it as a shield between himself and the enemy, he throws it down, bravely determined to fight to the death. He must know that he is committing suicide by leaving Dunsinane, but life has no value for him anymore and death is better than the dishonour of being taken prisoner:

> 'If this which he avouches does appear,
> There is nor flying hence, nor tarrying here.

I 'gin to be aweary of the sun,
And wish th' estate o' th' world were now undone. —
Ring the alarum bell! — Blow, wind! come, wrack!
At least we'll die with harness on our back'

(V. v. 47-52).

The irony is that now, as Macbeth's security begins to ebb away (he still has the Second Apparition's promise but he must have severe doubts about it), his courage, his real courage and not bravado or 'valiant fury', seems to be returning. (The same effect occurs in V. viii when the Second Apparition lets him down.) This is the Macbeth we knew in I. ii who 'carved out his passage' through the ranks of the enemy, 'with his brandished steel,/ Which smoked with bloody execution,/ Like Valour's minion' (I. ii. 17-19). A measure of respect for Macbeth is returning.

Act Five Scene VI

On open ground before Dunsinane Castle, Malcolm enters with old Siward, Macduff and their army, carrying branches in front of them. Malcolm says they are near enough to the castle and he tells the soldiers to throw down the branches. In deference to old Siward, Malcolm invites him and his son to head the army. Malcolm and Macduff will take charge of the rest, according to the plan they have devised. Siward bids farewell, adding that if they find Macbeth's army before nightfall, he wishes defeat upon his forces if they're not prepared to fight. Macduff calls for trumpets to sound; he describes these as the clamorous heralds of blood and death.

Commentary

As in V. iv. this scene emphasises the orderliness of Malcolm's army. In V. iv. 15-16, Macduff recommended the planning of a battle strategy. This has now been done, for the phrase 'According to our order' (line 6) means 'in accordance with the battle plan we have drawn up'. In contrast, Macbeth's men, pouring out of Dunsinane Castle with no other instructions than to fight (and none of them is keen to do this, V. iv. 13-14), are a rabble in dire straits against a disciplined army. Their only hope is to surrender or to join the other side — which many of them choose to do (see V. vii. 25). The sound of the trumpets as the scene closes creates an atmosphere of excitement and suspense.

Act Five Scene VII

Macbeth stands alone on another part of the plain. He compares himself to a bear tied to a stake (as in the sport of bear-baiting, which was popular in Shakespeare's day); he cannot run but must stand and fight. He asks himself what kind of man is not born of a woman. That's the sort he has to fear, and no one else.

Young Siward enters and asks Macbeth his name. Macbeth says he will be afraid to hear it. Young Siward says he won't; not even if Macbeth's name is hotter than any known in hell. Macbeth reveals who he is, and Young Siward says the devil himself could not pronounce a name more hateful to his ear. They fight and Young Siward is killed. Macbeth, standing over the body, says that Young Siward was born of a woman; he adds that he smiles at swords and laughs scornfully at weapons which are brandished by a man born of a woman. He exits.

Macduff enters. He has followed the noise of battle to where the fighting is most intense in the hope of finding Macbeth there. Macduff calls out, challenging Macbeth to show his face. He believes that the ghosts of his wife and childien will haunt him forever if Macbeth is killed by someone other than himself. He says that he cannot strike at wretched mercenaries who are hired to fight with staves. It is either Macbeth he will fight, or else he will sheathe his sword again unused. Hearing a noise somewhere in the distance, Macduff thinks Macbeth must be over there, for it indicates the presence of a man of high rank. Macduff exits, begging fortune to let him find Macbeth.

Malcolm and old Siward enter. Siward announces that the castle has surrendered without a struggle, and Macbeth's soldiers are fighting on both sides. He tells Malcolm that victory will soon be his, for there is little left to do. Malcolm says they have met with soldiers from the enemy forces who are fighting on their side. Siward invites Malcolm to enter the castle.

Commentary

> 'They have tied me to a stake: I cannot fly,
> But, bear-like, I must fight the course'
>
> (V. vii. 1-2).

Bear-baiting was a popular old English sport in which a bear was chained to a post where it was cruelly tormented by dogs; a 'course' was the name given to a bout, or round, between the bear and the dogs. The image is used here to suggest the following ideas: that Macbeth cannot escape; that he will be tormented by the foe; and eventually killed. But if Macbeth assumes he is going to die, what has happened to his faith in the Witches? The Third Apparition's prediction, that he cannot be vanquished until Birnam wood comes to Dunsinane, let him down earlier on (V. v), but he still has the Second Apparition's promise that 'none of woman born/ Shall harm Macbeth' (IV. i. 80-81). In lines 2-3, Macbeth, now a lot more sceptical about the Witches after V. v, seems to be questioning the possibility of the Second Apparition's promise:

> 'What's he
> That was not born of woman?'

His faith in the supernatural powers which protect him returns after he has killed Young Siward. He scornfully remarks: 'Thou wast born of woman' (line 11); then with renewed confidence he gloats:

> 'But swords I smile at, weapons laugh to scorn,
> Brandished by man that's of a woman born'
> (V. vii. 12-13).

Macduff's sole interest is in killing Macbeth. The deaths of his wife and children must be avenged by himself if their spirits are to rest in peace:

> 'Tyrant, show thy face:
> If thou be'st slain, and with no stroke of mine,
> My wife and children's ghosts will haunt me still'
> (V. vii. 14-16).

Macduff 'cannot strike at wretched Kernes, whose arms/ Are hired to bear their staves' (lines 17-18). These Irish soldiers fought for money and not for a cause; Macbeth has to rely on them because so few soldiers remain loyal to him and his cause — much as the rebel Macdonwald had to rely on them in his uprising against Duncan (see I. ii. 13).

As there is no scene division in the First Folio after V. vii, a few editors take V. vii and V. viii to be one scene. But as the action moves to another part of the battlefield at the start of V. viii, the majority of editors separate the two scenes.

Act Five Scene VIII

Macbeth is now at a different part of the battlefield. He

...asks himself why he should act like a foolish **Roman** (of ancient times) and die by falling on his own sword. Whilst he can see other people alive, wounds are more fitting on them (than on himself).

Macduff enters and, seeing Macbeth, cries 'Turn, hellhound, turn!' Macbeth says that of all men, he has been avoiding Macduff; too much blood of Macduff's is already on his soul. Macduff has nothing to say to Macbeth; his sword will speak for him. They fight.

Macbeth tells Macduff that he's wasting his energy; he could as easily wound the air with his sword as make Macbeth bleed. Macbeth says that he has a charmed life which cannot be taken by a man born of a woman. Macduff tells him to place no faith in his charm; he asks the fallen angel Macbeth has served to tell him this — that Macduff was cut from his mother's womb before her time.

Macbeth curses the tongue that tells him this, for it has disheartened his manhood. These devils, Macbeth says, who juggle with words are liars; they keep their promises in a literal sense while the real significance of their words is entirely different; they give hope only to destroy it. Macbeth refuses to fight Macduff.

Macduff tells Macbeth to surrender, calling him a coward. He says Macbeth can live to be exhibited, to be shown and gazed at: they will have Macbeth like one of their rare monsters, with his picture up on a pole and written underneath, 'Here you can see the tyrant'.

Macbeth refuses to surrender; he won't kiss the ground beneath young Malcolm's feet and be taunted by the curses of the rabble. Even though Birnam wood has come to Dunsinane, and Macduff was not born of a woman, he will fight to the end. Macbeth throws his shield in front of his body, crying 'Fight, Macduff. And damned be the one who first cries "stop, enough!"' They exit, then re-enter fighting, and Macbeth is slain.

Commentary

Although Macbeth refuses to 'play the Roman fool' by falling on his own sword, as Brutus, Mark Antony and Cato did, this does not mean that he is without honour and wishes to prolong the bloodshed for its own sake. He just has a different concept of honour: to him it means fighting to the death and not taking the easy way out by committing suicide. Such an act would be thought of as cowardice by Macbeth and, as the play draws to a close, Shakespeare wants us to regain some of the admiration we felt for Macbeth in I. ii. So, a moment later, after Macduff challenges Macbeth, we see Macbeth's humanity returning briefly (although this is the only time in the play Macbeth expresses remorse for the massacre of Macduff's family):

'...get thee back, my soul is too much charged
With blood of thine already'

(V. viii. 5-6).

Some critics have said this is the 'only touch of real remorse in Macbeth' in the entire play; others have suggested that Macbeth is actually frightened of Macduff and is using a guilty conscience to rationalise his fear to himself (i.e. he is telling himself that it isn't fear he feels but guilt). Macbeth was told by the First Apparition to 'beware Macduff;/ Beware the Thane of Fife' (IV. i. 71-72), so he has good reason to fear him.

When Macduff reveals that he 'was from his mother's womb/ Untimely ripped' (lines 15-16), we recall the form the Second Apparition took in IV. i, a bloody child. Whether we accept lines 5-6 as an expression of fear or not, once Macduff has dispelled the charm in lines 15-16, Macbeth readily admits to fear:

'Accursèd be that tongue that tells me so,

> For it hath cowed my better part of man'
>
> (V. viii. 17-18).

How do we explain this fear, when we recall the Captain's report of Macbeth's incredible feats during the battle in I. ii? The answer may be that Macbeth knows natural justice has caught up with him at last ('this even-handed justice/ Commends th' ingredients of our poisoned chalice/ To our own lips', I. vii. 10-12) and he has met his executioner. Another view is that Macbeth's courage has been bolstered so long by the illusion of invulnerability created by the Apparitions that, once they fail him, his courage collapses. It is only after lines 15-16 that Macbeth realises the full extent to which he has been fooled by the Witches and the Apparitions:

> 'And be these juggling fiends no more believed,
> That palter with us in a double sense,
> That keep the word of promise to our ear,
> And break it to our hope'
>
> (V. viii. 19-22).

He has been tricked by words, but the Witches are not to blame for Macbeth's downfall; they only influenced him in so far as he was already predisposed to being influenced. The future could have been different. Nothing that has happened to Macbeth was inevitable; it was a future of shadows, of 'might be', that the Witches looked into and held up to him as a prize. Had he made different choices (as he was always free to do), had he chosen virtue over evil, he could have made a glorious future for himself.

When Macbeth refuses to fight: 'I'll not fight with thee' (line 22), he sounds pathetic, like a young boy confronted with someone stronger. His manhood, which Lady Macbeth so often called into question, has deserted him ('it hath cowed my better part of man', line 18). However, he really has little choice; there is no walking away for Macbeth since Macduff can either kill him on the spot or take him prisoner. But when Macduff taunts him, calling him a coward and gloating over the humiliation Macbeth will face as a prisoner ('We'll have thee, as our rarer monsters are', line 25), his old courage, the courage of I. ii, returns (as it did in V. v. 46-52), and we hear a speech worthy of our admiration:

> 'I will not yield,
> To kiss the ground before young Malcolm's feet,
> And to be baited with the rabble's curse.
> Though Birnam wood be come to Dunsinane,
> And thou opposed, being of no woman born,
> Yet I will try the last: before my body
> I throw my warlike shield: lay on, Macduff;
> And damned be him that first cries, "Hold, enough!"'
>
> (V. viii. 27-34).

These are the last lines Macbeth speaks in the play and, as he dies fighting bravely like a soldier, they restore some of the sheen to Macbeth's tarnished image. There are three possible reasons why Macbeth loses the fight: he is tired of living (or of being King, for 'the sun' might refer to kingship, 'I 'gin to be aweary of the sun', V. v. 49); he knows he is doomed anyway — that this what the Apparitions were predicting all along — so he is demoralised and has no heart to fight; he feels guilty (about Macduff's family) and the burden of this guilt dulls the edge of his prowess. The stage direction, *Re-enter fighting,* emphasises the length of the struggle, so Macduff does not win an easy victory.

On the stages of Shakespeare's time, the fight would end on the inner stage where a curtain could be drawn to hide Macbeth's body, for the head has to be severed and carried on by Macduff in the next (and final) scene.

Act Five Scene IX

The final scene takes place inside Dunsinane Castle. Malcolm wishes that their missing friends were safely with them. Old Siward says that some must be killed; he looks at a list of the dead and says that from the few names written there, the day was won with little loss of life. Malcolm replies that Macduff is missing, as well as Siward's son. Rosse says that Young Siward died like a soldier; he had no sooner reached manhood than he proved his worth on the battlefield, fighting unyieldingly and dying like a man. Siward asks, 'Then he is dead?'; Rosse says yes, and his body has been carried off the field. Rosse tells Siward not to measure his sorrow by his son's worthiness, for then it would be infinite. Siward asks if his son's wounds were in front and when Rosse says they were, Siward says his son was a soldier for God, and if he had as many sons as hairs on his head, he couldn't wish a better death for them. Malcolm says that young Siward is worth more sorrow than this, and he will give it to him. But Siward denies this, saying his son is worth no more grief, for they say he died well and paid his score as a soldier, and so God be with him.

Macduff enters with Macbeth's head on a pike. He hails Malcolm as King and shows him the usurper's head. The world can breathe again, Macduff says. He looks at the thanes and says that he sees Malcolm surrounded by his country's pearls, and in their minds they speak his greeting. Macduff calls upon the thanes to join with him in saluting Malcolm aloud, and they all cheer: 'Hail, King of Scotland!' Trumpets sound.

Malcolm says that his thanes will not have to wait long before he assesses his debt to each one of them and pays them in full. He names his thanes and kinsmen Earls, the first use of that title in Scotland. The other things he has to do — such as calling home his exiled friends, who fled to escape Macbeth and his fiendish Queen, who took her own life — will be done at the appropriate time and place. Malcolm thanks everyone and invites them to his coronation at Scone.

Commentary

The *Retreat* in the stage directions is a trumpet-call which signals the end of the battle. Now, inside the castle with Malcolm as the new King, the last scene becomes more formal, an appropriate tone to end a royal play. The day has been 'cheaply bought', line 3, (i.e. victory has been gained with little loss of life) because so many of Macbeth's soldiers abandoned him to fight on the other side (V. vii. 25) and his army was depleted even before this by desertion (V. iii. 1-8).

The news of the death of young Siward and his father's reaction to it, gives human interest and thaws the cool formality a little. Old Siward's concern that his son should have died with his 'hurts before', line 11 (i.e. on his front) and his refusal to mourn any more than summarily ('so, his knell is knolled', line 16) show that he is a soldier of the old tradition who believes in death before dishonour and putting admiration for heroic sacrifice before grief and sentimentality.

Malcolm shows himself to be very human when he mildly reproaches Siward for being too stoic:

> 'He's worth more sorrow,
> And that I'll spend for him'
>
> (V. ix. 16-17).

If Malcolm seemed just a little insensitive at Macduff's loss in IV. iii, this goes some way to correcting that impression. Notice though that Siward gets the last word, 'He's worth no more;/ They say he parted well, and paid his score:/ And so, God be with him!' (lines 17-19); Siward is a throwback to the heroic age, and he's not going to let a young man, albeit his new King, tell him how a soldier should behave.

Macduff's entrance with Macbeth's head on a pike is a moment of high drama (and it becomes even more dramatic if the producer ignores the stage directions at the end of V. viii and has Macbeth killed offstage). It is Macbeth's final humiliation and Macduff's just revenge. Macduff's remark to Malcolm, 'I see thee compassed with thy kingdom's pearls' (line 22) compares Malcolm to the jewel in a crown surrounded by precious pearls. It is appropriate for Macduff to propose the salutation and be the first to pay allegiance to Malcolm as the new King, for he is the one who has slain the usurper, not just to seek revenge for himself, but to put Malcolm on the throne of Scotland where he rightly belongs.

We learn of Lady Macbeth's suicide in lines 35-37, 'his fiend-like queen,/ Who, as 't is thought, by self and violent hands/ Took off her life', but our thoughts have been away from her for some time and the point ties up a loose end which hardly seems to matter.

Malcolm closes the play on an optimistic note; appealing to God ('by the grace of Grace', line 38), he promises to reform the realm, and things are to be 'planted newly with the time' (line 31) — in other words, changed to suit the times. Once more, there is the promise of peace and harmony for Scotland.

8. The Characters

1. Macbeth

Macbeth is the play's central character and the story is about his rise and fall. Most of the time we exist inside his mind, seeing events through his centre of consciousness; we witness the struggle within him between good and bad, for Macbeth, like the day he describes in I. iii, the day of the battle against the rebel forces, is both 'fair and foul'.

In I. ii, praise is showered on Macbeth: the Captain refers to him as 'brave Macbeth: (well he deserves that name)', line 16; Duncan, his King and relation (kinsman), calls him 'valiant cousin! worthy gentleman!' (line 24); and Rosse gives him the flattering title of 'Bellona's bridegroom' (line 56). Macbeth's prowess on the battlefield, his immense courage against the rebels, impresses everyone, including ourselves. In the following extract the Captain is describing the incident where Macbeth hacked his way through the rebel lines to come face to face with the 'merciless Macdonwald':

'Disdaining Fortune, with his brandished steel,
Which smoked with bloody execution,
Like Valour's minion, carved out his passage,
Till he faced the slave;
Which ne'er shook hands, nor bade farewell to him,
Till he unseamed him from the nave to the chaps,
And fixed his head upon our battlements'

(I. ii. 17-23).

Then, Rosse and Angus ride out to tell Macbeth that praise 'As thick as hail' (I. iii. 97) has been heaped upon him, and to deliver his reward from a grateful King — he is to be made Thane of Cawdor.

However, before this, the Witches have intercepted Macbeth and Banquo on a heath and foretold that Macbeth will become both Thane of Cawdor and 'king hereafter' (I. iii. 50). Macbeth cannot conceal from Banquo his fear at having his innermost thoughts revealed, for, probably long before the play started, Macbeth has already considered murdering Duncan and taking his place on the throne:

'Good Sir, why do you start, and seem to fear
Things that do sound so fair?'

(I. iii. 51-52).

Before I. iii is over, Macbeth is already revealing his murderous thoughts to us:

'My thought, whose murder yet is but fantastical,
Shakes so my single state of man'

(lines 139-140).

He considers letting the prophecy fulfil itself without doing anything to make it happen, for, as he observes, if fate has predestined him to be King, fate can crown him: 'If Chance will have me king, why, Chance may crown me,/ Without my stir' (I. iii. 143-144).

But fate does not seem to be moving in that direction when Duncan makes his son, Malcolm, his heir and Prince of Cumberland. What Macbeth sees is fate placing an obstacle in his way to fulfilling his ambitions, and his murderous thoughts surface again:

'The Prince of Cumberland! — That is a step
On which I must fall down, or else o'erleap,
For in my way it lies. Stars, hide your fires!
Let not light see my black and deep desires;
The eye wink at the hand, yet let that be,
Which the eye fears, when it is done, to see'

(I. iv. 48-53).

Macbeth's fatal flaw, the imperfection in his character which comes to destroy him, is 'Vaulting ambition' (I. vii. 27). Apart from being courageous, Macbeth is very noble and aware of the moral consequences of the deed he must perform to seize the crown; so he vacillates between thoughts of murdering Duncan and getting what he wants so badly, and doing what he knows to be right. At one point he is prepared to sacrifice his soul for his ambition ('jump the life to come', I. vii. 7), but a little later he tells his wife:

'We will proceed no further in this business:
He hath honoured me of late; and I have bought
Golden opinions from all sorts of people,
Which would be worn now in their newest gloss,
Not cast aside so soon'

(I. vii. 31-35).

But Macbeth has another flaw in his character: he is too easily swayed (from virtue towards evil) by others and especially his wife (although we admire his fondness of her, which is evident in the letter in I. v, and in the speech of complete dejection at V. v. 17-28, after her death is announced). When she harangues him, calls him a coward and insults his manhood (I. vii. 35-54), Macbeth gives in to her: 'I am settled, and bend up/ Each corporal agent to this terrible feat' (I. vii. 80-81).

In II. i, just before the murder, Macbeth imagines he sees a dagger floating in the air, but he is in sufficient control of himself to know it is an hallucination; then he walks as though in a trance towards Duncan's bedchamber. But the murder, although it is accomplished, completely unnerves him: he hears voices (almost certainly hallucinations) calling 'Sleep no more!' (II. ii. 34) and is unable to say 'Amen' when the princes ask for God's blessing (II. ii 26-32). Worse still, not only does he forget to smear the grooms with blood — to make it seem as if they were the guilty ones — he even forgets to leave the daggers in Duncan's chamber (bringing them back with him) as he previously planned. Perhaps the words which best express Macbeth's troubled conscience immediately after the murder are:

'Will all great Neptune's ocean wash this blood
Clean from my hand? No, this my hand will rather
The multitudinous seas incarnadine,
Making the green one red'

(II. ii. 59-62).

Only moments after murdering Duncan, Macbeth is bitterly regretting the deed. A knocking is heard and he calls out: 'Wake Duncan with thy knocking: I would thou couldst!' (II. ii. 73). Macbeth is no good at hiding his feelings; his nerves are so frayed in II. iii that the insincerity in his words as he tries to explain to Macduff why he killed the grooms is obvious. Lady Macbeth has to faint to draw attention away from her husband (II. iii. 115). Even at this stage, the nobles can have few doubts about Macbeth's involvement, although no one dares accuse him.

Once Macbeth has the crown, he is uneasy. He fears Banquo because of the Witches' prophecy and Banquo's 'royalty of nature', the 'dauntless temper of his mind', and his wisdom (III. i. 49-53). These are a constant reproach to the evil in his own nature. The evil spirit that guards Macbeth is too weak to resist Banquo's good angel:

'under him
My genius is rebuked'

(III. i. 54-55).

So he plans to have both Banquo and Fleance murdered. Although in III. ii, Lady Macbeth should be able to guess her husband's intentions (see III. ii 39-44), he doesn't tell her what is going to happen ('Be innocent of the knowledge, dearest chuck,/ Till thou applaud the deed', lines 46-47), perhaps because Lady Macbeth has begun to show signs of strain (II. iii. 115 [?], III. ii. 4-7) and he is as worried about her giving them away as she is about him.

As King, Macbeth has absolute power and could quite easily have Banquo arrested and thrown in jail on a trumped-up charge of treason, and no one would dare gainsay him: 'I could/ With bare-faced power sweep him from my sight' (III. i. 117-118). So why doesn't he do so? Because Banquo poses a moral as well as a physical threat to Macbeth. He is a constant reminder of Macbeth's own evil nature. Instead, just as he tried to shift suspicion for Duncan's murder onto the grooms, he convinces two other underlings (the Murderers, who in III. iii are joined by a Third Murderer) that Banquo has persecuted them. By Macbeth's reckoning they now have a sufficient motive for Banquo's murder, which, if they are caught and tortured, will be revealed. He is confident that no one will dare accept their explanation that Macbeth put them up to it. It has been suggested that the Third Murderer in III. iii has been sent by Macbeth to kill the other two, once the job is over, to conceal the evidence. This presents a particularly devious, almost Machiavellian, streak in Macbeth — if it is to be believed.

The banquet is held as if to celebrate Macbeth's triumph over insecurity. His words about Banquo's absence are sheer hypocrisy:

'Here had we now our country's honour roofed,
Were the graced person of our Banquo present;
Who may I rather challenge for unkindness,
Than pity for mischance!'

(III. iv. 40-43).

When the Ghost enters, Macbeth's inability to hide or control his emotions lets him down once more. He gives himself away within seconds:

> (*To the Ghost*) 'Thou canst not say I did it. Never shake
> Thy gory locks at me'
>
> (III. iv. 50-51).

By the end of the banquet scene, we have learned other things about Macbeth: he is now a true tyrant who trusts no one, for he has a spy posted in every one of his lords' houses:

> 'There's not a one of them, but in his house
> I keep a servant fee'd'
>
> (III. iv. 131-132);

by this time he feels he has travelled so far down this bloody path that stopping and going back would be no easier than going on (so he is resigned to his career of evil):

> 'I am in blood
> Stepped in so far, that, should I wade no more,
> Returning were as tedious as go o'er'
>
> (III. iv. 136-138);

he even believes his inexperience is the cause of his fear:

> 'My strange and self-abuse
> Is the initiate fear, that wants hard use:
> We are yet but young in deed'
>
> (III. iv. 142-144).

What we sense from these words is that Macbeth is going to become more callous and brutal, and that gradually he will develop an immunity to the horror of his deeds — something which he recognises he has accomplished at V. v. 13-15:

> 'I have supped full with horrors:
> Direness, familiar to my slaughterous thoughts
> Cannot once start me'.

After Macbeth's visit to the Witches in IV. i, our glimpses of his humanity become fewer, but two outstanding examples still remain: his expression of life's futility after the announcement of his wife's death (V. v. 17-28) and his other expression of remorse in V. viii. 4-6, when he meets Macduff on the battlefield:

'Of all men else I have avoided thee:
But get thee back, my soul is too much charged
With blood of thine already'.

(Although it has been suggested that Macbeth is rationalising his fear here.) The massacre of Macduff's family is vile, and for us it is Macbeth's worst crime, motivated by his need to prove to himself that he can make 'The very firstlings' of his heart 'The firstlings' of his hand (IV. i. 147-148), and by jealousy and spite, because Macduff has children to succeed him:

'give to th' edge o' th' sword
His wife, his babes, and all unfortunate souls
That trace him in his line'

(IV. i. 150-152).

In the last act, Macbeth oscillates between 'valiant fury' (a desperate attempt to hide his fear from himself and others by frenetic activity), disgust at those around him who are showing fear or deserting him, and despair:

'I have lived long enough: my way of life
Is fall'n into the sere'

(V. iii. 22-23);

'I 'gin to be aweary of the sun'

(V. v. 49).

There comes a point when, in his moral inadequacy,

Macbeth appears like a dwarf, with blood on his hands, wearing the stolen robes of a giant:

> 'Now does he feel
> His secret murders sticking on his hands'
>
> (V. ii. 16-17);

> 'now does he feel his title
> Hang loose about him, like a giant's robe
> Upon a dwarfish thief'
>
> (V. ii. 20-22).

However suicidal he may feel, Macbeth scorns the idea of ending his own life ('Why should I play the Roman fool, and die/ On mine own sword?', V. viii. 1-2), preferring to fight to the death. He clings on desperately to the Second Apparition's promise that no man born of a woman can harm him, and when he meets Macduff and the power of that charm lets him down ('Macduff was from his mother's womb/ Untimely ripped', V. viii. 15-16), all his courage deserts him momentarily:

> 'I'll not fight with thee'
>
> (V. viii. 22).

But Macbeth redeems himself seconds later. As Macduff taunts him with the prospect of being humiliated as a prisoner ('We'll have thee, as our rarer monsters are', V. viii. 25), his former courage, the courage of I. ii, returns and he dies valiantly.

(N.B. For the reasons why Macbeth loses the fight, see Commentary to V. viii. If the ideas of Macbeth wanting to fight to the death in V. v. 52 and the knowledge that he is invulnerable because of the Second Apparition's promise seem contradictory, the best explanation is that Macbeth begins to doubt the validity of the promise after V. v. 42-46 when Birnam wood has come to Dunsinane.)

2. Lady Macbeth

If Macbeth's heart hardens as the play progresses, Lady Macbeth's softens. In I. v, when we first meet her, she is reading a letter from Macbeth in which he tells her of his meeting with the Witches. The letter makes no mention of murdering Duncan but her thoughts soon run to it, for she is a powerfully determined woman with wild ambitions for her husband and herself. She knows her husband's character well and fears that he is not ruthless enough to do what has to be done to seize the crown:

'Yet I do fear thy nature:
It is too full o' the milk of human kindness
To catch the nearest way. Thou wouldst be great;
Art not without ambition, but without
The illness should attend it: what thou wouldst highly,
That wouldst thou holily'

(I. v. 14-19).

Consequently, she makes up her mind to lash her husband with her tongue until any lingering doubts he has about murder are removed:

'Hie thee hither,
That I may pour my spirits in thine ear,
And chastise with the valour of my tongue
All that impedes thee from the golden round'

(I. v. 23-26).

This ruthless determination to ensure that nothing gets in the way of their plans extends even to herself. Accordingly, she

calls upon the spirits to drain all womanly kindness from her
and fill her with cruelty instead:

> 'Come, you spirits
> That tend on mortal thoughts, unsex me here,
> And fill me, from the crown to the toe, top-full
> Of direst cruelty!'
>
> (I. v. 38-41).

When Macbeth enters, her greeting to him echoes that of the
Witches (see I. iii. 48-50), and for a moment she appears to us
like the Fourth Witch:

> 'Great Glamis! worthy Cawdor!
> Greater than both, by the all-hail, hereafter!'
>
> (I. v. 52-53).

Duncan is honouring Macbeth by visiting his castle at
Inverness and Lady Macbeth gloats at the prospect, knowing
it will be Duncan's last day on earth:

> 'O! never
> Shall sun that morrow see!'
>
> (I. v. 58-59).

But her fear throughout the play is that her husband — with
his inability to hide his feelings — will give them away:

> 'Your face, my thane, is as a book, where men
> May read strange matters'
>
> (I. v. 60-61).

She tells him to act normally and conceal his evil intentions
within him:

> 'look like the innocent flower
> But be the serpent under 't'
>
> (I. v. 63-64).

It is in I. vii. that Macbeth starts having reservations about the murder and when he tells his wife, 'We will proceed no further in this business' (line 31), she scolds him, questioning his love for her ('From this time/ Such I account thy love', lines 38-39), calling him a coward (line 43), and mocking his manhood (lines 47-51). In a startling image, which clearly shows Lady Macbeth's mettle and the lengths to which she is prepared to go once her mind is made up, she says that if she had sworn to kill someone — as Macbeth has sworn to kill Duncan — even if it were her own child whom she had nursed and no matter how dear it was to her, she would still do it:

> 'I have given suck, and know
> How tender 't is to love the babe that milks me:
> I would, while it was smiling in my face,
> Have plucked my nipple from his boneless gums,
> And dashed the brains out, had I so sworn as you
> Have done to this'

(I. vii. 54-59).

She then devises a plan to kill Duncan while he is sleeping deeply after a hard day's ride and then put the blame on the drunken grooms (I. vii. 61-72). Macbeth is carried along enthusiastically by the way she makes it sound so simple, and he praises her for her courage:

> 'Bring forth men-children only!
> For thy undaunted mettle should compose
> Nothing but males'

(I. vii. 72-74).

In II. ii, immediately after the murder, Lady Macbeth's nerve is still strong, while her husband is almost hysterical with fear. Before he comes down from Duncan's bedchamber, though, Lady Macbeth says something that some critics take to be the first sign of her humanity:

'Had he not resembled
My father as he slept, I had done 't'

(II. ii. 12-13).

When Macbeth reappears, his mind on the verge of collapse, she takes control, telling him they should not think too deeply about what has happened lest it 'make us mad' (line 33), scolding him for being 'Infirm of purpose' (line 51) and returning the daggers, which Macbeth in his confusion has brought back with him, to the bedchamber. When she re-enters after doing this, she scorns her husband's fear that he will never be able to wash Duncan's blood off his hands, by saying prosaically:

'A little water clears us of this deed'

(II. ii. 66).

It is perhaps in II. iii that Lady Macbeth's nerve starts to fail her. When Macbeth is challenged by Macduff to explain why he killed the grooms, she faints and has to be carried off. This could indicate an attempt by her to draw attention away from Macbeth, or, the faint is a genuine sign of emotional strain and fatigue. Certainly in III. ii, her disillusionment with being Queen, because of her fear that their crime will be discovered, is beginning to show:

'Nought's had, all's spent,
Where our desire is got without content:
'T is safer to be that which we destroy,
Than by destruction dwell in doubtful joy'

(III. ii. 4-7).

Macbeth, possibly because he knows his wife is on the verge of a breakdown, doesn't tell her about his plan to murder Banquo.

In III. iv, the banquet scene, Lady Macbeth starts out

appearing a little subdued. When Banquo's Ghost enters and Macbeth's hysterical reaction begins to give him away, she tries to shame him out of his fear with the familiar attack on his manhood:

> 'O! these flaws and starts
> (Impostors to true fear) would well become
> A woman's story at a winter's fire,
> Authorised by her grandam. Shame itself!'
>
> (III. iv. 63-66).

When the Ghost reappears and all seems lost, she rallies to Macbeth's defence, using her last reserves of energy to excuse him to the others present by saying that he is ill, and then, with her last attempt at playing the gracious hostess, she ushers them all from the room. At the end of the scene, while Macbeth seems to be getting his second wind, she is exhausted. She has no strength left to scold her husband and can only answer meekly when he asks her why Macduff has failed to attend the feast:

> 'Did you send to him, Sir?'
>
> (III. iv. 129).

We don't see Lady Macbeth again until V.i, the sleepwalking scene. Here, all the fear locked away in her subconscious mind reveals itself and her thoughts wander back in time over their crimes. Even in this scene though, her callous streak is evident; she has no pity for Duncan — only a mild sense of surprise and disgust at the sight of his mutilated body:

> 'Yet who would have thought the old man to have
> had so much blood in him?'
>
> (V. i. 31-32).

The only religious statement (of sorts) that she makes in the play, comes in V. i. line 29, 'Hell is murky'. It briefly expresses her fear of damnation, a fear which has troubled Macbeth deeply (see I. vii. 1-7, 20) but which she seems to have been able to ignore up until this point. The rubbing motion with her hands, the attempt to wash away imaginary blood ('Here's the smell of blood still: all the perfumes of Arabia will not sweeten this little hand', lines 40-41) recalls the way she scoffed at her husband's fear that they would never be free of guilt (and that Duncan's blood would stick to his hands):

> 'A little water clears us of this deed:
> How easy it is then!'
>
> (II. ii. 66-67).

To whom does Lady Macbeth write (see V. i. 3-6)? The best explanation is that it is a letter to warn Lady Macduff of the attack on Fife Castle. The little doggerel, 'The Thane of Fife had a wife: where is she now?' (line 34) seems to express remorse at this atrocity. It has been suggested that this is the only expression of remorse Lady Macbeth gives in the play.

In Act V, Lady Macbeth is isolated from her husband, no longer exerting any influence over him. We don't see her again after V. i, and when her death is announced in V. v. 16, Macbeth has little time, with his castle facing attack, to mourn her. Instead, his statement in V. v. 17-28 is a more general comment on life's futility, and only in the last scene do we learn that Lady Macbeth has committed suicide:

> 'his fiend-like queen,
> Who, as 't is thought, by self and violent hands
> Took off her life'
>
> (V. ix. 35-37),

although the stage direction in V. v. 6, *A cry within, of women,* suggests her death was violent.

Just how evil Lady Macbeth really is, whether she justifies

the title, 'his fiend-like queen', is a matter of opinion, worthy of debate. There can be little doubt that had Lady Macbeth used her determination and strength of purpose for good rather than evil, she would have been an admirable character, instead of the cruel and even unnatural creature she appears to be for much of the story.

3. Banquo

Banquo is a foil to Macbeth. He is brave, wise, and has a regal nature, all of which disturb Macbeth for they are a constant reminder of his own evil nature, which is stained with blood:

> 'Our fears in Banquo
> Stick deep, and in his royalty of nature
> Reigns that which would be feared; 't is much he dares;
> And, to that dauntless temper of his mind,
> He hath a wisdom that doth guide his valour
> To act in safety. There is none but he
> Whose being I do fear: and under him
> My genius is rebuked'

(III. i. 48-55).

Macbeth and Banquo meet the Witches together in I. iii, but whereas Macbeth chooses to embrace evil to fulfil his ambitions, Banquo does not, although he thinks deeply about the Witches' prophecy, to the extent that it disturbs his sleep:

> 'A heavy summons lies like lead upon me,
> And yet I would not sleep: merciful powers!
> Restrain in me the cursèd thoughts that nature
> Gives way to in repose!'

(II. i. 6-9).

Notice how Banquo appeals to heaven ('merciful powers') to protect him from evil, while Macbeth sells his soul to the devil. Whatever evil ambitions are stirred in Banquo because of the Witches' prophecy — that his sons will be kings — they stay locked in his subconscious, only revealing themselves in nightmares ('cursèd thoughts that nature/ Gives way to in repose'). When Macbeth offers Banquo some advantage for himself if Banquo backs him when the time comes, Banquo insists that he will do nothing dishonourable:

> 'So I lose none (i.e. honour)
> In seeking to augment it, but still keep
> My bosom franchised, and allegiance clear,
> I shall be counselled'
>
> (II. i. 26-29).

Banquo is close to the King and they arrive at Macbeth's castle at Inverness together in I. vi. Like Duncan, Banquo is too ready to trust appearances. Banquo observed Macbeth's reaction when the latter was told he would be 'king hereafter' (I. iii. 50); he saw Macbeth jump and look scared:

> 'Good sir, why do you start, and seem to fear,
> Things that do sound so fair?'
>
> (I. iii. 51-52).

If Banquo has guessed that the Witches have touched upon Macbeth's secret hopes, he is a little naive to be taken in by the idyllic setting of Inverness Castle. In spite of the 'temple-haunting' martlets, danger lurks inside:

> 'This guest of summer,
> The temple-haunting martlet, does approve,
> By his loved mansionry, that the heaven's breath
> Smells wooingly here'
>
> (I. vi. 3-6).

After Duncan's murdered body is discovered in II. iii, Banquo says very little. He reproaches Lady Macbeth for her

inept remark, 'What! in our house?' with the retort, 'Too
cruel anywhere' (line 84). But not much else leaves his lips.
His comparative silence almost certainly denotes deep suspicion of Macbeth and disgust at the sham emotions Macbeth
is mouthing (II. iii. 103-115). Banquo expresses his suspicion
in a soliloquy in III. i:

> 'Thou hast it now, King, Cawdor, Glamis, all,
> As the weird women promised; and, I fear,
> Thou playedst most foully for 't'
>
> (lines 1-3).

But a question mark hangs over Banquo. If he suspects
Macbeth so deeply, why doesn't he expose him by telling the
other thanes what happened with the Witches and by describing the conversation he had with Macbeth in II. i. 20-29?
There are various possible answers: that there is nothing
Banquo can do, since no once can challenge the supreme
authority of the King (Macbeth can 'With bare-faced power
sweep him from my sight', III. i. 118); that Banquo has also
been corrupted by the Witches' promise and now embraces
evil with Macbeth — the ride in Act III being a visit to the
Witches to get them to look into 'the seeds of time' for him
once more. There are two reasons why this last idea seems
rather wild: if Banquo is now corrupt and wants his son to
take the throne, then it would be in his interest to expose
Macbeth, which would effectively get him out of the way so
that Fleance might replace him. Secondly, Banquo was an
ancestor of James I, who attended the play's première in
1606, and Shakespeare would hardly wish to insult his
monarch.

Banquo's virtue continues to unsettle Macbeth even after
he is dead. His Ghost haunts Macbeth in III. iv (the banquet
scene) and reappears in IV. i. 111, behind the show of eight
kings. There the Ghost's smile indicates exaltation at Banquo's

triumph over Macbeth, for the kings are all Banquo's offspring:

> 'the blood-boltered Banquo smiles upon me,
> And points at them for his'
>
> (IV. i. 123-124).

4. Duncan

Duncan is an old man. Although Malcolm and Donalbain are young men (Malcolm: 'I am young', IV. iii. 14, which probably means the brothers are in their twenties), two ideas suggest their father is well past middle-age: Lady Macbeth's remark, 'who would have thought the old man to have had so much blood in him?' (V. i. 31-32) and her impression that he looked like her father as he lay sleeping the night of the murder, 'Had he not resembled/ My father as he slept, I had done 't' (II. ii. 12-13). Another possible argument making the same point is that Duncan's lack of judgement can be put down to senility.

Duncan is a kind man and a virtuous King. When we first meet him, he is receiving news from the battlefront and he is quick to praise Macbeth ('valiant cousin! worthy gentlemen!', I. ii. 24) and reward him for his services to the nation by making him Thane of Cawdor. We see this gratitude and generosity again in I. vi, when Duncan arrives at Inverness Castle and is greeted by Lady Macbeth:

> 'Give me your hand;
> Conduct me to mine host: we love him highly,
> And shall continue our graces towards him'
>
> (lines 28-30).

Later on, while Duncan is at Inverness, he graciously presents Lady Macbeth with a diamond as a gift to his 'kind hostess' (the irony is cruel):

'This diamond he greets your wife withal,
By the name of most kind hostess'

(II. i. 15-16).

Duncan's virtue is one reason why Macbeth finds it so hard to murder him:

'this Duncan
Hath born his faculties so meek, hath been
So clear in his great office, that his virtues
Will plead like angels, trumpet-tongued, against
The deep damnation of his taking off'

(I. vii. 16-20).

Macbeth is saying that Duncan has used his powers with consideration ('born his faculties so meek') and that he is an incorruptible King ('So clear in his great office').

But Duncan, perhaps because he is a nice, gentle, unassuming man, cannot (or refuses to) see beneath the surface of things — to the rottenness hiding beneath — and so he is too trusting of others. The former Thane of Cawdor, who is executed for treason in Act I, was once a man Duncan had absolute faith in. Duncan admits that he can never tell what is going on in a man's mind by what is written on his face:

'There's no art
To find the mind's construction in the face:
He was a gentleman on whom I built
An absolute trust'

(I. iv. 11-14).

No sooner is the treacherous Thane of Cawdor dead than Duncan starts placing 'absolute trust' in Macbeth. There is considerable irony in the way that, as Duncan rides towards Inverness Castle where his murder awaits him, he comments on the castle's pleasant prospect and the salubrious air which surrounds it:

> 'This castle hath a pleasant seat; the air
> Nimbly and sweetly recommends itself
> Unto our gentle senses'
>
> (I. vi. 1-3).

This tendency to trust appearances too readily and his failure to develop a healthy scepticism, despite what has happened with the former Thane of Cawdor, proves fatal. Duncan goes to bed feeling completely at ease in Macbeth's castle ('shut up/ In measureless content', II. i. 16-17), no doubt with a good deal of wine inside him, without taking the obvious precaution of posting a proper guard at his bedchamber door. The two grooms have also enjoyed a rich meal with lots of wine and so fall easy prey to Lady Macbeth's cunning (she drugs their drinks). The grooms are useless guards and Duncan is an easy victim.

5. Macduff

Macduff is the one who discovers Duncan's body in II. iii and, as he has been commanded by Duncan to 'call timely on him' (II. iii. 41, i.e. 'wake him early'), we may assume that he is close to the King. Macduff is perceptive and brave. While the others may also have their suspicions of Macbeth in II. iii, Macduff is the first one to issue any sort of challenge to him when he asks why he slew the grooms:

> *Macbeth*
> O! yet I do repent me of my fury
> That I did kill them.
>
> *Macduff*
> Wherefore did you so?
>
> (lines 103-104).

Macduff can sense that Macbeth is lying and this is enough to convince him of Macbeth's guilt; he refuses to attend Macbeth's coronation, returning to his home at Fife Castle instead. He tells Rosse why he won't go to Scone:

'Well, may you see things well done there: — adieu! —
Lest our old robes sit easier than our new!'

(II. iv. 37-38).

Macduff is saying, and again his shrewdness and perception are obvious, that things may have changed for the worse.

The first we hear of Macduff in England is in III. vi. 29-30. His decision to leave his wife and family behind in Scotland seems so unwise as to be out of character. There is no evidence to suggest that he left in such great haste that he couldn't have taken them with him and left them safely in England. Macduff must assume that Macbeth is not such a butcher as to harm them, but relying on a tyrant's sense of fair-play is naive and irresponsible. In fact, Lady Macduff accuses her husband of cowardice, a lack of wisdom, and wanting the natural touch:

'All is the fear, and nothing is the love;
As little is the wisdom, where the flight
So runs against all reason'

(IV. ii. 12-14).

But these are words spoken in anger (because she doesn't know why he has abandoned them) and out of a sense of helplessness. Rosse replies that Macduff is, 'noble, wise, judicious' (IV. ii. 16), which is an accurate general description (although, as mentioned earlier, Macduff is not wise in leaving his family behind in Scotland).

The next time we meet Macduff is in England, in IV. iii, where Malcolm is testing him. Malcolm assumes the guise of an even greater villain than Macbeth to test Macduff's virtue and loyalty. Macduff is confused by Malcolm's words at first. He shows himself to be realistic and pragmatic in trying to accommodate certain of Malcolm's 'vices' (lust, lines 60-76; greed, lines 76-89) but when Malcolm claims that he has none of the 'king-becoming graces' to counterbalance these human failings, Macduff gives in to anger and despair, accusing Malcolm of being unfit to live, let alone govern:

> 'Fit to govern?
> Not not to live. — O nation miserable!'
>
> (IV. iii. 102-103).

Macduff is no puritan, and he knows that Malcolm is the rightful King of Scotland, but he loves his country and doesn't want Malcolm at any price, when convinced that all Malcolm's claims to vice are true.

When Rosse arrives in IV. iii and breaks the news of the massacre of Macduff's family, Macduff's initial reaction is stunned disbelief, the repetition of his questions at lines 211-219 indicating his shock. He tries to hide his anguish, but Malcolm tells him to give it utterance. Then words of grief pour out of him in which he expresses how much his family meant to him, how angry he is at heaven for letting it happen, and how angry he is at himself that his wife and children should die because of him:

> 'I cannot but remember such things were,
> That were more precious to me. — Did heaven look on,
> And would not take their part? Sinful Macduff!
> They were all struck for thee. Naught that I am,
> Not for their own demerits, but for mine
> Fell slaughter on their souls'
>
> (IV. iii. 222-227).

In Act V, Macduff is only interested in finding Macbeth and slaying him, for he believes that the souls of his wife and children will never be at peace unless he personally avenges their murders:

> 'If thou be'st slain, and with no stroke of mine,
> My wife and children's ghosts will haunt me still'
>
> (V. vii. 15-16).

When he meets Macbeth, he is the one who shows the Second Apparition's promise to be a quibble, for 'Macduff was from his mother's womb/ Untimely ripped' (V. viii. 15-16). Macbeth had taken the Second Apparition's words to mean that no one at all could kill him, whereas in another sense they mean that Macbeth would not be killed by a child born normally of a woman.

Macduff's revenge is complete when he carries Macbeth's severed head onto the stage in V. ix, and he, perhaps more than Malcolm in this scene, appears the saviour of Scotland as he greets his new King with these words:

> 'Hail, King! for so thou art. Behold, where stands
> Th' usurper's cursèd head: the time is free'
>
> (V. ix. 20-21).

6. Malcolm

Malcolm's part is small but significant in the play and Shakespeare defines his character sufficiently to let us know that Scotland will have a good King on the throne after Macbeth has been overthrown. We begin to judge Malcolm in II. iii, after his father's body has been discovered. When Macduff breaks the news to him, Malcolm's response is rather blunt and unemotional:

> 'O! by whom?'
>
> (line 96).

Is this insensitivity? No — it's caution and restraint, for

Malcolm knows that strong displays of emotion can be interpreted by others as hypocrisy:

'To show an unfelt sorrow is an office
Which the false man does easy'

(II. iii. 134-135).

These lines also show us that Malcolm can think quickly (and that he distrusts appearances, a point which will be developed later), for they tell us that he knows someone is lying in II. iii. He sees flight as his best course of action, and perhaps he is right, although it can be argued that the act of running away allows suspicion to fall on him and his brother, and so is a sign of inexperience and immaturity. If this is so, youth is his best defence. But Malcolm's wisdom is clearly seen in II. iii, when he tells Donalbain that whoever killed their father is likely to strike again, this time at them:

'This murderous shaft that's shot
Hath not yet lighted'

(lines 139-140).

As early on as I. iv. 48-50, Macbeth knew he would have to deal with Malcolm:

'The Prince of Cumberland! — That is a step
On which I must fall down, or else o'erleap,
For in my way it lies.'

In much the same way, Malcolm has anticipated trouble and by running away he is taking sensible evasive action.

The next time we meet Malcolm is in IV. iii, where he starts with the ploy to test Macduff's virtue and loyalty. Unlike his father, Malcolm distrusts appearances. After Macduff has proved his worth, Malcolm encourages him to join the fight against Macbeth, explaining why the deception was necessary:

> 'Devilish Macbeth
> By many of these trains hath sought to win me
> Into his power, and modest wisdom plucks me
> From over-credulous haste'

(IV. iii. 117-120).

In spite of his youth, Malcolm is wise enough to allow himself to be guided by Macduff: 'I put myself to thy direction' (IV. iii. 122); and being devout, he asks God to direct the relationship between Macduff and himself: 'God above/ Deal between thee and me!' (IV. iii. 120-121). Then, probably because this is the most economical way of doing it, Shakespeare allows Malcolm to relate his own virtuous nature:

> 'I am yet
> Unknown to woman; never was forsworn;
> Scarcely have coveted what was mine own;
> At no time broke my faith: would not betray
> The devil to his fellow; and delight
> No less in truth than life'

(IV. iii. 125-130).

At the beginning of IV. iii, Malcolm deliberately gave the false impression that his only answer to Macbeth's reign of terror was to weep:

> 'Let us seek out some desolate shade, and there
> Weep our sad bosoms empty'

(lines 1-2).

But Malcolm is not ineffectual; even before Macduff's arrival he was preparing to leave for Scotland with old Siward and an army of ten thousand men.

Malcolm may be a little insensitive when, after the news of the massacre of Macduff's family is announced, he tells Macduff to 'Dispute it like a man' (IV. iii. 220). Macduff rightly replies: 'I shall do so;/ But I must also feel it as a man' (lines 220-221). But Malcolm is right when he tells Macduff not to hide his grief, as locking it inside him can break his heart:

> 'Give sorrow words; the grief that does not speak
> Whispers the o'er-fraught heart, and bids it break'
> (IV. iii. 209-210).

So perhaps, rather than his remark showing insensitivity, Malcolm is trying to comfort Macduff by getting him to convert his grief into anger. Not only will this help their cause, it will allow Macduff to take positive action to avenge the death of his family and go some way to lessening his feelings of loss and helplessness. Certainly this is the point Malcolm is making in IV. iii. 228-229:

> 'Be this the whetstone of your sword: let grief
> Convert to anger; blunt not the heart, enrage it.'

Malcolm shows himself to be a good soldier versed in tactics in V. iv, for he is the one who thinks up the idea of camouflaging the size of their army as they approach Dunsinane Castle by using cut branches. Possibly Malcolm 's popularity as a future King contributes to the desertion of so many of Macbeth's soldiers. Rosse points out in IV. iii. 186-188 that Malcolm's presence in Scotland would be sufficient to cause a popular uprising against Macbeth:

> 'Your eye in Scotland
> Would create soldiers, make our women fight
> To doff their dire distresses'.

In the last scene, V. ix, Malcolm shows gratitude to his thanes by promising to repay them for their services with honours; he begins by making his thanes and kinsmen Earls.

He promises reforms to the realm, showing once again that far from being ineffectual, he is in fact a man of action:

> 'What's more to do,
> Which would be planted newly with the time,
>
> We will perform in measure, time and place'
>
> (V. ix. 30-31 & 39).

Malcolm's words here recall Duncan's promise to Macbeth in I. iv. 28-29:

> 'I have begun to plant thee, and will labour
> To make thee full of growing';

and Malcolm's display of gratitude to his thanes recalls his father's assurance that:

> 'signs of nobleness, like stars, shall shine
> On all deservers'
>
> (I. iv. 41-42).

9. The Examination

The 'O' level English Literature paper is 2½ hours long. In that time you have to answer five questions: two on Shakespeare (one context and one essay question) and three on at least two other texts. Allowing a few minutes to collect your thoughts, to read the paper and select the questions you want to answer, you have a little under half an hour left for each question.

The Essay Question

The essay question usually requires you to write a character study or to describe certain events in the play. So you must know the play in detail and be able to quote from the text to support the points you are making.

When you are quoting verse, you must retain the line formation of the text. You will know verse by the fact that every line starts with a capital letter, which is not the case for prose (of which there is very little in *Macbeth*). One way of quoting verse is down the page, like this:

'That which hath made them drunk hath made me bold.
What hath quenched them hath given me fire. — Hark! —
    Peace!
It was the owl that shrieked, the fatal bellman,
Which gives the stern'st good night. He is about it.
The doors are open, and the surfeited grooms
Do mock their charge with snores'

(II. ii. 1-6).

Notice that the quotation has a margin of one centimetre or so from the left hand side of the page. If you can give the act, scene and line numbers, so much the better. The other way of quoting verse is to show that a line in the text ends at a particular word by using a stroke or oblique-sign, like this: 'It was the owl that shrieked, the fatal bellman,/ Which gives the stern'st good night. He is about it./ The doors are open, and the surfeited grooms/ Do mock their charge with snores' (II. ii. 3-6). Remember to start each new word after the pen stroke with a capital letter. Also remember to preserve the punctuation mark (if any) at the end of the line, just before the stroke which shows a new line of verse is beginning.

When you are quoting prose, it doesn't matter if you follow the line formation of the text, and so no stroke is needed at the end of the lines, e.g.: 'If he were dead, you 'ld weep for him: if you would not, it were a good sign that I should quickly have a new father' (IV. ii. 59-60). In the text, line 60 starts at 'were a good sign' but there is no need to indicate this by putting a stroke between 'it' and 'were'.

How many quotations should you learn? As many as you can, within reason, but only learn by heart those quotations which describe characters and important events or ideas that you think might be useful in an essay. *Remember, a short, apt quotation is better (and easier to remember) than a long tedious one.* In other words, make your quotations just long enough to make your point. Go through the Scene Summaries, Commentaries, and the Character Studies in this book and jot down on a piece of paper or in a note book any useful quotations that you find, giving the act, scene and line numbers, and the point the quotation is making, as you understand it.

The Textual Question

This is a quotation from the Cambridge 'O' level syllabus for English Literature: *Candidates may be required to explain words and phrases, to rewrite passages in modern English, or to relate an extract to the work as a whole.* The last phrase, 'relate an extract to the work as a whole', means you might have to say what significance a particular passage has in the play — how it fits into the play. Whereas you are expected to know which act and scene the passage comes from, knowing the line numbers is not important.

Remember that each Textual Question (sometimes known as the 'Context' question) requires about ten responses from you. That gives you about three minutes for each answer, so don't get carried away and write over-long answers.

Here are three worked examples of Textual Questions:

1.
Lady Macbeth

That which hath made them drunk hath made me bold.
What hath quenched them hath given me fire. —
   Hark! — Peace!
It was the owl that shrieked, the fatal bellman,
Which gives the stern'st good-night. He is about it.
The doors are open, and the surfeited grooms
Do mock their charge with snores. I have drugged
   their possets,
That death and nature do contend about them,
Whether they live or die.

Macbeth (Within)
   Who's there? — what, ho!

Lady Macbeth

Alack! I am afraid they have awaked,
And 't is not done: — the attempt, and not the deed,
Confounds us. — Hark! — I laid their daggers ready;
He could not miss them. — Had he not resembled
My father as he slept, I had done 't.

(a) Briefly explain where this passage comes in the play, and what is happening.

(b) Explain the metaphor in which the shrieking owl is compared to 'the fatal bellman'.

(c) Re-write in modern English, 'the surfeited grooms/ Do mock their charge with snores'.

(d) What are 'possets'?

(e) What does Lady Macbeth mean by: 'the attempt, and not the deed,/ Confounds us'?

(f) 'I laid their daggers ready':
   (i) Whose daggers?
   (ii) What is Macbeth supposed to do with the daggers and why?
   (iii) What, in fact, does he do with them?

(g) Comment on the significance of these lines: 'Had he not resembled/ My father as he slept, I had done 't'.

Answers

(a) This passage comes at the beginning of II. ii. Duncan is sleeping in a bedchamber at Inverness Castle; his two attendants, the grooms, have been drugged by Lady Macbeth and are unconscious. While Lady Macbeth waits anxiously downstairs, Macbeth is in the process of slaying Duncan.

(b) In Shakespeare's day, when a body was being taken for burial, a man ringing a bell would lead the funeral procession. The owl is compared to this man — 'the fatal bellman'. So Lady Macbeth takes the owl's shriek as a signal, like the death bell, that Duncan is dead.

(c) The attendants, full of drink, make a mockery of their responsibility (to guard Duncan) by being fast asleep and snoring.

(d) Possets are hot, alcoholic drinks.

(e) Lady Macbeth means her husband has failed in his attempt to murder Duncan and been caught in the act;

she thinks this attempt on Duncan's life, rather than the actual murder, has destroyed them.

(f)   (i)   The grooms'.

(ii)   He and Lady Macbeth planned that the daggers should be smeared with Duncan's blood, or actually used in the murder, and then left in the bedchamber to point suspicion at the grooms.

(iii) Macbeth, in his confusion, brings the daggers back with him.

(g)   These lines are an indication that Lady Macbeth has a measure of humanity.

2.   *Macduff*
Your royal father's murdered.

                          Malcolm
                                    O! by whom?

                          Lenox
Those of his chamber, as it seemed, had done't:
Their hands and faces were all badged with blood;
So were their daggers, which, unwiped, we found
Upon their pillows:
They stared, and were distracted; no man's life
Was to be trusted with them.

                          Macbeth
O! yet I do repent me of my fury
That I did kill them.

                          Macduff
                          Wherefore did you so?

                          Macbeth
Who can be wise, amazed, temperate and furious,
Loyal and neutral, in a moment? No man:
The expedition of my violent love

>   Outran the pauser reason. — Here lay Duncan,
>   His silver skin laced with his golden blood;
>   And his gashed stabs looked like a breach in nature
>   For ruin's wasteful entrance: there, the murderers,
>   Steeped in the colours of their trade, their daggers
>   Unmannerly breached with gore. Who could refrain,
>   That had a heart to love, and in that heart
>   Courage, to make 's love known?
>
>   *Lady Macbeth (Fainting)*
>   Help me hence, ho!

(a) Comment briefly on Malcolm's reaction to the news of his father's murder here.

(b) Looking at Lenox's speech, explain in your own words why he thinks the grooms murdered Duncan.

(c) What does Macbeth mean by 'I do repent me of my fury/ That I did kill them'?

(d) What is the significance of Macduff's question, 'Wherefore did you so?'

(e) Explain the meaning of the phrase 'in a moment'.

(f) What does the word 'expedition' mean as it is used here?

(g) 'His silver skin laced with his golden blood':
   (i) Why is the word 'laced' used here?
   (ii) Suggest why Macbeth describes Duncan's blood as 'golden'.

(h) Explain why Lady Macbeth faints.

Answers

(a) Malcolm's reaction to the news of his father's death seems rather unemotional but this is because he knows how easily a liar shows a sorrow he does not feel. Rather than be thought a hypocrite by those who suspect him of the murder, he keeps his feelings to himself.

(b) Lenox thinks the grooms murdered Duncan because their hands and faces were covered with blood; so were their daggers, which lay unwiped on their pillows. Lenox says the grooms stared around them and looked demented, so he presumably thinks insanity drove them to murdering Duncan.

(c) Macbeth means that he regrets allowing his anger to get the better of him and killing the grooms.

(d) Macduff's question indicates his suspicion of Macbeth. He suspects Macbeth had some other motive than right-eous anger for killing the grooms.

(e) At the same time.

(f) The word 'expedition' here means 'speed'.

(g) (i) The word 'laced' metaphorically describes the way Duncan's 'golden blood' criss-crossed his 'silver skin' to form a pattern like lace.

(ii) Duncan's blood is described as 'golden' because it is not common blood — it is royal blood, the most pre-cious in the land. So Macbeth, rather than calling it a common 'red', calls it 'golden'.

(h) Lady Macbeth faints for one of two reasons: either she is trying to draw attention away from her husband, who she thinks is giving himself away by his lies about why he killed the grooms, or, this is a genuine sign of emotional strain and fatigue after the events leading up to Duncan's murder.

3.   *Lady Macbeth*
Glamis thou art, and Cawdor; and shalt be
What thou art promised. — Yet I do fear thy nature:
It is too full o' the milk of human kindness
To catch the nearest way. Thou wouldst be great;
Art not without ambition, but without

The illness should attend it: what thou wouldst highly,
That wouldst thou holily; wouldst not play false,
And yet wouldst wrongly win; thou 'dst have, great
     Glamis,
That which cries, "Thus thou must do, if thou have it";
And that which rather thou dost fear to do,
Than wishest should be undone. Hie thee hither,
That I may pour my spirits in thine ear,
And chastise with the valour of my tongue
All that impedes thee from the golden round,
Which fate and metaphysical aid doth seem
To have thee crowned withal.

(a) Briefly explain the circumstances in which this passage
     appears in the play.

(b) What does Lady Macbeth mean by, 'and shalt be/ What
     thou art promised'?

(c) 'Yet I do fear thy nature': What is Lady Macbeth saying?

(d) Explain the meaning of the phrase, 'To catch the nearest
     way'.

(e) What does the word 'illness' mean as it is used here?

(f) Re-write in modern English, 'wouldst not play false,/
     And yet wouldst wrongly win'.

(g) What is meant by 'the golden round'?

(h) 'metaphysical aid': What is Lady Macbeth referring to?

(i) How, according to Lady Macbeth's words here, is she
     going to help her husband become King? (You may
     quote from the text, but the bulk of your answer should
     be in your own words.)

Answers

(a) Lady Macbeth has just received a letter from her
     husband describing his meeting with the Witches.
     Wildly ambitious for her husband and herself, her

thoughts run to murdering Duncan as the quickest way to seize the throne, but she is worried that her husband is not ruthless enough to do this.

(b) She means Macbeth will be what the Witches have promised him, i.e. King.

(c) Lady Macbeth is worried about her husband's character, fearing that he is too soft-hearted to take a short-cut to the throne by murdering Duncan.

(d) The quickest way to the throne, i.e. murder.

(e) The word 'illness' means 'evil nature' here.

(f) (You) don't want to cheat and yet you want to win by unfair means.

(g) The crown.

(h) The 'metaphysical aid' refers to the supernatural forces, or the Witches, whom Lady Macbeth believes are going to help her husband become King.

(i) Lady Macbeth knows her husband's nature and, fearing that he is too tender-hearted to murder Duncan, she intends to overcome his scruples by encouraging him with brave words ('chastise with the valour of my tongue/ All that impedes thee from the golden round').

Essay Questions

(1) '... his fiend-like queen.' Just how evil, in your opinion, is Lady Macbeth?

(2) 'Fair is foul, and foul is fair.' Write an essay showing how this phrase aptly describes Macbeth and one other character in the play.

(3) It has often been observed that much of the play takes place in darkness. Show how this is true and explain why you think Shakespeare chose to do this.

(4) What part does the supernatural play in *Macbeth*?

(5) 'And be these juggling fiends no more believed,
That palter with us in a double sense,
That keep the word of promise to our ear,
And break it to our hope'

(V. viii. 19-22).

Show how Macbeth is tricked by words.

(6) Describe Macbeth's last meeting with the Witches (IV. i).

(7) Describe the scene in which Lady Macduff and her son are murdered, showing how Shakespeare varies the mood as the scene (IV. ii) progresses.

(8) Show how, and explain why, Lady Macbeth suppresses her natural instincts at the beginning of the play, but gradually loses her nerve as events progress.

(9) How does Macbeth's imagination show itself in the play? What do those incidents where his imagination manifests itself tell us about his character?

(10) What evidence is there that Duncan was a good King but a bad judge of character?

(11) In what ways are the characters of Macduff and Banquo both similar and different?

(12) Describe, with close reference to the text, the emotional relationship that exists between Macbeth and his wife. Are they, in your opinion, a loving couple from the beginning of the play to its end?

(13)   'this even-handed justice
Commends th' ingredients of our poisoned chalice
To our our own lips.'

Macbeth is saying that natural justice is always fair and that the harm we do to others always rebounds on us in the end. How does this show itself to be true in the play?

(14) What evidence is there that Malcolm will be a good King?

(15) There is a certain amount of confusion over whether or not the Macbeths have any children. Show how this confusion arises. Does it matter, in your opinion, whether or not they do have any children?

(16) Is there a scene in *Macbeth* that you think is missing? If so, write it for yourself in Modern English, using only those characters already in the play, and indicating in the stage directions where it comes in terms of the play's action.

(17) Discuss the symbolic significance of *either* feasting *or* sleeping in *Macbeth*.

(18) 'The Witches don't make Macbeth do anything,' says A. C. Bradley in his book *Shakespearean Tragedy*. Do you agree with him? Your answer must be based on close reference to the text.

(19) Describe the events of the banquet scene (III. iv), showing how Macbeth gives himself away and the change that comes over Lady Macbeth at the end of the scene.

(20) Write an essay on the theme of 'appearances versus reality' in *Macbeth*.

Essay Answers to Question 12, 18 and 20

Question 12: Describe, with close reference to the text, the emotional relationship that exists between

Macbeth and his wife. Are they, in your opinion, a loving couple from the beginning of the play to its end?

There are some lines in Macbeth's letter to his wife (I. v. 8-11) that indicate not only his love for her but also that everything he wants is as much for her sake as his own:

'This have I thought good to deliver to thee, my dearest partner of greatness, that thou might'st not lose the dues of rejoicing, by being ignorant of what greatness is promised thee.'

Later in the play, at III. ii. 46, having planned the murder of Banquo, Macbeth tells his wife: 'Be innocent of the knowledge, dearest chuck.' Both the term of endearment, 'dearest chuck', and his desire to save Lady Macbeth any more emotional strain, indicate his deep fondness for her (other terms of endearment can be found at III. ii. 29 and III. ii. 36).

Some take the view that his tender feelings are not reciprocated, and that the relationship is one-sided. They argue that there is no evidence of any love for her husband on Lady Macbeth's part. True, she knows his nature well, but what she knows about it, she doesn't seem to like or respect. She considers his virtues (kindness, a sense of honour, moral awareness etc.) as signs of weakness in his character. When Macbeth tells her, 'We will proceed no further in this business' (I. vii. 31), because Duncan has just honoured him and he wants to preserve the value of that honour, Lady Macbeth chooses to interpret this as cowardice:

'What beast was 't then
That made you break this enterprise to me?
When you durst do it, then you were a man'

(I. vii. 47-49).

These insults, aimed at her husband's manhood, are so frequent in the play that they dispel any impression of love. Here are a few more examples:

'My hands are of your colour; but I shame
To wear a heart so white'

(II. ii. 63-64);

'Are you a man?'

(III. iv. 58);

'Fie, my lord, fie! a soldier, and afeard?'

(V. i. 29-30).

Those who hold this view would point out that, even allowing for rhetoric in I. vii. 54-59, and despite her dubious claim to 'know/ How tender 't is to love the babe that milks me' (V. vii. 54-55), it is hard to imagine a woman who is prepared to dash out the brains of her baby as capable of loving anyone. They would conclude that Lady Macbeth is totally selfish, her interest in her husband being simply what he can do for her in terms of fulfilling her ambition to be Queen, and, despite a limited display of conscience in V. i, she is insensitive to others to the point that would preclude a capacity to love.

On the other hand, there are those who argue that Lady Macbeth is not motivated by personal ambition. Unlike Macbeth, who openly wants to be King, she never expresses the desire to be Queen. Her ambition is on her husband's behalf; she wants him to achieve what he so much desires and, being the stronger character of the two, she knows that she must bolster his determination. This is the measure of her love for him.

They would point out that, in addition to constantly rallying and reassuring him ('Come on;/ Gentle my lord,' III. ii. 26-27), she comes to his rescue twice: at II. iii. 115, when she faints to draw attention away from him when he is in a tight spot over explaining why he killed the grooms; and in the banquet scene (III. iv), when she hastily resorts to the story of Macbeth's strange malady since childhood to explain his hysterical behaviour.

Similarly, they would argue that the shocking image of dashing out the brains of her baby (I. vii. 54-59) is merely to emphasise her determination to carry out her word, not a literal declaration of intent.

In the end, it is Macbeth who hardens his heart against conscience and deliberately embraces evil, and Lady Macbeth who is driven to despair and suicide by her sense of guilt. Perhaps the realisation that her husband no longer needs or heeds her contributes to her despair.

Whatever our interpretation of Lady Macbeth's feelings towards her husband at the beginning, it is clear that soon after Macbeth becomes King, the couple are no longer close to each other. In fact, Lady Macbeth does not appear again on stage after Act Three, except in the brief sleep-walking scene.

In V. iii, Macbeth seems to be reminded of her only when he notices the Doctor (line 37); then he doesn't refer to her as 'my wife' but 'your patient', as though he no longer feels any responsibility towards her. It is possible to argue, of course, that Macbeth has other and more pressing problems on his mind — the coming battle with Malcolm. But he obviously no longer needs his wife's support and she, in any event, is no longer capable of helping him.

He is saddened by her death, which brings home to him the brevity and futility of life, but, hard-pressed by his enemies, he barely has time to grieve.

> 'She should have died hereafter:
> There would have been a time for such a word'
> (V. v. 17-18).

Question 18: 'The Witches don't make Macbeth do anything,' says A. C. Bradley in his book *Shakespearean Tragedy*. Do you agree with him? Your answer must be based on close reference to the text.

The essential feature of Shakespeare's tragedies (though not necessarily the tragic plays of his contemporaries) is that his tragic heroes and heroines have freedom of will; the ability to decide freely whether or not they want to follow a path leading to good or evil. Such is the choice Macbeth has.

The argument that if the Witches can see into the future and know what Macbeth's fate will be, then he has no freedom of choice because his fate has been predetermined by forces beyond his control, is not valid. This would make Macbeth a puppet of the Witches, or an automaton. He is neither of these. The Witches influence Macbeth, but only in so far as he is already predisposed to be influenced by them: they know what he wants to hear and they tell him just that. Even before he meets them in I. iii, his ambition to be King exists like a seed in his mind, a seed the Witches water with their words of encouragement. He has thought about murdering Duncan to fulfil this ambition, which explains his guilty reaction at I. iii. 51-52, which Banquo notices:

'Good sir, why do you start, and seem to fear
Things that do sound so fair?'

All the Witches do is to hold a mirror up to the evil thoughts already planted deep in Macbeth's mind, hence his guilty reaction when they are exposed.

The Witches make no mention of murder, but Macbeth is thinking about it in I. iii. 139, 'My thought, whose murder yet is but fantastical'. This is the first mention of the idea, but it has been with him longer than this.

Macbeth freely chooses to commit murder. Right up to the slaying of Duncan in II. ii, he is confronted, as a free, moral agent, with a choice between good and evil. The first example of him examining these options comes when, after contemplating murder in I. iii. 133-142, he looks at the alternative, which equally promises to fulfil his ambition for kingship:

> 'If Chance will have me king, why, Chance may crown
>   me,
> Without my stir'

> (I. iii. 143-144).

What changes this resolve, to let fate make him King without helping it along, is when fate appears to be putting obstacles in his way, i.e. Duncan's declaration of Malcolm as his heir ('We will establish our estate upon/ Our eldest, Malcolm; whom we name hereafter/ The Prince of Cumberland', I. iv. 37-39). This destroys Macbeth's faith in 'Chance' (or fate) and he decides to look after his own future:

> 'The Prince of Cumberland! — That is a step
> On which I must fall down, or else o'erleap,
> For in my way it lies. Stars, hide your fires!
> Let not light see my black and deep desires'

> (I. iv. 48-51).

Even after this, he wavers between murdering Duncan and calling the whole thing off:

> 'We will proceed no further in this business'

> (I. vii. 31).

Macbeth could have stopped himself at this point, but within forty or so lines he has allowed himself (for he could have walked away from his wife or refused to listen to her) to be persuaded into going on with the murder. He even seems quite excited about it, congratulating his wife for her courage and adding his ideas to her plan:

> 'Bring forth men-children only!
> For thy undaunted mettle should compose
> Nothing but males. Will it not be received,
> When we have marked with blood those sleepy two
> Of his own chamber, and used their very daggers,
> That they have done 't?'
>
> (I. vii. 72-77).

(Using the grooms' daggers, smearing the grooms with blood, and killing them, are Macbeth's ideas, though the last, killing the grooms, comes to him after Macduff has discovered the murder in II. iii and Macbeth returns with Lenox to the bed-chamber.) Macbeth is also aware that the consequence of his crime will be damnation but he is prepared to accept this ('We'd jump the life to come', I. vii. 7) as part of the price he has to pay, the other part being the avenging hand of natural justice:

> 'this even-handed justice
> Commends th' ingredients of our poisoned chalice
> To our own lips'
>
> (I. vii. 10-12).

The Witches don't tell Macbeth to murder Banquo; they don't even say that Banquo is a threat to him. All they say is that Banquo will be 'Lesser than Macbeth, and greater' (I. iii. 65) and they tell Banquo, 'Thou shalt get kings, though thou be none' (I. iii. 67). Banquo is murdered because Macbeth chooses to perceive him as a threat, although he might not be one at all, for Banquo doesn't do anything to expose Macbeth after announcing his suspicions at III. i. 1-3:

> 'Thou hast it now, King, Cawdor, Glamis, all,

> As the weird women promised; and, I fear,
> Thou playedst most foully for 't.'

Macbeth fears Banquo's 'royalty of nature', the 'dauntless temper of his mind', and his wisdom (III. i. 49-53), but most of all Banquo unnerves him because his virtue is a standing reminder of his own evil nature, now stained with Duncan's blood:

> 'There is none but he
> Whose being I do fear: and under him
> My genius is rebuked'
>
> (III. i. 53-55).

One cannot argue that the Witches' remarks in I. iii push Macbeth towards his attempt on Fleance's life; Macbeth's fixation with 'No son of mine succeeding', III. i. 63 (if he has any) is entirely of his evil mind's own making:

> 'For Banquo's issue have I filed my mind;
> For them the gracious Duncan have I murdered;
> Put rancours in the vessel of my peace
> Only for them; and mine eternal jewel
> Given to the common enemy of man,
> To make them kings, the seed of Banquo kings!'
>
> (III. i. 64-69).

But Fleance escapes the Murderers' clutches and flees (which might be said to be the turning point of the play, as evil begins to fail in its purpose).

The Witches might be responsible for giving Macbeth a false sense of security, or, to be precise, the Apparitions might be accused of doing this:

> 'laugh to scorn
> The power of man, for none of woman born
> Shall harm Macbeth'
>
> (Second Apparition, IV. i. 79-81);

'Macbeth shall never vanquished be, until
Great Birnam wood to high Dunsinane hill
Shall come against him'

(Third Apparition, IV. i. 92-94).

But it can be argued that Macbeth places his own construction on these words, finding in them the meaning he wants, and so he deceives himself. The First Apparition tells Macbeth to 'beware Macduff' (IV. i. 71) and Macduff's family are slaughtered in IV. ii, but Macbeth has already begun to fear Macduff at III. iv. 128-129 and the slaying of Macduff's family is not so much a consequence of the Apparition's warning (how could it be, for it told Macbeth to fear Macduff and not his wife and children) as it is a need for Macbeth to prove to himself that 'The very firstlings of my heart shall be/ The firstlings of my hand' (IV. i. 147-148).

To shift any part of the responsibility for Macbeth's crimes to the Witches is to let Macbeth off too lightly. It is better to see the Witches, not as malevolent pranksters who trick Macbeth into committing murder after murder, nor as the mouthpieces of unalterable fate, but as the symbolic representatives of the evil and the evil intentions already in Macbeth. A. C. Bradley is right; the Witches don't make Macbeth do anything he hasn't already thought of doing before he meets them. The decisions to act are entirely his.

Question 20: Write an essay on the theme of 'appearances versus reality' in *Macbeth*.

'Appearances versus reality' means that the way things seem to be in the play (to the characters or, sometimes, to ourselves) is different from the way they actually are. This theme, because deception of one sort or another fills *Macbeth* to overflowing, is perhaps the most prevalent in the play, and we come across it in practically every scene.

Of all the characters in the play, Duncan is the one who places the greatest trust in appearances, and he is, consequently, the one most easily fooled by them. When we first meet him in I. ii, he is busy praising Macbeth, 'O valiant cousin! worthy gentlemen!' (line 24), and yet Macbeth has already begun to think — or will very soon begin to think — of murdering him in order to seize the crown ('My thought, whose murder yet is but fantastical', I. iii. 139).

In I. iv. 13-14, Duncan tells us that the treacherous Thane of Cawdor was a man on whom he 'built/ An absolute trust'. He says, 'There's no art/ To find the mind's construction in the face' (I. iv. 11-12), meaning there is no skill by which one can fathom what is going on in a man's mind by his facial expression, but Duncan is, of course, referring to himself here more than anyone else and to his own tendency to trust others too easily.

A little later on in the same scene, after Duncan has pronounced Malcolm his heir and Prince of Cumberland, he praises Macbeth to Banquo ('he is full so valiant', line 54) even as Macbeth is harbouring 'black and deep desires' (line 51). Duncan is once again placing 'absolute trust' in a man whose intentions towards him are malign. And as Duncan rides up to Macbeth's home at Inverness Castle, where his murder awaits him, he somewhat incongruously praises the place for its pleasant position and the salubrious air that surrounds it:

'This castle hath a pleasant seat; the air
Nimbly and sweetly recommends itself
Unto our gentle senses'

(I. vi. 1-3).

Then Duncan is greeted by his 'Fair and noble hostess' (I. vi. 24), Lady Macbeth, to whom he later gives a diamond for being a 'most kind hostess', II. i. 16, (and which, with cruel irony, Macbeth carries with him as he creeps into Duncan's bedchamber to murder him). Of course, Lady Macbeth is anything but a 'kind hostess' and as she leads Duncan by the hand (I. vi. 28) into the castle, she appears to us to be luring her prey to its fate. Duncan has just escaped one attempted rebellion and yet he goes happily to bed ('shut up/ In measureless content', II. i. 16-17) without taking the obvious precaution of placing an adequate guard at his door. He is naive.

In I. iii, the Witches seem to be promising Macbeth something highly desirable, the crown. The fulfilment of the first two of the Witches' promises, that he will be Thane of Glamis and Cawdor, he sees as 'happy prologues to the swelling act/ Of the imperial theme' (lines 128-129). But the honour of being King, implied in the phrase 'the swelling act/ Of the imperial theme', will be short-lived. The more lasting impression that he leaves is either of a dwarfish-thief wearing the stolen robes of a giant ('now does he feel his title/ Hang loose about him, like a giant's robe/ Upon a dwarfish thief', V. ii. 20-22) or as 'this dead butcher' (V. ix. 35).

Lady Macbeth contributes to the theme of 'appearances versus reality' when she tells Macbeth to hide his evil thoughts and intentions beneath a sweet exterior:

> 'look like the innocent flower
>
> But be the serpent under 't'
>
> (I. v. 63-64).

In I. vii, the plan to alter appearances at the scene of the crime, to make it look as if the grooms murdered Duncan, is hatched (lines 63-77). Then in II. i we have Macbeth's hallucination of the airborne dagger, something which at first appears real to him but which, as he still has a certain amount of self-control left, he knows to be a mere figment of his overworked imagination:

'A dagger of the mind, a false creation,
Proceeding from the heat-oppressèd brain'

(lines 38-39).

Another hallucination follows in II. ii — the voice that cries 'Macbeth does murder sleep' (lines 35) — but this time, because Macbeth is hysterical with fear and guilt, he accepts it as real and not a product of his imagination.

After Duncan's body has been discovered, Macbeth and Lady Macbeth must, of course, disguise all appearances that point to their guilt. Macbeth pretends horror and grief at Duncan's death. He falsely claims to have killed the grooms in righteous anger, and when Macduff questions this, Lady Macbeth pretends to faint to distract attention from her husband. If any of the others suspect that she is acting, Macduff and Banquo in particular, they dare not say so.

Appearances and reality are at odds in the relationship between Macbeth and Banquo, who voices his suspicions of Macbeth:

'Thou hast it now, King, Cawdor, Glamis, all,
As the weird women promised; and, I fear,
Thou playedst most foully for 't'

(III. i. 1-3),

and yet pledges loyalty to him:

'Let your highness
Command upon me, to the which my duties
Are with a most indissoluble tie
For ever knit'

(III. i. 15-18).

On the other hand, in spite of this pledge, Macbeth fears Banquo: 'Our fears in Banquo/ Stick deep' (III. i. 48-49). In a false show of friendliness, he says to Banquo, 'Fail not our feast' (III. i. 27), having arranged for Banquo to be murdered before then.

In III. vi. 3-20, in a bitterly ironical speech, Lenox questions the general falseness of appearances. He says that Macbeth seemed to mourn Duncan's death and to have killed the grooms in righteous anger; Fleance seems to have been responsible for his father's murder; Malcolm and Donalbain seem to be similarly guilty of their father's murder. However, Lenox makes it clear that he does not believe in any of these deceptive appearances.

Above all, appearances prove misleading in Macbeth's dealings with the three Apparitions. They deceive him, firstly in the form they take, and secondly, by the promises they make.

The First Apparition, an armed head, is probably taken by Macbeth to be Macduff's, whereas it represents his own head, severed from his body by Macduff.

The Second Apparition, a bloody and seemingly helpless child, urges Macbeth to:

'Be bloody, bold and resolute; laugh to scorn
The power of man, for none of woman born
Shall harm Macbeth'

(IV. i. 79-81).

The Third Apparition, a crowned child holding a tree, promises that:

'Macbeth shall never vanquished be, until
Great Birnam wood to high Dunsinane hill
Shall come against him'

(IV. i. 92-94).

Macbeth is misled by these assurances into believing himself invincible. However, Birnam wood *does* seem to move as Malcolm's soldiers each carry a branch to camouflage their numbers; and Macbeth discovers that 'Macduff was from his mother's womb/ Untimely ripped' (V. viii. 15-16). The shattering of Macbeth's apparent certainties brings home to us, perhaps more than anything else, the special role which the theme of 'appearances versus reality' plays in Macbeth.

10. Revision Questions

Say who is speaking, give the Act and Scene Numbers, and the missing words.

(1) 'She should have died ... '

(2) 'Fit to govern?/ No, not to ... '

(3) 'To show an ... sorrow is an office/ Which the ... man does easy.'

(4) 'Stars, hide your ... !/ Let not light see my ... and ... desires.'

(5) 'And be these ... fiends no more believed,/ That palter with us in a ... sense,/ That keep the word of ... to our ear,/ And break it to our ... '

(6) 'I pull in resolution, and begin/ To doubt th' ... of the fiend,/ That lies like ... '

(7) 'There's not a one of them, but in his house/ I keep a servant ... '

(8) 'But here upon this bank and ... of time,/ We'd ... the life to come.'

(9) 'this even-handed justice/ Commends th' ingredients of our poisoned ... / To our own lips.'

(10) 'art thou but/ A dagger of the mind, a false creation,/ Proceeding from the ... - ... brain?'

(11) 'The Thane of Fife had a ... : where is she now?'

(12) 'Go, get some water,/ And wash this filthy ... from your hand.'

(13) 'Will all great ... ocean wash this blood/ Clean from my hand?'

(14) 'O! yet I do repent me of my ... / That I did kill them.'

(15) 'Thou canst not say I did it. Never shake/ Thy ... locks at me.'

(16) 'O proper stuff!/ This is the very ... of your fear:/ This is the ... - ... dagger which, you said,/ Led you to Duncan.'

(17) 'If it were done when 't is ... , then 't were well/ It were done ... '

(18) 'I have no spur/ To prick the sides of my intent, but only/ ... ambition.'

(19) 'Let us seek out some desolate shade, and there/ ... our sad bosoms ... '

(20) 'Your face, my thane, is as a ... , where men/ May ... strange matters.'

(21) 'Come, you spirits/ That tend on mortal thoughts, ... me here.'

(22) 'screw your courage to the ... - ... '

(23) 'Some say he's mad; others, that lesser hate him,/ Do call it ... fury.'

(24) 'now does he feel his title/ Hang loose about him, like a ... robe/ Upon a ... thief.'

(25) 'There is none but he/ Whose being I do fear: and under him/ My ... is rebuked.'

(26) 'laugh to ... / The power of man, for none of woman ... / Shall harm Macbeth.'

(27) 'Meet we the ... of the sickly weal;/ And with him pour we, in our country's ... ,/ Each drop of us.'

(28) 'Here's the smell of blood still: all the ... of Arabia will not ... this little ... '

(29) 'My thought, whose murder yet is but ... '

(30) 'this dead butcher, and his ... - ... queen.'

(31) 'This diamond he greets your wife withal,/ By the name of most kind ... , and shut up/ In ... content.'

(32) 'but, for your husband,/ He is ... , ... , ... , and best knows/ The fits o' th' season.'

(33) 'From this moment/ The very firstlings of my ... shall be/ The firstlings of my ... '

(34) 'Infected be the air whereon they ride;/ And ... all those that trust them!'

(35) 'merciful powers!/ Restrain in me the cursèd ... that nature/ Gives way to in ... !'

(36) 'There's no art/ To find the mind's ... in the face:/ He was a gentleman on whom I built/ An absolute ... '

(37) 'Duncan is in his grave;/ After life's ... fever he sleeps well.'

(38) 'We have ... the snake, not killed it:/ She'll close and be herself; whilst our poor ... / Remains in danger of her former ... '

(39) 'Thou hast it now, King, Cawdor, ... , all,/ As the weird women promised; and, I fear,/ Thou ... most ... for 't.'

(40) *(Macbeth)* 'Fail not our ... ' *(Banquo)* 'My lord, I will not.'

(41) 'We will proceed no further in this business:/ He hath honoured me of ... ; and I have bought/ ... opinions from all sorts of people,/ Which would be worn now in their newest ... ,/ Not cast aside so soon.'

(42) 'I have given suck, and know/ How ... 't is to love the babe that milks me:/ I would, while it was ... in my face,/ Have plucked my nipple from his ... gums,/ And ... the brains out, had I so ... as you/ Have done to this.'

(43) 'This castle hath a pleasant ... ; the air/ Nimbly and sweetly ... itself/ Unto our ... senses.'

(44) 'Here had we now our country's ... roofed,/ Were the graced person of our ... present.'

(45) 'I hope, in no place so ... ,/ Where such as thou may'st find him.'

(46) 'No son of mine succeeding. If 't be so,/For Banquo's ... have I ... my mind;/For them the ... Duncan have I murdered.'

(47) 'How now, you secret, black and ... hags!'

(48) 'Wake Duncan with thy ... : I would thou couldst!'

(49) 'My strange and self- ... / Is the ... fear, that wants hard use:/ We are but ... in deed.'

(50) 'I dare do all that may ... a man;/ Who dares do more is ... '

(51) 'This murderous ... that 's shot/ Hath not yet ... , and our safest way/ Is to avoid the aim.'

(52) 'by the clock 't is ... ,/ And yet dark night ... the travelling lamp.'

(53) 'Macbeth shall never ... be, until/ Great Birnam wood to ... Dunsinane hill/ Shall come ... him.'

(54) 'Macbeth! Macbeth! Macbeth! beware ... '

(55) 'By the pricking of my ... ,/ Something ... this way comes.'

(56) 'A great perturbation in ... , to receive at once the benefit of ... , and do the effects of ... '

(57) 'Give sorrow ... ; the grief that does not ... / Whispers the o'er-fraught ... , and bids it ... '

(58) 'Who then shall blame/ His ... senses to recoil and start,/ When all that is within him does ... / Itself for being there?'

(59) 'Now does he feel/ His secret murders ... on his hands.'

(60) 'Lechery, Sir, it provokes and unprovokes: it provokes the ... , but it takes away the ... '

(61) 'Nay, had I power, I should/ Pour the ... milk of ... into hell.'

(62) 'Yet I do fear thy ... :/ It is too full o' the milk of ... kindness/ To catch the ... way.'

(63) 'Come to my woman's breasts,/ And take my milk for ... '

(64) 'He has ... me, mother:/ Run away, I ... you!'

(65) 'To dew the ... flower and ... the weeds./ Make we our march towards Birnam.'

(66) 'look like the innocent ... / But be the ... under 't.'

(67) 'New honours come upon him/ Like our strange ... , cleave not to their ... / But with the aid of use.'

(68) 'The west yet ... with some streaks of day:/ Now spurs the lated ... apace,/ To gain the timely ... '

(69) 'To Ireland, I: our separated fortune/ Shall keep us both the ... '

(70) 'Not so sick, my lord,/ As she is troubled with thick-coming ... ,/ That keep her from her ... '

(71) 'Your ... in Scotland/ Would create soldiers, make our ... fight/ To doff their ... distresses.'

(72) 'He needs not our ... , since he delivers/ Our ... , and what we have to do,/ To the direction ... '

(73) 'Cousins, I hope the days are near at hand,/ That ... will be safe.'

(74) 'What rhubarb, senna, or what purgative ... ,/ Would ... these English hence?'

(75) 'Why should I play the ... fool, and die/ On mine own sword?'

(76) 'The tyrant's people on both ... do fight.'

(77) 'If thou be'st slain, and with no stroke of ... ,/ My wife and children's ... will ... me still.'

(78) 'But wherefore could not I pronounce " .. "?/ I had most need of blessing, and " ... "/ Stuck in my ... '

(79) 'Bring forth ... - ... only!/ For thy undaunted ... should compose/ Nothing but males.'

(80) 'I have almost forgot the ... of fears./ The time has been, my senses would have ... / To hear a night-shriek.'

Answers to Revision Questions

(1)   Macbeth; V. v. (17); hereafter.

(2)   Macduff; IV. iii. (102-103); live.

(3)   Malcolm; II. iii. (134-135); unfelt, false.

(4)   Macbeth; I. iv. (50-51); fires, black, deep.

(5)   Macbeth; V. viii. (19-22); juggling, double, promise, hope.

(6)   Macbeth; V. v. (42-44); equivocation, truth.

(7)   Macbeth; III. iv. (131-132); fee'd.

(8)   Macbeth; I. vii. (6-7); shoal, jump.

(9)   Macbeth; I. vii. (10-12); chalice.

(10) Macbeth; II. i. (37-39); heat-oppressèd.

(11) Lady Macbeth; V. i. (34); wife.

(12) Lady Macbeth; II. ii. (45-46); witness.

(13) Macbeth; II. ii. (59-60); Neptune's.

(14) Macbeth; II. iii. (103-104); fury.

(15) Macbeth; III. iv. (50-51); gory.

(16) Lady Macbeth; III. iv. (60-63); painting, air-drawn.

(17) Macbeth; I. vii. (1-2); done, quickly.

(18) Macbeth; I. vii. (25-27); Vaulting.

(19) Malcolm; IV. III. (1-2); Weep, empty.

(20) Lady Macbeth; I. v. (60-61); book, read.

(21) Lady Macbeth; I. v. (38-39); unsex.

(22) Lady Macbeth; I. vii. (60); sticking-place.

(23) Cathness; V. ii. (13-14); valiant.

(24) Angus: V. ii. (20-22); giant's, dwarfish.

(25) Macbeth; III. i. (53-55); genius.

(26) Second Apparition; IV. i. (79-81); scorn, born.

(27) Cathness; V. ii. (27-29); medicine, purge.

(28) Lady Macbeth; V. i. (40-41); perfumes, sweeten, hand.

(29) Macbeth; I. iii. (139); fantastical.

(30) Malcolm: V. ix. (35); fiend-like.

(31) Banquo; II. i. (15-17); hostess, measureless.

(32) Rosse; IV. ii. (15-17); noble, wise, judicious.

(33) Macbeth; IV. i. (146-148); heart, hand.

(34) Macbeth; IV. i. (138-139); damned.

(35) Banquo; II. i. (7-9); thoughts, repose.

(36) Duncan; I. iv. (11-14); construction, trust.

(37) Macbeth; III. ii. (22-23); fitful.

(38) Macbeth; III. ii. (13-15); scotched, malice, tooth.

(39) Banquo; III. i. (1-3); Glamis, playedst, foully.

(40) Macbeth; III. i. (27-28); feast.

(41) Macbeth; I. vii. (31-35); late, Golden, gloss.

(42) Lady Macbeth; I. vii. (54-59); tender, smiling, boneless, dashed, sworn.

(43) Duncan; I. vi. (1-3); seat, recommends, gentle.

(44) Macbeth; III. iv. (40-41); honour, Banquo.

(45) Lady Macduff; IV. ii. (78-79); unsanctified.

(46) Macbeth; III. i. (63-65); issue, filed, gracious.

(47) Macbeth; IV. i. (48); midnight.

(48) Macbeth; II. ii. (73); knocking.

(49) Macbeth; III. iv. (142-144); abuse, initiate, young.

(50) Macbeth; I. vii. (46-47); become, none.

(51) Malcolm; II. iii . (139-141); shaft, lighted.

(52) Rosse; II. iv. (6-7); day, strangles.

(53) Third Apparition; IV. i. (92-94); vanquished, high, against.

(54) First Apparition; IV. i. (71); Macduff.

(55) Second Witch; IV. i. (44-45); thumbs, wicked.

(56) Doctor; V. i. (7-8); nature, sleep, watching.

(57) Malcolm; IV. iii. (209-210); words, speak, heart, break.

(58) Menteth; V. ii. (22-25); pestered, condemn.

(59) Angus; V. ii. (16-17); sticking.

(60) Porter; II. iii. (24-25); desire, performance.

(61) Malcolm; IV. iii. (97-98); sweet, concord.

(62) Lady Macbeth; I. v. (14-16); nature, human, nearest.